MAGGIDIM & HASIDIM:
THEIR WISDOM

BOOKS BY LOUIS I. NEWMAN

JEWISH INFLUENCE ON CHRISTIAN REFORM MOVEMENTS

STUDIES IN BIBLICAL PARALLELISM
(In Collaboration with William Popper)

THE HASIDIC ANTHOLOGY AND THE TALMUDIC ANTHOLOGY
(In Collaboration with Samuel Spitz)

THE JEWISH PEOPLE, FAITH AND LIFE
A Manual of Instruction for Newcomers into Judaism

TRUMPET IN ADVERSITY, *a Book of Poems*

THE LITTLE ZADDIK
A Three-Act Play on the Baal Shem Tov and the Wolf

THE WOMAN AT THE WALL
A Three-Act Play on Genesis 38

PANGS OF THE MESSIAH
And Other Plays, Pageants and Cantatas

LIVING WITH OURSELVES

THE SEARCH FOR SERENITY

BITING ON GRANITE, *Sermons and Addresses*

A JEWISH UNIVERSITY IN AMERICA?

A "CHIEF RABBI" OF ROME BECOMES A CATHOLIC
A Study in Fright and Spite

MAGGIDIM & HASIDIM: THEIR WISDOM

A NEW ANTHOLOGY OF THE PARABLES, FOLK-TALES, FABLES, APHORISMS, EPIGRAMS, SAYINGS, ANECDOTES, PROVERBS, AND EXEGETICAL INTERPRETATIONS OF THE LEADING MAGGIDIM (FOLK-PREACHERS), AND THE HASIDIC MASTERS AND THEIR DISCIPLES

A Companion Volume to "The Hasidic Anthology"

Translated from the Hebrew, Yiddish, and German,
Selected, Compiled and Arranged by

LOUIS I. NEWMAN

AUTHOR OF "THE LITTLE ZADDIK"; "PANGS OF THE MESSIAH"; "THE JEWISH PEOPLE, FAITH AND LIFE," ETC.

IN COLLABORATION WITH

SAMUEL SPITZ

WITH AN INTRODUCTION ON "THE MAGGIDIM AND HASIDIM; THEIR PREACHING METHOD AND ART"

BLOCH PUBLISHING COMPANY
"The Jewish Book Concern"
NEW YORK
5722–1962

Copyright, 1962, by

LOUIS I. NEWMAN

JUL 15 1963

PRINTED IN THE UNITED STATES OF AMERICA

AMERICAN BOOK-STRATFORD PRESS, INC., NEW YORK

TO
MY GRANDCHILDREN
AND THEIR PARENTS

TABLE OF CONTENTS

PAGE

INTRODUCTION

MAGGIDIM AND HASIDIM:
THEIR PREACHING METHOD AND ART

by Louis I. Newman

The late Samuel Spitz who collaborated with me in the preparation of the basic manuscript of the items selected for *The Hasidic Anthology* (Scribner's, New York, 1934), helped also to prepare the translation from the Hebrew and the Yiddish of the items selected for this new Anthology: *Maggidim and Hasidim: Their Wisdom.* The work was done in the late 1930's and the early 1940's. Since 1934 the Hasidic movement has come into wide public attention in the Western world, and the literature of Hasidism and concerning it has attained great popularity. In 1960, the 200th anniversary of the death of Israel ben Eliezer, the Baal Shem Tov, or the Besht, the founder of Hasidism, was generally observed.[1] (This author has published a three-act play on the story of the boy Besht and the Wolf, entitled: *The Little Zaddik.*) *The Hasidic Anthology* continues to have an appeal, apparently because of the selection of the material from the writings of the Hasidic Sages, and also because of the arrangements of its contents into Rubrics, with a detailed Index. As originally intended, it has proved to be a sourcebook for preachers, speakers and teachers, and selections from it have been printed in many collections since its appearance.

Believing that material not included in the *Hasidic Anthology* may be of interest, the items left in my hands by the late Samuel Spitz, have recently been re-worked, arranged and made ready for publication. It is hoped that this compilation will have an appeal similar to that of the initial collection. While it has not been possible in this printing to furnish a detailed Index, according to the model in the *Hasidic Anthology*, nevertheless the nature of the numerous Rubrics should make the use of this volume relatively easy. The same method of arrangement has also been followed in the *Talmudic Anthology* (Behrman's; New York, 1945). In a later edi-

[1] See Louis I. Newman, "The Baal Shem Tov," in *Great Jewish Personalities in Ancient and Medieval Times,* New York, 1959, pp. 287-306.

tion of *Maggidim and Hasidim: Their Wisdom,* a detailed Index, so valuable for the preacher, may be furnished.

The Four Divisions of Material

There are four general divisions of material included in this Anthology, as follows:

1. The first contains items chosen from the works of the folk-preachers, known as Maggidim, who specialized in sermons and addresses of interest to the common people, particularly during the 18th, 19th, and early 20th century.

2. The second division contains items from the works of the Hasidic Maggidim, namely, those, who in their preaching, emphasized the teachings of Hasidism, the great popular movement, called into being about the year 1735 by the Baal Shem Tov (1699-1760).

3. The third division presents aphorisms, epigrams, reflections and comments of the Zaddikim, namely, the Saintly, Righteous spiritual leaders of Hasidism. The material gathered for this volume is similar to that of the companion volume: *The Hasidic Anthology,* but is not a repetition of it. The items selected have the characteristic Hasidic approach, underscoring joy, enkindlement, humility, democracy, compassion and other ideals representative of the movement of the Besht and his followers.

4. The fourth division of material has been culled from the writings of distinguished Rabbis and scholars, who, in addition to being authorities in the domain of Halakah or Jewish jurisprudence, were also outstanding preachers. They utilized Aggada and Midrash, but their emphasis was primarily upon the ethico-spiritual aspects of Jewish religious law. They were masters of Biblical exegesis, and of Talmudic legalism, but they also appreciated the value of the *Mashal* or Parable, and, like the Maggidim, drew upon the experiences of ordinary, everyday life.

While a pronounced similarity will be perceived in the selections from the works of these four groups of Jewish preachers, teachers, commentators and authors, nevertheless each has its own unique quality. The sum-total of the wisdom of these instructors of the people is a compendium of utterances and writings expressive of Jewish teaching at its highest and best. The nuances and variations of narrative, interpretation and comment contribute to the many-sidedness of the Jewish message. If utilized aright, they can vastly enrich the substance and spirit of contemporary Jewish preaching in all circles of Jewish life.

Origin and Development of the Word: Maggid

The word: Maggid is the Hiphil or Causative participle of the root: N-G-D, namely, Higgid, and means: to declare, announce, or preach. The Maggid is one who declaims, announces or preaches. The root is found in the word Haggadah which signifies a Narrative, and is the name given to the Order of Service for the Seder at Passover time recounting the story of the Exodus from Egypt. The narrator at the Seder Services is known as the Maggid.

The word: Hasid is derived from the root H-S-D, which is found in the word: Hesed, meaning Grace or Lovingkindness. It is found in the text in the Ethics of the Fathers (*Pirkei Avot*), ii, 5: "Lo am-ha-aretz Hasid", namely, "an ignorant man cannot be pious." This text is at the basis of the Hasidic movement, since the Baal Shem Tov expressed a view opposite to the dictum of Hillel, asserting that a man untutored in the Law could be as pious as the scholar. The Zaddik, or the Righteous Man, became the leader of the Hasidim or Pious Disciples, by striving to attain to spiritual and moral perfection. (See my introduction in *The Hasidic Anthology*, pp. lvii-xc, entitled: "The Hasidim; Their History, Literature and Doctrines".)

In Zechariah ix:12, occurs the phrase: "*Maggid Mishneh.*" The usual translation is: "Even today do I declare that I will render double unto thee." But there are scholars who translate the phrase to mean: "The Maggid repeats," saying that it applies to the popular Prophet of Biblical days. In the Talmudic-Rabbinic period two major types of preacher became active: one was the Darshan, the other the Maggid. The Darshan was usually the scholarly Rabbi accustomed to deliver at intervals a "Derashah" or a Searching of the Scriptures based both on Aggada or narrative items and Halakah, the latter being predominant. The Darshan drew heavily upon the Midrash or imaginative lore based upon a literary or psychological interpretation of Biblical sources (see Edmond Fleg, *The Life of Moses*, New York, 1928; William G. Braude: *Midrash Tehillim*, New Haven, 1959). Though the Darshan was recognized as the authoritative type of preacher in Jewry, the second type, namely, the Maggid, gained widespread popularity even before the close of the Bible Canon. The Maggid avoided lengthy discussions of legalistic, ritualistic and pilpulistic elements in Jewish learning, and sought to speak in simple terms directly to the hearts of the masses. It is not surprising that oftentimes the Maggid or folk-preacher proved more appealing than the expounders of the Halakah. There is the well-known story of the dilemma of Rabbi Isaac Nappaha (4th Century C.E.) as to whether he should accede to a request to preach a popular Haggadic instead of a scholarly Halakic discourse (*Baba Kamma,*

60b; see my poem, "Single-Blessedness" in *Trumpet in Adversity*, New York, 1948, pp. 113-114). R. Abbahu, the Maggid (c. 279-320), was acknowledged to be more popular with the masses than R. Hiyya, the Darshan (fl. 3rd century C.E.), without any diminishment of the latter's importance (*Sotah*, 40b; see my poem, "Quality, Not Numbers" in *Trumpet in Adversity*, p. 126). So extensive was the activity of the Maggidim that Levi ben Sisi (c. 190-210 C.E.), his son, Joshua ben Levi (first half of the 3rd century C.E.) and others, conducted formal schools for the training of Maggidim.

Jesus of Nazareth must be included among the Maggidim. Joseph Klausner describes him as "a great teacher of morality and an artist in parable." (*Jesus of Nazareth*, Macmillan, New York, 1925, p. 414). He gives considerable attention to the role of Jesus as "the preacher of parables" (pp. 259 ff.; see also Israel Abrahams, *Studies in Pharisaism and the Gospels*, 2 vols., Cambridge, 1917-1924). Jesus disclosed himself, according to Klausner (pp. 254-255), as "a 'Rab' and simple Galilean preacher. A wandering Galilean 'Rab' and preacher was a common sight and specially known by the title of 'Galilean itinerant' (*Over Galilah*)." (The phrase is in *Sanhedrin*, 70a; *Hullin*, 27b. (*Darash Over Galilah*). Later the Disciples of Jesus attributed to him other attributes. In other words, in one of his chief manifestations it is possible to regard Jesus as a wandering Galilean Maggid.

In the period of the Geonim (6th to the 11th centuries), the function of the Maggid was to preach to the common people in the vernacular tongue whenever the occasion required, usually on Sabbath afternoon, between the Minhah or Afternoon Service, and Maariv, the Evening Service. The Rabbi, however, would preach on Shabbat ha-Gadol, the Great Sabbath, just before Passover. In the 15th and 16th century, no less a personage than Don Isaac Abravanel (1437-1508), who played a memorable role at the time of the Expulsion of Spanish Jewry, became known as a Master Maggid. His homiletic commentary on the Bible served as a major source for later Maggidim in their discourses on the Sedrah or the Weekly portion of the Pentateuch. Moses Alshech was a renowned Maggid in Safed, Palestine (c. 1508-1600). Asher Lemmlein in Germany and Austria (c. 1502) and Solomon Molko (1500-1532) in Italy and Turkey, announced the advent of the Messiah in discourses which followed the Maggidic method. An interesting use of the word: Maggid appears in the activities of the Pseudo-Messiahs. They considered their inner Mentor or Guide a "Maggid" who prompted them to proclaim the coming of the Messiah. The ordinary folk-preacher or Maggid, however, would reserve the expression of the traditional Messianic hope for the conclusion and climax of his discourse.

—

It was in the 16th century that the title: *Maggid Mesharim* became important, referring to the "preacher of uprightness." The title was later applied to the Maggid who in the community served as a Rabbinical Judge. Oftentimes he was known as a *Maggid Mesharim u-Moreh Tzedek*, namely, a "preacher of uprightness and a teacher of righteousness." The latter phrase: *Moreh Tzedek* brings to mind an identical title found in one of the Scrolls of the Dead Sea area. An authentic Maggid who delighted large audiences was Rabbi Hoeschel of Cracow (d. 1663).

In the 18th century the art of the Maggidim underwent a considerable development. For example, Elijah ben Solomon Abraham ha-Kohen (d. 1729), the Dayyan of Smyrna, became known as a "Terror Maggid," preaching, as his foremost work: *Shevet Musar* (Constantinople, 1712) indicates, fierce sermons on moral and religious conduct. He sought to forefend the terrible punishments on the *Yom ha-Din*, the Day of Judgment, in terms similar to those of the American Puritan preacher, Jonathan Edwards and others of the same type. At Constantinople, Judah Rosanes (d. 1727) sought to fuse the method of the Darshan with the technique of the Maggid, striving to harmonize the acts of Biblical personalities with the legalistic views of recognized Talmudic scholars. It was, as we shall see, Jacob ben Wolf Kranz of Dubno (c. 1740-1804) who brought the Maggid's art to its highest form. Herman A. Glatt has written of the Dubner Maggid, as Kranz came to be known, in his admirable work: *He Spoke in Parables: The Life and Works of the Dubno Maggid* (New York, A. Jay Bithmar Publication), 1937.[2] Later Maggidim include Abraham Berush Plahm (1804-1873), a pupil of the Dubner Maggid (Glatt, p. 205); Levi of Vardaslau, a Polish Maggid; Jacob Israel of Kremnitz; Judah Loew Edel of Slonim; Hayyim Abraham Katz of Moghilev; Ezekiel Feiwel of Deretschin, and others. In Lithuania some of the visiting Maggidim included the Kamenetzer Maggid; the Skidler Maggid and others. The title: Maggid was prized by many Jewish scholars, and both Joseph ben Meir Tummim and Solomon Kluger (1783-1860) preferred it to that of Rabbi.

Moses ben Isaac ben Noah Darshan (1828-1899) was perhaps the most celebrated Maggid of the 19th century, being known as the Kelmer Maggid. He was active in Lithuania and traveled throughout the then Pale of Settlement; he also lived for a time in London. He studied under Rabbi Israel Salanter (Israel Lipkin) (1810-1883) at Kovno, and became an emissary of the *Musar* or Ethics movement, emphasizing the moral teachings of Judaism.

[2] See also Israel Bettan, "The Dubno Maggid" in the *Hebrew Union College Annual*, Part 2, pp. 267-293.

The Kelmer Maggid belonged to the "Terror" or *Shevet Musar* School of preachers, stirring his listeners to moral and religious fervor by his portrayal of torments to attend the wicked on the *Yom ha-Din*. Other 19th century Maggidim included Hayyim Zedek, known as the "Rumsheshker"; Enoch Sundal Luria, a noted "philosophical Maggid" who preached sermons based on Arama's *Akedat Yitzhak* and Bahya ibn Pakuda's *Hobot ha-Levavot*. Meier Leibush Malbin (1809-1879) wrote commentaries which furnished the popular Maggidim with fruitful homiletical suggestions.

Out of the group of "Terror Maggidim" developed the "Penitential Maggidim" who, especially during the month of Elul at Selihot time, and during the *Aseret Yemei Teshuvah*, the Ten Days of Penitence between Rosh ha-Shanah and Yom Kippur, would urge their listeners to repent of their sins and to petition God for pardon, using imagery of extraordinary emotional power. For example, Rabbi Jacob Joseph (1848-1902), formerly Maggid of Vilna and later chief Rabbi of the Russian Jewish community of New York, had immense skill as a preacher of penitential ideals. In the middle of an impassioned discourse, he would pause to recite the *Sh'ma Koleinu* and the *Ashamnu*, thereby raising the audience to a high pitch of religious fervor.

As the group of emissaries from Palestine, known as *Meshullahim* expanded their activities during the 19th century on behalf of charitable institutions in the Holy Land and Europe, a number of them became authentic Maggidim. Another type of Maggid was the so-called "Stadt-Maggid," as in Vilna and in early 19th century American Jewish communities, who would preach in several synagogues in one city; some would travel to other cities with large Jewish settlements. Still another type of Maggid appeared, known as the *Maskil Maggid*, who followed the teachings of the Haskalah or Enlightenment movement in 19th century Jewry. He became known as a "Volksredner" or "People's Orator," utilizing the method of the German "Prediger."

Another type was the so-called "Nationalistic" or "Zionistic" Maggid, who sought to arouse the people on behalf of the redemption of Palestine as the Jewish Homeland. One of the first of these was Zevi Hirsch Dainow (1830-1877) also known as the Slutzker Maggid. When Russian Jewry began to look with suspicion upon him for preaching in terms of the Haskalah, he settled in London, and won the esteem of the immigrant Russian and Polish Jews there. Joseph Zeff won renown as a Maggid, particularly in New York City. In the person of Zevi Hirsch Masliansky (1856-1943), long associated with the Educational Alliance of New York City, the preaching art of the modern Maggid found one of its most eloquent representatives. He was an advocate of the *Hibbat Zion* movement in the 19th century, and later of contemporary Zionism; he advocated the rebuilding of Zion both in Russia and the United States. Several volumes of his sermons have been published.

From time to time modern religious movements in Jewry have produced impressive "People's Orators." The foremost of these was the late Rabbi Stephen S. Wise (1874-1949). While he did not utilize *Meshalim* or Parables, he was adept in the coining of epigrams, in the use of highly dramatic phraseology, and in pungent, fiery utterances which drew great audiences to hear him. His themes covered the outstanding problems of Jewish, American and world life, and because of his far-flung influence among non-Jews as well as Jews, he must be accounted as one of the greatest preachers in the annals of Jewry.

The Hasidic Maggidim

Among the Hasidim, a number of Zaddikim, or Righteous Men (Saints) performed the functions of the Maggid in the communities with which their names became identified. They are better known, therefore, as Maggidim of the particular places where they were active than by their individual names. Among the outstanding Hasidic Maggidim were the following:

"The Great Maggid" or the "Mezeritzer Maggid," namely Dov Ber (c. 1710-1772). Originally he was an austere Maggid, but he became the chief Disciple of the Baal Shem Tov, and after the latter's death, the recognized leader of Hasidim. In addition to being a notable preacher himself, he sent his pupils into many communities of the Ukraine, Lithuania and Galicia, in order to spread the doctrines and practices of Hasidism. The Mezeritzer wrote no books himself, but his teachings were assembled and published by his Disciple, Rabbi Solomon of Lutzk, himself a famous Maggid (d. 1800). The latter was Maggid in Sokal and therefore was called the Sikubler Maggid (*Hasidic Anthology*, Index, p. 569). Isaac, the Maggid of Drohobycz was another pupil of the Baal Shem Tov; so, too, was Yechiel Michel, the Zlotzover Maggid (d. 1781) whose writings have a vital appeal (*Hasidic Anthology*, Index, p. 573). Israel of Koznitz, the Koznitzer Maggid (d. 1814) was a leading Disciple of the Mezeritzer (*Hasidic Anthology*, Index, p. 567). Nahum Tzernobiler (d. 1798) was likewise a Disciple of the Mezeritzer (*H.A.*, Index, p. 572). His son, Mordecai (Motele) Tzernobiler (d. 1837), was a Maggid (*H.A.*, Index, p. 572). Mordecai had two sons: Aaron and Abraham, the latter being known as the "Trisker Maggid" (Abraham Tversky, d. 1887; *H.A.*, Index, p. 572).

Other important Hasidic Maggidim were: the Byalystoker Maggid (*H.A.*, Index, p. 564); Solomon Kluger, the Broder Maggid (*H.A.*, Index, p. 563); the Kelmer Maggid (*H.A.*, Index, p. 566); the Voydislaver Maggid, father of Rabbi Simhah Bunam (*H.A.*, Index, p. 572).

The Dubner Maggid

In the activities of Jacob ben Wolf Kranz of Dubno (c. 1740-1804), the so-called Dubner Maggid, the mastery of the preacher's art came to its greatest efflorescence. The Dubner officiated in Poland, Galicia and finally in Dubno (Volhynia), but he traveled extensively, gaining a deserved reputation as the outstanding preacher of his era. He was called "The Jewish Aesop" by the German Jewish philosopher Moses Mendelssohn, and was highly praised by Elijah, the Gaon of Vilna, a vigorous opponent of the Hasidim. The sermons of the Dubner Maggid were "spiced" with parables and epigrams, drawn chiefly from ordinary daily life. As we shall see, they deal with the relationship between parents and children; between employers and workers, masters and servants, the rich and the poor, the city-dwellers and the village-dwellers, the bridegroom and the bride, and the *Mehuttanim* or contracting parties or relatives by marriage. The Dubner compared human relationships to those between Israel and God, as the Rabbis were accustomed to do their exposition of *Shir ha-Shirim*, the Biblical "Song of Songs." The non-Jewish "Arabian Nights," the fables of Aesop and other non-Jewish story-tellers, as well as secular stories drawn from many sources, furnished him with homiletical suggestions, with which he illustrated a Bible text or a Midrash.

The parables of the Dubner Maggid, included in this work, have been selected, condensed, paraphrased and re-written, on the basis of the material in two volumes in Yiddish by Israel J. Zevin (Tashrak), issued by the Hebrew Publishing Company, New York, 1925, entitled: *Alle Meshalim von Dubner Maggid.* The sources cited are the Dubner's works: *Ohel Yaakov; Kol Yaakov; Kokav Yaakov; Emet le-Yaakov,* and *Sefer ha-Middot.* In each instance an endeavor has been made to sharpen the point of the tale. It was the custom of the Dubner to conclude his *Mashal* with a paragraph or two, beginning with the word: *Nimshal,* in which he drew the lesson from the parable. The word *Nimshal* is translated by Herman A. Glatt in *He Spoke in Parables,* as "Application." In our translation and paraphrasing of the parables, we have not used the word: "Application," but, for the most part have said: "From this we learn, etc."

It must also be mentioned at this point that no translations of the Dubner's *Meshalim* have been taken from Dr. Glatt's volume, inasmuch as the manuscript containing our material from the Dubner's works, was prepared, as we have already indicated, in the late 1930's and early 1940's, many years before *He Spoke in Parables* appeared (namely, 1957). Even when our compilation was reworked and arranged for printing in the late 1950's, no items were drawn from Dr. Glatt's work, though it is heartily recommended for its scholarship and readability. It is without doubt the authoritative volume in English on the illustrious folk-preacher.

It will be noted by consultation with *Alle Meshalim von Dubner Maggid* and other works, that only a small segment of the abundant writings of the Dubner has been presented in our compilation. There are treasures of wisdom yet to be culled from the Dubner's writings, and it is to be hoped that in due time, a writer dedicated to the improvement of contemporary preaching will make available the homiletical riches still untapped and unrevealed.

Rabbinical Scholars and Their Preaching

Among the great company of Rabbinical scholars a number have distinguished themselves as well as preachers of influence. In the Talmudic-Rabbinic period such preachers drew heavily upon the Midrash, and their discourses were in the form of Derashot. Many were Halakic in content, emphasizing the legalistic, dialectic and pilpulistic elements. In their concluding paragraphs the discourse took on a Haggadic quality, with a climax voicing the Messianic hope of Israel. These Halakic discourses were motivated by a desire to impress the audience with the Rabbi's profound knowledge and penetration, and were understood by only the well-informed among the large gatherings assembled to hear them, usually on Shabbat ha-Gadol. This type of preacher appears in every century of Jewish history.

In this Anthology we have selected in particular the works of Israel ben Meir Kahan (Kagan) (1838-1933), known as the "Hafetz Hayyim" after the title of one of his foremost works; Rabbi Moses Sopher (1762-1839), Rabbi Akiba Eger (1761-1837), Rabbi Israel Salanter (Israel Lipkin) (1810-1883) and others. Moses Sopher (Moses ben Samuel Schreiber; see *Jewish Encyclopaedia*, xi, 110-111) was known as the "Hatham Sopher" from his great work of the same name (6 vols., Pressburg, 1855-1864). In addition to being famous as a Talmudic scholar, he was acclaimed as a distinguished ethical lecturer and teacher. While in his early days, he utilized extensively the method of Pilpul, he later discarded this approach, and presented his message in lucid, simplified form, easily comprehensible to his listeners. He was accustomed to vehement denunciation of transgressors, regardless of their influence in the community. He was a fond and sympathetic instructor of his pupils, and was known for his modesty and charity. The selections quoted from his writings reflect these traits. Others, bearing the name Sopher were Abraham ben Ephraim, Hayyim ben Mordecai Ephraim Fischl Sopher (1821-1886), an authority on Responsa, and their kinsfolk.

The selections from the writings of the Hafetz Hayyim have been drawn from the *Mikhtevei ha-Rab Hafetz Hayyim*, published by his son, Aryeh Leib Pupko, at Warsaw in 1937. (A reprint of this work has been issued in New York in 1953). The Hafetz Hayyim was a renowned Talmudist, whose major work *Hafetz Hayyim* ("He Who Desires Life") was published at Vilna in 1873. The Hafetz Hayyim was an authority on Jewish ethics, his works dealing with the laws against slander and tale-bearing. He was an authority, also, on the religious customs and practices of Judaism, his work: *Mishnah Berurah* (Warsaw, 1892-1896), dealing with the writings of legal scholars, is still used by many Rabbis as a Manual of Jewish observances. Though primarily a Talmudic scholar, the Hafetz Hayyim was an eminent teacher and moralist. His works abound with incisive exegetical interpretations, and with homiletical material of the highest order. But, as we note in the selections included in this Anthology, the Hafetz Hayyim, like other Talmudists, was a master of parable, a commentator on life's experiences in ethical terms, and a sage with keen insight into the human heart and spirit. While the Hafetz Hayyim did not seek contemporary popularity as a folk-preacher, nevertheless his writings have a permanent place in the literature of Jewish ethical and spiritual instruction, as well as in Jewish jurisprudence in particular and Jewish literature in general.

The Preaching Style of the Maggidim

The great reputation of the Maggidim was not undeserved for they were eloquent, versatile and psychologically acute in the pursuit of their calling. Just as the Hasidic movement arose in the 18th century because the masses yearned for an interpretation of Judaism closer to their capacity to understand it, so the Maggidim became increasingly effective because of the scholasticism of the learned Rabbis. The people appreciated discourse which would enlighten and edify them in terms within their ken, and they sought religious guidance in the light of the circumstances attending their personal and group problems.

Though the Maggidim were not usually attached to any established synagogue or community, and oftentimes were given only the most meagre payment for their efforts, they built up a large following in the places to which they went to deliver their sermons. In addition to his title as Maggid, the folk-preacher became known as a "Baal Darshan" or "Master of Preaching," a title condensed in popular usage to "Baldarsher." The more skilful Maggidim had the respect of Talmudic scholars, and would be invited by the local Rabbis to display their homiletical art in the synagogues. Most of the Maggidim, however, were only scantily remunerated, sometimes by money donated by members of the audience, or by gifts collected after the lecture. Having no fixed position, they led an uncertain existence as itinerants, and their livelihood was necessarily precarious. A few exceptions can be noted, however, among them the beloved Zevi Hirsch Masliansky at the Educational Alliance in New York City, whose discourses at Zionist conventions won him vast appreciation.

The very nature of the Maggid's profession as an itinerant without the duties of pastoral ministration or synagogue and community leadership enabled him to concentrate upon the task of stirring and delighting his listeners. Thus he could perfect his preaching technique in a manner pleasing to his audiences. It must not be thought, however, that the Maggid was predominantly an entertainer. The representative Maggidim would seize upon the opportunity to reprove and admonish their hearers, and sometimes, in the role of the "Maggid Mochiah" or "Musar Sager," a folk-orator would rouse his hearers to open sobs and tears. The Maggid would draw upon the Aggada, or the Oral Law, and upon the plentiful Midrash through which he would find new meanings, in addition to the literal one, in the Scriptures. He would make adroit use of popular sayings current at the time; he would draw upon allegorical allusions, wise words of comfort to the stricken, and upon the enduring hope of Jewry for a better future. Though the Maggid couched his instruction in terms easily understood by the *Amei ha-Aretz*, the commoners and plebeians in society, nevertheless, he addressed his ethical injunctions towards the rich and the powerful. The Hasidic Maggidim in particular sought to moderate the arrogance of the well-placed; in fact the typical Hasidic emphasis upon *Shiflut Ruach* of "lowliness of spirit" was directed at the magnates and the intellectually-proud scholars of the community.

The language of the Maggid was pithy, pungent and epigrammatic, even though at time the discourses were of long duration. The words the Maggid chose were well-known, avoiding the formal, pedantic phrases of the Talmudist's vocabulary. While the Maggidim rarely wrote down their utterances for posterity, a number of chroniclers arose who preserved their discourses from hearsay, and in this way transmitted them in a fashion similar to that of the Disciples of the Zaddikim. (See my Introduction to the *Hasidic Anthology*). The Maggid's images, similes and metaphors were usually taken from the personal experience of his hearers, so that he could build a forensic bridge between them and himself; thus they could be instructed on the basis of the conditions they shared with others of their economic class as well as those members of the community with whom they had less frequent contacts. The *Baal Agalah* or teamster and his horse, cart or sleigh appears frequently in the Maggid's illustrations. Men of commerce also received the preacher's attention, and he built many a lesson upon the give-and-take of business and mercantile life. The Hafetz Hayyim drew ethical lessons from experiences with censors and military men. The King, the Prince, their courtiers and subjects are often cited, with appropriate lessons. Match-making, the discussions regarding the dowry, the arrangements for the wedding, the plans for the couple's future, and their experiences in married life—all were subject matter for the Maggid. The beggar, the tavern-keeper, the store-keeper, the tax-assessor, and the civic official were personalities who entered into the Maggid's sermons. He had an uncanny insight into the tribulations of those in front of him; he possessed extraordinary intuition and imagination, which prompted him to the ingenious use of topics, illustrations and phraseology. This clairvoyance enabled the competent Maggid to reach the inmost soul of his patrons.

In the *Nimshal,* or "application," namely, an implementing of the lessons learned from a parable, the Maggid sought, as far as possible, to relate his material to a situation growing out of the Torah and Israel's history. Frequently the question arises whether the parable enters as an illustration in immediate human terms, of a Bible text or narrative, or whether the parable was first hewed out by the Maggid, and then placed in its appropriate Biblical setting. The Dubner in his *Mishlei Yaakov (The Parables of Jacob)* furnishes parables attached to or growing out of verses in the Sedrahs or Weekly Portions of the Pentateuch. Undoubtedly these were included in his discourse after the recitation of Prayers in the synagogue or in the *Beit ha-Midrash,* on Sabbath afternoons, or on a suitable week-day evening, when he could address a very large audience. The Dubner, however, declares that oftentimes he would make note of a *Mashal,* and retain it in his memory until he could use it aright. There is an amusing story of a little boy's marksmanship; he shoots the arrows and then draws the target around them. The intrinsically Jewish nature of the fables and tales of the Dubner, the Mezeritzer, the Koznitzer and other preachers in various walks of Jewish life, is to be found in their "application" to the Biblical texts and narratives regarding personalities and events. Moses Mendelssohn must have had this in mind when he praised the Dubner not merely as a superb raconteur in the mood of Aesop, but also as an exponent of pristine Jewish tradition through the medium of his quaint anecdotes and imaginative lore.

The *Mashal,* as we have seen, was not confined to the professional Maggidim who journeyed from town to town. Settled and established Rabbis in their own pulpits made adroit use of the *Mashal,* finding it a worthwhile instrument of instruction, as they expounded the Rabbinic codes. Rabbi Sopher, the Hafetz Hayyim and others employed the parable for its own sake, and not in imitation of the Maggidim.

It was natural that humor should be found in the utterances of the Maggidim, who sought to give a witty turn to their illustrations and interpretations. These witticisms were oftentimes very subtle, and were employed perceptively and drolly. The Maggidim enjoyed punning; they did not turn aside from Gematria and Notarikon, namely, a play upon numbers and letters. The understanding of human foibles was admirable, as in the case of the Rabbi who reminded his Disciple that he is truly vain, inasmuch as he blushes when praises of him are spoken in his hearing. The satires of human frailties were offered in a kindly and sympathetic spirit. If they could drive home a point which otherwise seemed intricate, by means of a delicate and amusing epigram or word-picture, they did not hesitate to do so. As for Bible exegesis among the Maggidim, both non-Hasidic and Hasidic, they made no effort to indulge in the technicalities of scholarship. The Bible was for them a volume of ethical and spiritual inspiration; its contradictions and omissions in the Hebrew text were of no concern to them. Therefore the preachers of all derivations showed very few variations in their approach to Bible hermeneutics. Their analogies, similes and metaphors were almost identical in character. Again it must be said that the key to an appreciation of the distinction between Hasidic and non-Hasidic preaching lies in the fact that the general Maggidim did not look to the Zaddikim or Hasidic masters for guidance; nor did they underscore the special set of spiritual and ethical values which give to Hasidism its individuality. The Maggidim sought to utilize the totality of Jewish law, lore and literature, and while they appealed to the commoners and the populace, they encouraged the development of learning among the masses. The Hasidim were freer, more spontaneous and ebullient than the non-Hasidic Rabbis and laity. In time they evolved a cult and a way of life arousing the antagonism of the erudite Mitnagedim or Opponents. The ethical stress, however, the *Musar,* remained the same in all Jewish groups; the lessons which emerged were universal in scope: namely, inwardness in worship, sincerity in faith, humility of heart, generosity in charitable, communal and personal affairs, forgiveness for the sinner, whole-heartedness in the attainment of the good life—in short, all the basic excellencies present in the complete armory of Jewish moral teachings from the earliest times to the present. The Zaddikim, to be sure, did not urge upon their adherents the strict and compelling discipline of the Law; they condemned asceticism and rigorous abstinence from the amenities of living; they were willing to accept as genuinely pious those persons unlettered in Jewish scholarship but whose direct and earnest piety opened up a clear avenue of communication with the Sovereign of the Universe.

This Anthology is presented to readers in the hope that it may augment the treasuries of new homiletical material. Every Rabbi today can take a leaf from his predecessors among the Maggidim of all classifications; he can strive to emulate their ability to furnish sound spiritual nourishment in a form which the masses can accept and digest. Modern preachers must do as the Maggidim did, namely, to seek to reach the heart of the multitudes, not by grandiloquence or high-flown oratory, but by the intelligently-chosen and skilfully introduced epigrams, fables, tales, exegetical interpretations, parables, and other weapons in the equipment of the folk-preachers. Vivid utterance is always welcome, without any sacrifice of the intellectual, and it is believed that the method, style and art of the Maggid furnish admirable patterns for contemporary men of the pulpit and rostrum. We must never lose sight of the Rabbinic dictum: *Mik-kol melameday hiskalti:* "from all my teachers, I have learned."

I take this opportunity to express again my gratitude for collaboration in years past on the part of the late Samuel Spitz, who aided in gathering the ore from which the polished jewels of Hasidic and Maggidic wisdom have been fashioned. I wish also to express my appreciation for assistance in technical matters to Mrs. Joseph Lerner, Miss Judy Wackstein and others. I am deeply appreciative of the cooperation given me by members of the staff of the American

Book-Stratford Press, including Mr. Bernard Kass, Mr. Sidney Fein-
berg, Mr. Marvin Dori and others in the completion of this volume
in printed form.[3]

[3] Much of the information for this Introduction has been selected from the
Jewish Encyclopaedia, the *Universal Jewish Encyclopedia,* the *Standard Jewish
Encyclopedia* and other general volumes.   No pretense has been made that
this Introduction is anything more than a statement in general terms regarding
the subject; those interested in pursuing the theme further may consult the
extensive bibliographies available.   Notation is made at the appropriate point
of those specific volumes which have been used as references.

Louis I. Newman

November, 1961
New York City

1. ABUSE

1. Too Easy a Way

Once the Medzibozer issued a declaration to the effect that any Rabbi who abused the Berditschever Rabbi in a sermon would surely receive a goodly portion in the World-to-Come. Rabbi Joseph Landau of Jassy chanced to be visiting the Medzibozer at the time, and loudly announced unwillingness to abuse the Berditschever. Rabbi Baruch, the Medzibozer, thereupon inquired: "Do you doubt the validity of my promise?" "Not at all," responded Rabbi Joseph. "But I do not care to acquire the *Olam-ha-Bah* in so easy a fashion. I wish to work for it." The Medzibozer was delighted with this clever answer.

M. B., p. 25.

2. Belittling the Saint

The Medzibozer often spoke derisively of the manner in which the Berditschever prayed. When the latter died, the Medzibozer explained himself as follows: "By belittling the Berditschever I really aided him and helped to prolong his life. When the Lord discovers that everyone agrees that a certain person is perfect and is beyond improvement, the Lord dispatches His Angel of Death to transport him to Heaven. But if one man remains unconvinced regarding another's perfection, the latter is permitted to continue in life and to strive for improvement."

M. B., p. 25.

3. Suffering and Insult

When the Hafetz Hayyim lay ill in bed, he said to a relative: "A man's sins are washed away by means of two things: one is suffering, and the other is subjection to abuse and insult. Inasmuch as I have never been insulted, I am forced to suffer often from illness."

Pupko, p. 19.

4. No Comment

Rabbi Isaac of Ziditchov related that his grandfather, the Safrin scholar, never made a comment regarding another person, either in

1

favorable or derogatory terms. Said Rabbi Isaac: "I find myself able
to refrain from speaking ill of another person. But never to speak
favorably of anyone—that I cannot do."

Braver, p. 8.

5. Without Abuse

Said Rabbi Abraham Sopher: "He who answers abuse with abuse
demonstrates that he has deserved the initial abuse. A good man
does not permit unclean words to cross his lips. It is for you to understand, also, that the man who has abused you has disclosed in
himself the very thing of which he is guilty; he has revealed his own
disgrace."

Sopher, p. 32.

6. Excusing Their Offenses

The Hafetz Hayyim said to his son: "Always strive to leave behind you an excellent name. I caution particularly against abusing
students of the Torah, inasmuch as this is a profanation of God's
Name." His son responded: "But, father, this applies only to illustrious scholars!" The Rabbi answered: "Usually the common folk
will not accept you as a great man to be emulated. But when they
offend and are reproved, they recall your slightest misdeed and say:
'Why blame me? Did not this eminent scholar, the greatest in our
generation, do exactly the same thing as I have done?'"

Pupko, p. 58.

7. Cursing the Subtle

The Hafetz Hayyim: "The man who deems himself to be exceedingly wise is frequently the target for fierce malediction. The Bible
describes the serpent as 'very subtle,' but also as 'cursed above all
others.'"

Pupko, p. 75.

8. A Mistake in Identity

The Hafetz Hayyim came to a certain town on behalf of his
books. A young man met him in the synagogue and inquired
whence he came. The Rabbi replied: "I reside in Radin." "Then
you must know the illustrious Hafetz Hayyim," continued the young
man. "Yes, I know him," replied the Rabbi, "but he is like other
men." The youth commenced to abuse the visitor for belittling the
Hafetz Hayyim. Later when the youth was made aware of the

identity of the visitor, he contritely asked his pardon. The Rabbi replied: "Come now, young man, should I pardon you for paying honor to my fame?"

Pupko, p. 75.

9. *Measure for Measure*

Said the Hafetz Hayyim: "The Lord deals with us in conformance with the rule: measure for measure. If you have accused no one and have spoken evil of no one, God will not permit the Prosecuting Angel to speak evil against you at the Seat of Judgment."

Pupko, ii, 60.

2. ACCOUNTS

1. *Settling Our Accounts*

Said the Hafetz Hayyim: "A man of integrity makes a periodic visit to his creditors in order to settle his accounts. Likewise, a man should make a periodic investigation of his spiritual accounts, and make payment for his defects through repentance and good deeds."

Pupko, p. 119.

2. *Our House and Garment*

Said the Hafetz Hayyim: "Do not forget, oh man, that the day will come when you must take off your garment of flesh and appear at the Heavenly Tribunal. You will be asked: 'Have you brought the house which you have built?' This refers not to a house of brick and mortar, but an edifice of Torah. For he who labors in Torah erects a house acceptable in the After-Life. You will also be asked: 'Where is your garment?' This refers not to a garment of cloth, but one of Mitzvot. And the less the Mitzvot have been performed correctly, the more they will constitute a garment filled with holes."

Pupko, ii, 5.

3. *Rendering an Account*

Two Rabbis came to the home of the Hafetz Hayyim late at night. They were directed to his room in the garret. At the door they overheard the Rabbi rendering an account of the manner in which he had spent each waking hour. As he spoke, it became clear that he had forgotten what he had done during a certain hour, despite his effort to recollect. Later the Rabbi described to the Lord the immense correspondence he was conducting, and He implored the Almighty to vouchsafe His mercies to those who were in suffering. So impressed were the listening visitors that they dared not enter the Rabbi's room, and postponed the matter which had brought them until the next day.

Pupko, p. 82.

4. *Achieving a Balance*

The Hafetz Hayyim thus commented upon the verse in Isaiah 1:18 which reads: "Come now and let us reason together, saith the Lord; though your sins be as scarlet, they shall be as white as snow; though they be red like crimson, they shall be as wool." "The meaning of these words may be illustrated by the story of a storekeeper to whom a leading customer was greatly in debt. The customer stopped coming to the storekeeper, and one day, when the merchant saw him passing by, he called to him and said: 'Why do you treat me as an enemy? Come in, and let us arrange matters, so that you may settle your debts by small payments from time to time. In the meantime, you can buy from me what you need. If you and others avoid me, it will bring about my bankruptcy.' This is what the Lord desires to say. He will provide the means whereby we can wipe away our sins, even as one wipes away snow. He will arrange a balance for our transgressions by accepting good deeds in their place."

Pupko, p. 80.

3. ADORNMENT

1. *Unwanted Adornment*

The Hafetz Hayyim insisted on having his home simply furnished. He found adornments highly distasteful, saying: "The money spent on ornamentation can be far better used for the purchase of worthy books."

Pupko, p. 14.

4. ADVANCEMENT

1. *Advancement in "This Life"*

Said the Hafetz Hayyim: "In some respects 'This World' is better than the 'World-to-Come.' The matter may be compared to the wish of a king to reward two favorites who had pleased him. To one he donated a handsome estate whereby he received a comfortable income. To the other he awarded an appointment as governor of a province with the right to retain a share of the taxes collected from its inhabitants. It was unanimously conceded that the second favorite had received a higher reward. If he as governor took steps to develop the resources of his province so that it would enhance its wealth, his own return would be correspondingly larger. From this we learn that while there is no provision in the 'After-Life' for increased reward, in 'This Life' advancement is always possible."

Pupko, ii, 56.

5. ADVERSITY

1. Prayer in Adversity

Said the Bratzlaver: "The Psalmist advises us how to pray amid the torment of pain and anxiety. He says: 'To Thee will I bring a thank-offering and then I shall call upon the name of the Lord.' (Psalm 116:17). In other words, it behooves us to thank the Lord for the benefits which we have previously received. After we have done this we will discover that we are able to pray for relief from our present tribulations."

H. H. N., p. 5a.

6. ADVICE

1. Enjoying Good Advice

Said the Leover: "Offer no advice which your own experience has not proved to be beneficial. If the advice is good, you should be the first to enjoy the benefits it confers."

Guttman, p. 25.

7. AFTER-LIFE

1. Only During Life

Said the Hafetz Hayyim: "The verse in Numbers 5:10: 'And every man's hallowed things shall be his' is a suggestion that only hallowed things are in truth a man's property. These are the things he takes with him for his existence in the 'After-Life,' whereas all other possessions really do not belong to him, inasmuch as he owns them only during his life on earth."

Pupko, p. 47.

8. THE AGED

1. Counsel from the Aged

The Lelever Rabbi once walked in a forest which led to Lizensk.
An old man met him and entered into conversation. Before he left
the old man said to the Rabbi: "My son, remember two things: the
first is this: in order to tie two logs firmly together, it is wise to cut
away the 'upper part' of the logs; the second is this: rather than to
see into another man's face, take care that thine own face be not
seen by the other person." The Lelever often repeated this counsel,
and added: "In making friends the old man's words aided me immensely." *

Selected.

* By "upper part" the old man intended to advise against thinking oneself
superior to another person. The word: "see" in the second sentence of counsel
is meant to signify: "searching out faults in the other person."

9. ALTRUISM

1. Finding Time to Aid

Said the Tzanzer: "We read in Genesis 32:25: 'And there wres-
tled a man with Jacob until the breaking of the day.' Rashi makes
the comment: 'It was the Protecting Angel of Esau.' We also read
in Genesis 37:15: 'And a certain man found Joseph . . . wandering
in the field.' On this text Rashi makes the comment: 'It was the
Angel Gabriel.' What led Rashi, we may ask, to make these two
differing comments? The answer doubtless is this: the first angel
found time to wrestle with Jacob the entire night, but when he
was asked to bless his adversary, he pleaded lack of time. Only the
Protecting-Angel of Esau would act in this fashion. The second
angel, however, found the time needed to aid the wandering youth,
Joseph. This could only have been the Angel Gabriel."

Tzanzer Hasidut, p. 244.

10. ANGELS

1. The Three Angels

Rabbi Baruch of Medziboz said: "The three angels who came to
Abraham were symbols of the Three Patriarchs. How is this explained? The symbol of Abraham was kindness, and one of the
angels possessed a nature of kindness. Isaac symbolized strength in

his person, and this was the nature of the second angel. Jacob symbolized Holy Splendor, and this was the nature of the third angel."

M. B., p. 11.

2. *The Accusing Angel*

Said the Hafetz Hayyim: "The sins committed under cover create the Angels of Punishment. These Angels do not appear openly to initiate the accusation against the sinner. But the transgression of public thievery does create an Accusing Angel who comes to the fore with open accusations, to be followed by other Accusers at the Heavenly Tribunal."

Pupko, ii, 36.

11. ANGER

1. *No Loss Through Delay*

The Rozdoler Rabbi said: "When I feel angry against a person, I delay the expression of my anger. I say to myself: 'What will I lose if I postpone my anger?'"

Walden, p. 94.

2. *Comprehending Ears*

A distinguished scholar came to the Sabbath table of Rabbi Isaac of Ziditchov, and was invited by the Zaddik to sit next to him. Later the Rabbi's son told him that his chief benefactor and Disciple was chagrined to have been asked to yield his seat to the scholar. Rabbi Isaac replied: "I am sure he will not remain angry. It was my intention to hold a discussion on a profound subject of Torah; I needed ears that would hear. My good friend will appreciate the fact that the discussion would have been too intricate to interest him, and he will forgive me."

Braver, p. 46.

3. *The Common Level*

Said the Leover: "When Moses beheld the Golden Calf, he became enraged and broke the Two Tablets into fragments. But the Talmud teaches us that he who smashes something in the moment of his wrath is comparable to an idolater. Why, then, did Moses commit such an act? The answer is as follows: Moses wished to uplift the people, and a Zaddik cannot give spiritual aid, if he feels himself to be high above the sinners. He must descend to their moral level if he is to prove helpful."

Guttman, p. 26.

12. ANIMALS

1. Animal and Man

Said the Bratzlaver: "Both a man and an animal receive the necessaries for their existence. The difference, however, lies in this: that a man is able to ask God to meet his needs. Be, therefore a man! Ask your God for everything you need!"

H. H. N., p. 4b.

2. A Lawsuit with a Horse?

Once the Lelever paid a visit to the Lubliner on Rosh ha-Shanah. When the time came for the blowing of the Shofar, the Lelever was missing. The Lubliner thereupon ordered a delay, and sent out messengers to search for his guest. He was found in a stable feeding a horse. The Lelever explained: "His owner had gone early to the synagogue and neglected to feed the poor beast."

On another occasion, the Lelever saw a teamster whipping his horse mercilessly. He approached him and said: "After your demise, the horse will place your soul on trial before the Heavenly Tribunal. Do you consider it a suitable thing that you should be compelled to engage in a lawsuit with a horse?"

H. Hak., p. 19.

3. The Melamed and the Goat

The Gaon of Vilna once welcomed the Dubner Maggid, and as he was descending from his wagon, asked him: "Have you brought any fresh parables?"

The Maggid replied: "Here is one: a Melamed purchased a she-goat, and brought her to his home, leaving at once for the synagogue. His wife was delighted at the prospect of having milk, cream, butter and cheese. Immediately she took a pail and commenced to milk the goat. Not a drop of milk came forth. When the Melamed returned, his wife exclaimed: 'What kind of a goat have you brought? She gives no milk.' The husband answered: 'You must remember that the goat is tired and hungry. Feed her and let her rest. You will see that she will give you milk.' In the same way, my friend, permit me to rest; give me some refreshment, and then I will give you of my milk."

Dubner, i, 30-31.

13. ANXIETY

1. Anxious to Reward

Said the Hafetz Hayyim: "A man is not aggrieved if his work-man does not appear to receive his payment. But God is always eager to give rewards to those who labor in His behalf.

Pupko, p. 103.

14. ASCETISM

1. Austerity for Approval

"Asceticism and austerity," said Rabbi Baruch of Medziboz, "are essential for a spirit that is haughty and worldly by nature. A spirit inclined by nature to matters spiritual should have nothing to do with asceticism. Too often asceticism is practiced in order to gain the approval of the populace, not to please our Maker on high. Asceticism tends to implant pride and hypocrisy unless we are on guard."

M. B., p. 14.

15. ASPIRATION

1. Rising or Descending

Said the Hafetz Hayyim: "Jacob dreamed of a ladder standing on the ground. I interpret this as follows: Jacob dreamed of man's estate on earth. Man never stands still. He either ascends, or he descends."

Pupko, p. 94.

2. Holy Ground

Said the Hafetz Hayyim: "We read in Exodus 3:5: 'Put off thy shoes from off thy feet, for the place whereon thou standest is holy ground.' Every man needs to attain a higher position in the realm of goodness. Do not say: 'I can uplift myself only under different circumstances.' No, the place whereon thou standest is holy ground, namely available for moral uplift. It is necessary only to put off thy uncleanness, and to strive to ascend to holier ground."

Pupko, p. 94.

3. A Gradual Ascent

Said the Hafetz Hayyim: "We have learned this instruction: when a man is standing in a land outside of Palestine, let him turn his face during the Amidah towards Palestine. If he is in Palestine, let him turn towards Jerusalem. If he is in Jerusalem, let him face towards the Temple site. Why are we not enjoined always to turn towards the Temple site? The answer is: we must learn that a person may ascend only one step at a time in the ascent towards holiness."

Pupko, p. 95.

4. Spiritual Wealth

Said the Leover: "Man's wants are many because his understanding is narrow. Man feels that he should aspire to something. He aspires wrongly, if he seeks to achieve riches and honors, rather than wealth of the spirit."

Guttman, p. 26.

5. A Diplomatic Answer

An adherent of the Lizensker Zaddik left him and became a follower of the Lubliner Rabbi. The Lizensker soon after was passing through the town where his former Hasid resided, and asked him the reason for his departure. The clever Hasid responded: "You were too lofty of mind, Rabbi, for my understanding. It seemed to me wise first to climb up on the shoulders of your Disciple, and from this point, to make the attempt to reach your heights."

Walden, p. 28.

6. The Central Point

Said the Hafetz Hayyim: "It behooves you to think of the Lord having His residence at a central point. If you serve Him well in your own way, you will be certain to reach Him. And others, too, will reach Him, each according to the way each one chooses."

Pupko, ii, 22.

7. "Still Higher"

Aryeh ben Pinhas took his little granddaughter into the synagogue. She walked down its center aisle, her hand in his. Together they walked up the steps to the Bimah, and then took their place in front of the Aron ha-Kodesh. They walked up the steps before the Ark of the Covenant, and the grandfather opened the doors of the Aron ha-Kodesh, to show the child the Sifrei Torah, clad in their velvet mantles. The little granddaughter looked at them raptly, and then exclaimed: "I want to go still higher."

The grandfather bent down and kissed her, and said: "May you always wish to go higher in life!"

Selected.

16. ASSURANCE

1. Make Sure of Your Possession

Said the Hafetz Hayyim: "He who carries with him on his person a valuable object, is accustomed to touch it frequently to make sure he still has it. Do the same with respect to your faith and your reverence for Heaven."

Pupko, ii, 37.

17. ATHEISM

1. A Wealthy Atheist

A Hasid overheard the lamentation of the wife of Rabbi Baruch of Medziboz because of the heavy debt the family had incurred. The Hasid collected from well-to-do Hasidim the amount required to erase the indebtedness. The Rabbi gave him his blessing and said: "May the Lord grant you ten thousand rubles for your labors in my behalf. If the Lord asks me whether He can take away so large a sum from another person, without subjecting Himself to a complaint against His dispensation of justice, I shall give Him this counsel: 'take the money from a wealthy atheist, O Lord. Surely one who does not believe in Thine existence cannot complain against Thee.' "

M. B., p. 20.

2. Gradations of Piety

Moses ben Maimon wrote in his Code that a Jew does not deny his Creator by one step only. First he derides the God-fearing man; then he speaks evil of the learned man, of the great man, of those who are departed, of the Talmudic Sages and of the Prophets, until he concludes by becoming an atheist. "I believe," said Rabbi Moses Sopher, "that the very steps enumerated by Moses ben Maimon are needed, in reverse order, to attain the power to cleave unto the Lord. First he should associate with God-fearing men, then with learned men, and so forth, until his mind becomes close to the ideals of holiness and he feels himself in intimate communion with God."

Sopher, p. 30.

3. No Question; No Solution

Said the Hafetz Hayyim: "The believer refuses to question or doubt; the unbeliever refuses to listen to a proferred solution." *

Pupko, ii, 42.

* Another version is: "For the believer there is no question; for the unbeliever, there is no solution."

18. ATONEMENT

1. The Red Heifer

Said the Vorker: "According to tradition, Rabbi Moses ha-Darshan in the tenth century explained the Red Heifer as an atonement for the sin of the Golden Calf. The question arises: if we know a good reason, why is the commandment of the Red Heifer regarded as an unreasonable statute? The answer is as follows: the Golden Calf indicated a lack of faith where a reason was not forthcoming. Because the Israelites lacked faith and could not tell by reasoning why Moses had delayed to return from Mount Sinai in good time, they fashioned the idol. Now, however, the Red Heifer is prepared despite the dictates of reason, but as an act of our faith in the value of God's ordinances. Therefore the Mitzvah which depends upon faith alone atones for the sin due to a lack of faith."

Zammlung, p. 27.

19. ATTRIBUTES

1. "Zemah" and Its Initials

The Leipniker Rabbi said: "In the Prophet Zechariah 3:8 we read: 'I will bring forth My servant Zemah.' Zechariah thus alludes to the words of the Prophet Hosea 2:21: 'Yea, I will betroth thee unto Me in righteousness, justice and loving-kindness.' The initial letters of these three attributes, *Zedek, Mishpat* and *Hesed*, are Z M H, forming the word *Zemah*."

Eibeshitz, p. 72.

20. AUDACITY

1. Cobwebs from the Walls

Said the Bratzlaver: "Some people hesitate to speak to the Lord in an intimate manner. They lack the audacity that accompanies holiness. Let them recollect, however, that they must constantly battle a mighty enemy, their Evil Impulse. Should then an insignificant thing restrain them? It is like a general who orders an attack on a fort only to retreat because some cobwebs hang down from the walls."

H. H. N., p. 21a.

21. BAR MITZVAH

1. The Soul of a Mystic

When Rabbi Leib Saras as a boy of thirteen became Bar Mitzvah, he was taken by his father to the Mezeritzer Maggid to receive the Zaddik's blessing. The Maggid blessed him, saying: "I have given thee this day a blessing of supreme value." At the time the lad did not comprehend the Maggid's meaning, but later he came to understand that he had been made the recipient of an "additional soul" (*Neshamah Yeteirah*), the soul of a mystic.

G. A., p. 6.

22. BENEFITS

1. "Why Do It?"

Said the Hafetz Hayyim: "When we are about to perform a certain deed, or to say something, we should ask ourselves: 'Will our soul benefit by my deed or my words?' If so, then act or speak. You can also add the question: 'Will my body profit in health by my deed or word?' If so, do the deed, or speak the word. But if what you wish to do or say is no benefit to either your body or your soul, why do or say it?"

Pupko, ii, 7.

23. BLESSINGS

1. An Acceptable Hour

A Hasid petitioned the Tzortkover to grant him his blessing so that a son might be born unto his wife. After the Rabbi had pronounced the blessing, the Hasid informed him that he had been blessed several times by the Tzortkover, but no child had as yet been born unto him. The Rabbi commented: "May the Lord assist you to gain the merit whereby my blessing may come to you in an hour acceptable to Him!"

Margulies, p. 23.

2. The Truly Blessed

The Mirapoler Rabbi said: "We read in Genesis 24:1: 'And the Lord had blessed Abraham in all things.' The Midrash explains that God had endowed Abraham with the power to rule his own desires. Thereby we learn that the person who must continually combat his desires cannot be called 'blessed'. To be 'blessed' a man must be stable in his behavior, without being under the necessity of waging a perpetual struggle against his impulses."

Kaufman, p. 27.

3. A Mere Blessing is Inadequate

A Jew asked the Hafetz Hayyim to offer a blessing in his behalf so that his children might become God-fearing men and women. The Rabbi replied: "In these days we cannot accomplish this goal merely by virtue of a blessing. It requires the sacrifice of your very life, almost equivalent to martyrdom."

Pupko, ii, 41.

4. The Value of the Blessing

The Berditschever once made a long journey on foot and entered a town tired and hungry. He went to the residence of the local Rav and found him absorbed in a complicated passage in the comments of the *Tosafot* on a Talmudic portion. The Rav invited the aid of his guest in unravelling the passage. The Berditschever remarked: "It is impossible for me to peruse this volume while I am weary and famished." Food was set before him, but he declined to partake of it. "It is Jewish law that everything belongs to the Lord until a man recited a blessing over it. Since you, my host, have recited no blessing over the food, it is not yours to give to me." The Rav begged the Berditschever's pardon and recited the blessing and partook of a small amount of it. Thereupon the Rabbi ate sufficient to appease his hunger. Following the meal he offered a prayer that the passage be made clear to him, and, having perceived its meaning, he explained it to the Rav.

Szlamovitz, p. 35.

5. The Householder's Blessing

The second son of Rabbi Isaac of Ziditchov was not a Rebbe. Some Hasidim, however, regarded him as a holy man and offered him gifts frequently. He said: "I am a common householder and can command no special favors in Heaven. But our Sages offer the good counsel that whatever your householder (or host) invites you to do, you must accede to his request. May I, therefore, not request that the Lord do as I, the householder, strive to do, namely, pronounce a blessing upon those who present gifts to me?"

Braver, p. 109.

24. BOOKS

1. The Eye, the Ear and the Book

Said the Mezeritzer: "In the period of the First Temple, we had the 'Seeing Eye' of the Prophets. In the period of the Second Temple, we had the 'Hearing Ear' of the Divine Echo (*Bat Kol*). Now, in Exile, we resort to the third item mentioned by Rabbi in *Ethics of the Fathers* (2:1): 'And all thy deeds are written in a book.' By consulting our Holy Books we are able to give counsel."

BDH., p. 72.

2. The Danger of Printing

Rabbi Moses Sopher declined to permit the printing of his Responsa during his lifetime. He said: "I am acquainted with a Rabbi who during his early years printed his immature opinions; when he grew older, he had greater knowledge, but he was unable to recall the printed word. The great Alfassi ordered erasures and corrections in all copies of his writings, but he could not have done so if, in his generation, printing had already been invented."

Sopher, p. 34.

3. Seven Years in Paradise

Rabbi Phineas of Frankfort-on-the-Main was famous for his charities. Herr Brodelheim, a non-Jewish judge, invited the Rabbi's assistance for a priest who required an operation. The Rabbi donated a handsome sum. When Rabbi Phineas published his renowned work: *The Haflaah,* the Neskizher Rabbi exclaimed: "For seven years the author's mind has dwelt in Paradise and the fruit thereof is the book which he has written."

Walden, Y. A., p. 44.

4. The Book of God

Said the Hafetz Hayyim: "The life of a man and his conduct are indeed of utmost value. For this reason his deeds are recorded in the Book of God, where insignificant things are given no place in the Celestial Records."

Pupko, p. 99.

5. A Poorly Printed Talmud

In the presence of the Hafetz Hayyim some persons spoke critically of the Hasidim, and condemned their ideas as foolish and ignorant. The Rabbi reproved them, saying: "A man came to Rabbi Hayyim, Head of the famous Volozhyn Yeshivah, and informed him that he had gone through the Talmud several times. Rabbi Hayyim arose and gave him the tokens of great esteem. When he had left, however, some of the Rabbi's learned students declared: 'He knows the words, but comprehends little of their meaning.' Rabbi Hayyim answered: 'Even so, he has studied the Talmud repeatedly. He is a person of saintliness, even though his understanding of it is a little obscure. Do we not regard a poorly printed set of Talmud volumes to be as holy as a well-printed set? The Hasidim, too, despite their obscure knowledge of Judaism, preserve the Torah in holiness, rear their children to reverence God and display other virtues which should prompt us to overlook their defects.'"

Pupko, p. 18.

6. Seizing the Holy Books

Said the Hafetz Hayyim: "The Communists were permitted by Heaven to seize the Holy Books from their Jewish owners, because these Jews held them in light esteem."

Pupko, ii, 65.

25. BUILDING

1. Mansions and Men

There is a similarity between the sayings of the Bratzlaver and the Leover. Said the Bratzlaver: "Give me bricks and mortar, and I will build therewith wonderful mansions." Said the Leover: "Give me men endowed with suitable traits and habits, and I will build therewith the ideal Hasidim."

Guttman, p. 18.

26. BUSINESS

1. Direct Advice

A Hasid came to Rabbi Hirsch of Ziditchov asking advice on a "speculation" he might make in order to find a solution for his business difficulties. The Rabbi replied: "'Speculation' is an alien word, unsuited to an Israelite. I can give you direct advice, rather than the involved and intricate counsel you have sought."

Braver, p. 69.

27. CALMNESS

1. The Rabbi's Sagacity

A young man who visited Rabbi Abish put down his purse, and despite every effort, could not recall the place where he had left it.

He told the Rabbi of his plight with great distress of spirit. The Rabbi calmed him, and said: "I give you my assurance that you will find your purse. First you must recite your prayers." The young man did so, and while saying his prayers, he recollected where he had left the purse. During an interlude in the Services he recovered it. After the Services he came to the Rabbi's Study to inform him, and Rabbi Abish commented: "Please note that I sought to calm you by my advice to engage in prayer, and the calmness which you achieved aided your memory so that you could regain what you had lost."

Michelson, p. 14.

28. CENSORSHIP

1. *A Censor Without a Home*

The Hafetz Hayyim said to the Warsaw Censor of Hebrew books: "I cannot help but pity you. I am convinced that your openly impious deeds will not win for you the admittance of your soul to a place of eternal rest. I once knew a buyer who was accustomed to visit Lodz for several months each year, in order to fulfil the commissions entrusted to him by the merchants of his native town. I met him, later, in a melancholy frame of mind. He remarked to me: 'My wife has died, and I have no home to which I may return.' In my eyes, you have also no place to go when you have taken your departure." The anti-religious Censor died soon after as the result of an accident, and it seemed to the Hafetz Hayyim and his followers that he had received his punishment in this life.

Pupko, ii, 18.

29. CHARACTER

1. *At the Boundary Line*

The Koretzer was informed that the Jews residing at the boundary line between two countries were guilty of smuggling and other offenses. Their conduct was by all means worse than the behavior of Jews residing in other places. The Rabbi remarked: "Every people has its own patron-angels, one good and the other evil. The Jews dwelling at the boundary line are under the influence of two such angels, since they are near two countries. Hence they are either better or worse than other Jews."

Migdal David, p. 83.

2. The Missing "Ach"

A householder sent back a Yeshivah Bachur to the Rabbi, with a note that the youth lacked the "Ach" in the word "Bachur". The Rabbi replied: "It is true that without 'Ach', the word remains 'Bur' or 'boor'. But you profess to be a supporter, a 'Machazik'. Please note that without the 'Ach' in your title, the word becomes 'Mazik' or 'Evil Spirit.'"

Sopher, p. 62.

3. Suitable Receptacles

The Tzortkover said: "O Lord! We are told that Rabbi Schmelke received excellent wine in excellent receptacles when he was inducted as Rabbi. May we not, also, receive from Thee suitable receptacles wherein to receive a portion of Thine Abundance, so that it may endure?"

Margulies, p. 25.

4. Twofold Character

The Ladier Rabbi said: "A man should so master his nature that he can habituate himself to both the positive and negative aspects in every character trait. For example, he should be both a conservative and a progressive; a man without fear and yet a man of peace; a man of strong personality, and yet a meek one."

Teitelbaum, p. 49.

5. The Four Lords

Said a Hasid: "The Riziner was the lord of splendor; the Bershider, the lord of humility; the Berditschever, the lord of service, and the Lubavitzer, the lord of understanding."

Berditschevky, p. 55.

6. Four Qualities

Said Rabbi Sopher:
"He who is wise and knows it is not a humble man.
"He who is a fool and knows it not is a happy man.
"He who is wise and knows it, disdains and is disdainful.
"He who is a fool and knows it is liked and has the power to like others."

Sopher, p. 35.

7. Ben Zakkai

The youngest son of Rabbi Mordecai Tzernobiler, by name, Rabbi Johanan, was told that a friend had overheard his father describing him as the owner of a soul like unto that of Rabbi Johanan ben Zakkai. "Without doubt this is correct," retorted the Rabbi. "My name is Johanan and I am the son of a Zakkai, a man of merit, innocent of offenses."

Twersky, p. 69.

8. *Utilize Your Endowment*

Said the Hafetz Hayyim: "Every man enters this world with a certain endowment. It behooves him to make use of his endowment, for he will be held accountable regarding it."

Pupko, p. 51.

9. *All We Can Be*

Rabbi Uri used to say: "I am not afraid that I will be judged for not being like the Patriarch Abraham. I am not Abraham and can never be. What I fear is that I will be judged for not being all I could be."

I. K., p. 9.

10. *A Good Quality*

A Hasid said to the Bratzlaver: "You say one should apply every Psalm to himself. Is it proper for me to apply to myself the verses wherein the Psalmist praises himself; for example, when he declares he is a pious man?" The Rabbi replied: "Every person is pious and observant in one matter or another. Look for a good quality in yourself, and it will help you in your endeavor to banish your bad qualities and improve your character."

H. H. N., p. 18b.

11. *Appreciation for Qualities*

The Dubner Maggid said: "A traveler found hospitality at the home of a good-hearted man. He gave the guest some excellent liquor, to which the guest helped himself too freely. The liquor intoxicated him, and he became abusive and insulting towards his host. When the guest had grown sober, he begged his host's pardon, stating that the delectable liquor had gone to his head. The good-hearted host replied: 'In truth I find it hard to forgive you. Yesterday when you abused me, I said nothing, for I thought you to be a coarse lout unable to appreciate any good qualities in me. But now, that I perceive you are acquainted with liquor and can discern its excellence so clearly, I am vexed at you. You should have shown me respect at least for my knowledge of good liquor and my choice of it for my home.'"

The Dubner drew the moral, saying: "The Lord declares to the impious: 'Your denial of a spiritual world with a place of reward and punishment after death, I can understand and forgive. You are spiritually undeveloped, and too coarse to comprehend holy matters. But you do not deny the existence of This-World and you enjoy living in it. Why, then, do you not have some respect for Me, at least as the Creator of This-World?' "

Dubner, i, 61-62.

12. A Strong Wall

Said the Hafetz Hayyim: "In the *Song of Songs* we read: 'If she be a wall, we will build upon her a turret of silver . . . I am a wall . . . then I was in his eyes as one who found peace.' (8:9). Under all circumstances it behooves us to remain firm and strong, for upon firm and strong qualities of character, tall turrets of achievement can be built."

Pupko, p. 114.

30. CHARITY

1. All Is Dust

Rabbi Leib Saras heard of a Jew who had been imprisoned for his inability to pay his debt to a nobleman. The Zaddik began a tour of the region in order to collect sufficient money to free the prisoner. In one town he asked a servant at the tavern to go to the richest man in the community, and, in the Rabbi's name, to petition him for a donation of a hundred gold coins. The servant hesitated because the magnate was not a Hasid and would not, he thought, be responsive, to the appeal of a Hasidic Rabbi. The Zaddik, however, said to him: "Go and declare to him: 'You are dust; I am dust; gold is dust. What is higher than dust? A Mitzvah. And by the power of a Mitzvah I have come to you.' "

The servant did as the Zaddik enjoined him to do, and his appeal was effective. The rich man proved generous, and the prisoner was released.

G. A., p. 16.

2. "Give on Week Days"

A rich but miserly Jew went to visit his Rabbi on a Festival and greeted him with the words: "Git Yom Tov, Rabbi." The Rabbi exclaimed: "Git on week days, too, my affluent friend!" *

Zlotnik, p. 91.

* Among Polish and Ukrainian Jews, the vowel "u" is pronounced "ee." The Rabbi therefore was punning on the word: "Gibt," "Give."

3. Giving and Receiving

Said Rabbi Baruch of Medziboz: "A person may be said to be deserving of life only when he both gives and receives of material and spiritual things. Give food and shelter to the needy. Make gifts to God by directing your free will into proper channels. Only giving as well as receiving is called life."

Migdal David, p. 85.

4. Wandering Ways

In a year of famine, Rabbi Abraham Abish of Frankfurt (d. 1768) distributed all that he possessed among the hungry. He said: "Did not the Sages lay down the rule that a man should never give to charity more than a fifth of his property?" Rabbi Abraham replied: "I read in Proverbs 5:6 the words: 'So that she cannot balance the path of life, her tracks are unsteady, and she knoweth it not.' * I understand this verse to mean: 'when it is a matter of saving lives, do not calculate and do not balance, but let thy ways wander as if thou didst not know the rules.'"

Michelson, p. 12.

* Leeser translation. The Jewish Publication Society translation reads: "Lest she should walk the even path of life, her ways wander, but she knoweth it not."

5. Giving Aid Yourself

Said the Leover: "If someone comes to you for assistance and you say to him: 'God will help you,' you become a disloyal servant of God. It is for you to understand that God has sent you to aid the almoner, and not to refer him back to God."

Guttman, p. 27.

6. A Distant Relationship

Rabbi Shalom of Stripkov narrated this story: "Rabbi Naftali Katz of Frankfort learned that a certain Jew was very ill. The sick man had a distant relative who was very wealthy. The Rabbi journeyed to Vienna where the man of wealth resided and asked him to donate a sum sufficient to cure his relative. 'But ours is a very distant relationship,' protested the rich man. This incident occurred in the Selihot period before the coming of Rosh ha-Shanah. Early next morning the Selihah prayer was recited: 'O, remember Thy covenant with Abraham.' Both the Rabbi and the magnate were present at the Services. At their conclusion, the Rabbi said to the rich man: 'Isn't it a fact that your relationship to the Patriarch Abraham is far more remote than your kinship with the sick man. Yet you offer supplication to God that He be merciful to you for the sake of Abraham.' The wealthy man recognized the force of the Rabbi's argument and donated the sum required."

Michelson, p. 58.

7. *The Opportune Gift*

A man came to the Radziminer, petitioning him for a blessing that a son be granted his wife and himself. The Rabbi demanded that the suppliant present him with 150 rubles. Though the man protested that he did not possess this sum, the Rabbi would accept no excuse. Eager for the Rabbi's blessing, he sold almost all his possessions and brought the money to the Rabbi. A son was born to the man's wife, much to the petitioner's joy. When the lad became twenty years of age, his father betrothed him to a lovely but poor girl. The father had no money to give his son on his approaching marriage and again went to the Rabbi. The Radziminer promptly instructed his Warden to bring him a package from a certain closet, and this package he gave to the father. In it were the 150 rubles which the Rabbi had received for his blessing years before. The sum was sufficient to meet the requirements of the groom and bride, and an amount was left over whereby the father might make a fresh beginning in his work. Happily good fortune attended them all henceforth.

Zammlung, p. 51.

8. *Snow on the Hills*

The Hafetz Hayyim repeated a Maggid's parable regarding those persons who refuse to share their wealth with the poor. Once, he narrated, during the winter season, a teamster brought merchandise to town in a sleigh. When he was ready to depart with a return cargo, the sun shone brightly and the snow underfoot melted. The sleigh proved a grievous burden to the teamster, and frequently he was obliged to push it himself. Exhaustion overtook him, and he lifted his eyes to the nearby hills, saying: "O Lord! On the hills I perceive abundant snow. Of what use is it there? Why not place some snow here on the roads so that my soul may be revived?" In similar fashion we may say: "Of what use is wealth in the hands of misers? Give it to those whose hearts are full of compassion towards their fellow-beings."

Pupko, p. 45.

9. *Tears and Substance*

Said Rabbi Sopher: "Unto the Lord give of your tears; unto the poor give of your substance. Follow this rule and salvation will be yours."

Sopher, p. 35.

10. Charity Unto God

The Kaminker Rabbi translated Genesis 15:6 as follows: "And Abraham caused the Lord to believe and the Lord accepted this as charity." ("And he believed in the Lord and He counted it to him for righteousness.") In Job 15:15, we read: "Behold, He putteth no trust in His holy ones; Yea, the heavens are not clean in His sight." Thus it appears that God does not believe in the constancy even of His holy ones. He finds a trace of disloyalty in every person. But when God observed the perfection of Abraham's piety, He regarded Abraham as an exception, since he was a truly loyal servant. Now charity," continued the Kaminker, "implies a gift to him who is lacking. God lacked belief in the perfection of man. When, however, Abraham gave Him this belief, God received it as if it were in truth charity from Abraham."

Kaufman, p. 17.

11. Snatching a Benefit

Aaron Leib Frankel, brother of the Leipniker, was a prosperous importer of lumber. It chanced, however, that once a shipment of lumber was lost. The lumber merchant thereupon compiled a list of the poor known to him and made up packages of money to be sent each one. His wife wished to know the reason for this act, seeing that he had just suffered a severe loss. Aaron Leib Frankel replied: "Have I not seen that my wealth is being snatched away from me by the will of Heaven? Therefore I wish to snatch a part of it for a benefit to myself, a benefit on behalf of my soul."

Eibeshitz, p. 62.

12. Adding a Blessing

Rabbi Feivel Gritzer remarked: "We read in Deuteronomy 15:11: 'Therefore I command thee, saying: "Thou shalt surely open thy hand unto thy poor and needy brother, in thy land."'" The word: 'saying' seems to be unnecessary, but it does broaden the commandment as follows: 'when you give charity, add words; bless the recipient to the end that he may deserve the merit of being able to give charity himself before long.'"

Zammlung, p. 39.

13. Believing in a Cause

Said the Dubner: "A man was gathering donations for a worthy cause. He encountered a man unfriendly to him and asked him to make a contribution. The other man refused to do so. Thereupon the philanthropically-minded man said: 'You do me no favor by

making a donation, nor a disfavor by refusing it. But if you believe
in the merit of the cause, then give to it.' The unfriendly man
thereupon made a donation, and his attitude changed from hostility
to good will.

"From this we learn: when a man prays for himself, his petition
may be unheard. But if he prays for another, he will be heard,
and it may be that he himself will be benefitted."

Dubner, i, 158-159.

14. Nothing but Abuse

Said the Dubner: "A charitable man who was gathering money
to assist a needy person came to a certain citizen for a donation.
The latter abruptly refused, without, however, offering any reason.
The man of charity went to another citizen, and the latter began to
abuse the man in need for whom the collection was being taken.
'He is a shiftless, lazy creature,' said the second citizen. 'Otherwise
he would not be in such circumstances. I refuse to give a single
penny to a worthless drunkard.' The man of charity replied: 'Your
neighbor gave nothing but he kept silent; you, however, not only
give nothing, but you also abuse and insult a needy man.'

"From this we learn that a wicked man invents false accusations
against those to whom he gives nothing."

Dubner, i, 171-172.

15. The Returning Orphan

In Horodok a Jew returned from America and distributed a
considerable sum of money among its citizens in repayment for the
community's care of him in his boyhood. The Hafetz Hayyim, on
hearing of this, praised the donor greatly, saying: "Be assured that
the Lord is even more anxious than he has been, to pay well-merited
rewards to those who manifest their love for Him."

Pupko, p. 110.

16. The Reason for Tears

Said the Dubner: "A wealthy Jew returned to his home town for
a visit. He announced his desire to assist the needy members of the
community but he requested each applicant to ask for one thing only.
A particular resident of the town was sick; he was immersed in poverty, and his little cabin required many repairs to make it habitable.
In his distress he took a position near the door of the wealthy visitor's
room and commenced to weep. The kindly man approached him
and invited him to state his greatest need. The indigent suppliant
replied: 'I have so many pressing needs I feel unable to select the
most pressing one. Therefore, all I can do is to weep.'"

"The moral of the story is that other nations know what they lack and they ask the Lord to meet their needs. We Jews, however, lack so many things we do not know what to ask first, and therefore we can merely make our plea before the Lord through our tears."

Dubner, i, 196-197.

31. CIRCUMCISION

1. From Milah to Heaven

The Besht said: "We find the word Milah, meaning circumcision, in the initial letters of the verse in Deut. 30:12: 'Mi Yaaleh lanu ha-Shamayemah?' ('Who shall go for us to Heaven?'). This furnishes us with an indication of the fact that those inducted into the Covenant of Abraham may attain to Heaven."

M. B., p. 7.

32. CLEANLINESS

1. Measure for Measure

Said the Dubner: "A teacher handed his pupil his diploma, but when the student's father read it, he was vexed to see that the paper on which a commendation of the pupil was written was very soiled. Soon afterwards the young man married. The father thereupon took some cake, placed it on a soiled platter, together with a banknote wrapped also in a soiled paper. He then sent the package to the bridegroom's teacher. The latter could not understand why the gift, which he appreciated, had been sent in this untidy fashion. When he met his pupil's father, he thanked him, but added the words: 'Your gift was most welcome, but it came to me in an unclean covering. I would have enjoyed it more if it had been packed nicely.'

"The father replied: 'I, too, appreciated your praise of my son's abilities, which you attached to his diploma. But I would have enjoyed it more if it had been written on clean paper.'

"From this we learn that before complaining of a friend's treatment of you, you should search your own memory. Perhaps you deserve his treatment of you because of your treatment of him."

Dubner, i, 212-213.

33. CLEAVING

1. Attachment on High

Said the Strelisker: "You, O Hasidim, come to visit me, your Rabbi, and you pour out your hearts before me. I, too, go on visits. I visit my Maker on High and I strive to attach myself to Him."

I. K., p. 36.

34. COMFORT; DISCOMFORT

1. Comforting God

Said the Koznitzer Maggid: "God Himself feels the pain experienced by every one of His children. The comfort of God depends upon the comfort granted His children. During the Penitential Period we pray: 'Remember us unto life, O King, who delightest in life; inscribe us in the Book of Life, for Thine own sake, O God of Life'. Therefore when His children partake of a life that is worthwhile and pleasing, we thus grant a more pleasing life to our Father in Heaven."

Rosenfeld, p. 117.

2. The Nature of Our Comfort

Said Rabbi Solomon Sopher: "Isaiah, the Prophet, tells us: 'As one whom his mother comforteth, so will God comfort you, and ye shall be comforted in Jerusalem.' (66:13). A mother's comfort is acceptable and welcome because she understands the sufferer's anguish. Likewise God knows our sorrow and will truly comfort us. A sign or omen of our comfort is the fact that no other nation has rebuilt Jerusalem as an important world center. It still awaits the return of Israel to restore Jerusalem's grandeur. Therein lies our comfort."

Sopher, p. 86.

3. Comfort from a Psalm

Rabbi Simeon Deutsch vigorously opposed Rabbi Bunam's wish to become a Hasidic Rebbe because he had previously been an apothecary and a business man. Once he wrote Rabbi Bunam: "Do you not know that you should show me respect, since I am exalted in the Temple of Love?" Rabbi Bunam answered: "It is true that you occupy a high place therein, and I a lowly. But I remember the verse in Psalm 138:6: 'For though the Lord be high, yet He regardeth the lowly, and the haughty He knoweth from afar.'"

Ẓammlung, p. 9.

4. Discomforts on Earth

Said the Hafetz Hayyim: "A friend of the Gaon of Vilna became so disturbed of mind on hearing the Gaon's description of Divine Punishments that he fell grievously ill. The Gaon visited him and said: 'Divine Punishment takes place for the most part in this existence. If you have not greatly sinned, your earthly discomforts may suffice, and you will enter Paradise without a sojourn in Purgatory.'"

Pupko, ii, 34.

35. COMMONERS

1. A Veritable Flood

In a year of drought, Rabbi Abish ordained a special Service of prayer for rain. On his way to the synagogue he encountered a Jew of low repute, and invited him to join in the Services. The man answered: "How can the prayer of a person like me avail at all?" The Rabbi promptly replied: "Men like you have brought down not merely rain but a veritable flood."

Michelson, p. 44.

2. The Common Soldier

Said Rabbi David Mirapoler: "Concerning Genesis 49:6: 'Unto their assembly, let my glory not be united', Rashi makes the comment: 'Jacob prayed that his name be not mentioned in connection with rebellious assemblies like that of Korah. Only in connection with worthy things should it be mentioned.' I offer this parable to illustrate Rashi's comment: a common soldier who offends is punished only slightly; by the same token his excellent performance of a duty is but slightly rewarded. The reverse is true of a general. Jacob prayed: 'When my sons sin, I beseech Thee, O Lord, to punish them as if they were common soldiers. When, however, they serve Thee well, I beseech Thee to reward them as my sons.'"

Kaufman, p. 55.

3. The Leader's Worries

Said the Strelisker: "A soldier stood guard and mused: 'How fortunate is the general! But, no; he bears many responsibilities which wear down his strength. How fortunate is the king! But no; he is filled with anxieties over the welfare of his people. Perhaps it is best, after all, to be a common soldier.' By the same token, Hasidim, do not aspire to overload yourselves with the worries of the leader!"

I. K., p. 32.

4. The Beggar's Vote

Said the Dubner: "A certain politician ran for office, and in order to gain votes, he became friendly with every voter in his district. His wife protested: 'I saw you speaking in a cordial and friendly manner to a ragged man. Is is not beneath your dignity to do so in public?'

" 'By no means', replied her husband. 'He has a vote, and it might be the very vote which will bring about my election.'

"From this we learn that we must combat even the least transgression and strive to perform the least Mitzvah. In the scales on which our good deeds and misdeeds are weighed on Judgment Day, these may decide the balance in our favor."

Dubner, i, 214-215.

36. COMMUNION

1. An Intimate of God

Said the Hafetz Hayyim: "The mere fact that you may address God as 'Thou' manifests His desire that you be His intimate."

Pupko, ii, p. 4.

37. COMMUNITY

1. Zaddikim in the Community

Said the Hafetz Hayyim: "We read in Genesis 18:26: 'And the Lord said: "If I find in Sodom fifty righteous within the city, then I will forgive all the place for their sake." ' From this we learn that the righteous persons were expected to be within the city, sharing in its regeneration, if they were to be effective in the effort to save it from perdition. If they, the Zaddikim, separate themselves in their way of life from civic affairs, they can exercise no influence whatsoever, even if they exist."

Pupko, ii, 45.

38. COMPASSION

1. "The All-Merciful"

Said the Hafetz Hayyim: "At the conclusion of the main portion of Grace after Meals we may add the words: 'May the All-Merciful sustain us in a dignified manner'. We also add other such petitions, thereby indicating that a request to God after the performance of a Mitzvah is acceptable before Him."

Pupko, ii, 65.

39. CONCENTRATION

1. The Sheaf of Grain

The Lubliner asked Rabbi Bunam: "How is it possible for us to fulfil the duty not to forget God when our mind is usually engrossed in other matters?" Rabbi Bunam replied: "Only something which is of minor value can be forgotten. Something of major value may be overlooked for a few moments, but it is eventually remembered. Thus a large sheaf of cut grain is not placed in the category of a forgotten sheaf and need not be given away to the poor." The Lubliner commented: "You have placed new life within me, Rabbi Bunam."

Rokotz, ii, 17.

2. Binding the Tefillin

Said the Hafetz Hayyim: "We read in the Sh'ma: 'Thou shalt bind them (the Tefillin) for a sign upon thy hand.' We also read: 'Thou shalt love the Lord.' From this we learn that we should strive to acquire a love of God with the same concentration we manifest in binding the Tefillin on our arm and forehead. Both require actual performance rather than mere contemplation."

Pupko, p. 113.

40. CONDUCT

1. The Many and the Few

The Ropshitzer was accustomed to say: "Many come to my house, but few come to me." Rabbi Solomon Sopher explained this as follows: "Many come to the Zaddik to seek his prayer in their behalf. But few come to seek to know his holy conduct, and to learn from spiritual perfection."

Sopher, p. 31.

2. The Zaddik and His Conduct

Said Rabbi Leib Saras: "A Zaddik is not a person who preaches Torah, but rather lives Torah. Not his words but his actions should teach Torah to the people. I visit Zaddikim not to listen to their interpretations of Torah, but to observe how they conduct themselves from the time of their arising in the early morning until the time of their lying down to rest at night."

G. A., p. 7.

41. CONFESSION

1. Confessions by the Alphabet

Rabbi Mordecai Bennett asked Rabbi Israel Isaac of Vork to explain to him why the Confessions on Yom Kippur and other occasions are arranged in alphabetic order. The Vorker replied: "If it were otherwise, we would not know when to stop." Rabbi

Mordecai exclaimed: "Only a Disciple of Rabbi Bunam is able to give so shrewd an explanation!"

Zammlung, p. 18.

42. CONFIDENCE

1. *True Confidence*

Said the Hafetz Hayyim: "Have confidence in those leaders who guide us on the way to the Lord, and give to them your loyalty. When blind men are led by men who have their sight, can the blind men protest that they are being led along the wrong way?"

Pupko, p. 57.

2. *Well-Placed Confidence*

Said the Hafetz Hayyim: "Even the impious, with little knowledge of the Lord, can be saved if he places his trust in God. The *Yalkut* to Psalm 25 illustrates this with a parable: 'A man in Caesarea was seized by the royal police on suspicion of being a criminal. He told the police that he was a representative of the Emperor and was brought before the monarch. The Emperor expressed surprise and asked the prisoner: "Do I know you personally, as you have declared?" The prisoner replied: "If I had not said this, the police would have beaten me severely." The Emperor was impressed and said: 'Inasmuch as you have placed your confidence in me, I herewith release you.'"

Pupko, p 5.

43. CONSIDERATENESS

1. *The Considerate Employer*

Said the Dubner: "A clerk tried his best to secure employment from a small storekeeper who was charitably inclined. The clerk was an excellent salesman and could easily have associated himself with a larger establishment, but he resolved to await an opportunity to work for the less affluent merchant. When a friend asked the reason, the clerk replied: 'I chanced once to go to the merchant for a small article. I found him and his family at supper, their clerk being seated with them at the same table. When the clerk left the table to secure the article I wished, I observed that the family waited to serve the next course of the meal until he returned. It is because I am thus convinced he is a most considerate employer that I wish to work for him.'"

Dubner, i, 284-285.

44. CONTENTMENT

1. The Perfection of Torah

Said the Hafetz Hayyim: "If a man truly believes that the Torah is perfect, it has the power to revive his soul and, at the same time, to grant him contentment of spirit."

Pupko, ii, 50.

45. CONTRACTS

1. A Permanent Contract

Said the Dubner: "A young man sought employment from a certain business man. The merchant agreed on condition that he first demonstrate his abilities, and accept a nominal salary during the probationary period. The clerk's services proved satisfactory, whereupon the employer said: 'Until the present you have worked irregular hours and have been paid wages accordingly. From now on I wish to sign a contract with you and regulate your hours and salary in accordance therewith.'

"From this we learn: when Abraham's services proved satisfactory to the Lord, He ordered him to undergo circumcision as a sign of a Covenant. The Lord declared: 'From now on I am your steady employer; therefore let us make a contract. Henceforth you shall be my steady employee and you shall do regular work.'"

Dubner, i, 168-169.

46. CONTROVERSY

1. A Dislike of Debating

The Hafetz Hayyim had an intense dislike of arguments and debates. He suspected the participants of being more concerned with winning over their opponents than in discovering the truth.

Pupko, p. 14.

47. CORRECTION

1. No Correction for Nothing

A miserly man remarked to the Dubner Maggid: "How can you reconcile it with your sense of justice that you correct people, and then take their money?" The Maggid instantly replies: "God also does not correct for nothing." *

Dubner, i, 31.

* A play on words is present here: "Correct" means both to "admonish" and to "punish." There is also a play upon the word: "for nothing."

48. COURTESY

1. Postponing Conversation

The Hafetz Hayyim reproved his son for engaging in conversation during the study period. The son protested: "But, father, how can I show discourtesy when a friend comes over and begins a conversation?" The Rabbi replied: "Have you not observed at market that when a relative walks over to a merchant who is surrounded by customers, the merchant says: 'Pardon me, but I shall converse with you this evening.' It is for you to do the same."

Pupko, p. 55.

49. CREATION

1. A By-product of Purpose

Said the Hafetz Hayyim: "God created the sun and the moon in order to enable men to perform the Mitzvot. Only as a by-product of their mission in the universe do they illumine and warm the world. Do we not read in Psalm 104:19: 'who appointedst the moons for seasons', namely, the festivals of the seasons?"

Pupko, ii, 44.

50. CREDIT

1. Prayers on Credit

Said the Bratzlaver: "A storekeeper is accustomed to trust his customers and extends them credit on condition that they will pay later. Why not be like the storekeeper and give unto God on credit some sincere prayers, some earnest and holy study, and some good deeds? Let the Lord be indebted to you. Trust Him; eventually He will repay you." *

H. H. N., p. 22a.

* A variation of this simile is to be found in the idea of making daily deposits in a bank, the money to be withdrawn when need for funds arises.

2. The Final Word

Said the Dubner: "A man came into a store to make a purchase. When he was told the price of the article he desired, he loudly exclaimed that the price was too high, and that others had paid less.

"After considerable bargaining, a price was set below which the merchant would not go.

"The would-be purchaser then whispered: 'I wish to have the article on credit, because I have no money with me today.'

"From this we learn that on the Awesome Days we loudly entreat the Lord in many paragraphs: 'Our Father, our King'. We ask
for more and more as we go forward. But finally we say in a low
voice: 'We have no merits; pity us and answer us.'"

Dubner, i, 126-127.

3. Deserving Credit

Said the Dubner: "A man came to a city and opened up a very
large store. When communal taxes were assessed, this man's assess-
ment proved to be the highest. He complained that he was not as
rich as he seemed because his stock had been obtained on credit.
'Yes,' retorted the assessor, 'but you must be a wealthy man indeed
to have been found deserving of so much credit. A poor man is not
trusted in this way.'

"From this we learn: Joseph declared that his wisdom had been
derived from God. Without God's desire to grant him wisdom, he
would have been no wiser than any ordinary person. Pharaoh replied: 'When the Almighty vouchsafed you so much wisdom, it
proved that you are truly a very wise man. For God "gives wisdom
to the wise" (Daniel 1:21.)'"

Dubner, i, 153-154.

51. CROWDS

1. Fire and Water

Rabbi Phineas of Kotzk said: "I had hoped to draw to myself a
few earnest Disciples, and through them to become as a flame. But
a multitude came to me, and transformed me into water."

Guttman, p. 17.

52. DEATH

1. A Minor Day of Judgment

In 1839 Rabbi Moses Sopher fell ill and realized that he would
not recover. He said: "My case resembles that of a soldier who
survived major battles but fell in a minor skirmish. I have survived
the major Days of Judgment, on Rosh ha-Shanah and Yom Kippur,
but I was laid low on a minor Day of Judgment, namely, Hoshanah
Rabbah."

Sopher, p. 54.

2. Why a Zaddik Dies

The "Yud" said: "The Lord would be pleased to keep the Zaddik
alive indefinitely. He rejoices to hear the Zaddik's sincere prayers

and to observe his profound learning. But it is the Zaddik himself who requests death, since a soul bounded by a body cannot overstep a prescribed comprehension of divinity."

H. Hak., p. 15.

3. Spacious Mansions

Rabbi Meyer of Premislan said to Rabbi Hayyim of Tzanz who was visiting him: "Tzanzer Rav, is it not fitting that I should move to a more spacious mansion?" The Tzanzer replied: "To be sure, Rabbi Meyer. "Very well, then," remarked the Tzanzer: "since you agree with me, I shall soon move." A few weeks later, the Tzanzer did move. He died.

Szlamovitz, p. 14.

4. As One Who is Dead

Said the Hafetz Hayyim: "In the Talmud, *Berakot* 63 we read: 'Words of Torah remain only in the man who behaves like a dead man with respect to them'. But in Rabbinical law we find the axiom regarding the words of Torah that we are to 'live by them and not to die by them.' Is there not a contradiction here? A parable will explain it. An elderly storekeeper resolved to spend two hours a day in the synagogue studying the Torah. His wife complained that she could not attend to the customers if she were alone. The man replied: 'Why should you complain? Suppose I died for two hours! Fortunately I return to the store alive after my two hours of study.' "

Pupko, ii, 14.

53. DECEIVER; DECEPTION

1. Jacob and Laban

Rabbi Moses Sopher said: "Every Jacob, namely, every sincere, God-fearing person, meets his Laban, namely a deceiver with an evil heart. But seldom indeed does Laban, the deceiver, meet his match, and more, in a Jacob."

Sopher, p. 31.

2. Pathways that Deceive

Said the Hafetz Hayyim: "One cold winter day a villager was driving his wagon through the snows. He halted at an inn and purchased several drinks in order to warm himself. When he took his driver's seat, he was more drunk than sober. The horse dragged the wagon through the falling snow the entire night. In the morning when the villagers saw the path the wandering horse had made, they followed it in the belief that it was the correct road.   Later they discovered that it led nowhere.   Hence they might well have said: "Our fathers have inherited nought but lies . . . Shall a man make unto himself gods, and they are no gods?" (Jeremiah 16:19-20)"

Pupko, ii, 2.

54. DECORUM

1. *Decorum Breeds Respect*

A Rabbi in a small town complained to Rabbi Isaac of Ziditchov that his fellow-townsmen did not show him respect.   Rabbi Isaac replied: "Perhaps you are a restless person, and are accustomed to walk about the synagogue during Services.   If you change your habits into more decorous conduct, you will gain the respect you crave."

Braver, p. 63.

55. DEDICATION

1. *Less with Intensity*

Said the Dubner: "A bride's father boasted that he would order three costly dresses to be made for her.   The bridegroom replied: 'I know that you are not a man of means, and I therefore prefer that you make for my wife one excellent garment rather than three shoddy ones.'

"From this we learn that it is preferable to study less but with greater intensity."

Dubner, i, 266.

56. DEFORMITY

1. *A Crooked Foot*

The young man, who later became the famous Tzanzer Rabbi, had a deformed foot.   He married the daughter of the Leipniker Rav, who remarked: "My son-in-law has a crooked foot, but a straight head."

Eibeshitz, p. 36.

57. DELAY

1. *The Delayed Ritual Immersion*

On the Eve of Yom Kippur the Berditschever Rabbi undertook his ritual immersion quite late in the afternoon, explaining his tardiness by the following story: "A woman who is required by the laws of the Torah to take her ritual immersion at a specified time had refused to do so. He husband chided her, but she defended herself on the ground that her husband gave her too meagre an allowance for food. I justified her in this protest, and her husband promised to increase the household allowance. I then bethought myself: why should not I, like this woman, refuse to take my ritual immersion until the Lord assures me that he will grant an increased allowance of benefits for His people. And this I have obtained from Him."

Guttman, p. 13.

58. DELIBERATION

1. Deliberation and Diligence

Said the Hafetz Hayyim: "Before a decision is reached, be deliberate; after the decision, be diligent. There is a tradition that Boaz lived only a brief time after his marriage to Ruth. If he had delayed longer in his decision to marry Ruth, neither David nor the Messianic line would have come to pass."

Pupko, p. 90.

59. DESIRES

1. The Spiced Foods

Said the Dubner: "Two travelers halted at an inn. One ordered plain foods, but the other chose highly spiced dishes. The second traveler suffered a severe gastric upset. He then understood that the seasoned and spiced foods, though appetizing, were neither fresh nor wholesome.

"From this we learn that man has desires in this world. If he be wise, he will satisfy his legitimate desires in a plain, wholesome fashion, and happiness will be his portion. But if he be unwise, he will be misled by the attractive and appetizing lures which disguise his unwholesome desires. After they bring him suffering, he comes to understand that their attractiveness was a masquerade of the true nature of these desires."

Dubner, i, 127-128.

2. The Use of Desires

Said the Hafetz Hayyim: "Man is endowed with desires. But these were given to him in order that he might employ them for the acquisition of Torah, not to indulge in follies."

Pupko, p. 114.

3. Desiring Wisely

Said the Hafetz Hayyim: "In Psalm 145:19 we read: 'He will fulfil the desire of them that fear Him.' But we must first express a wise desire. Ask yourself, do you offer prayer voicing your desire for fine children, acute in the learning of Torah, and endowed with a lofty soul?"

Pupko, p. 108.

60. DESTINY

1. Our Steps are Decreed

Said the Hafetz Hayyim: "We read in Job 14:16: 'Thou numberest my steps'. A decree is sent forth regarding the number of steps a person shall make during his lifetime. But it rests within his choice to determine whether his steps shall lead him to good deeds or direct him in an opposite path."

Pupko, p. 102.

61. DEVOTION

1. Devotion Breeds Devotion

Said the Bratzlaver: "If you are a sincere penitent, and, repeating the formal of confession, you exclaim: 'Woe is me!', you will soon feel more deeply the gravity of your offenses. Then you will exclaim: 'Indeed, woe is me, me in particular.' In the same way that one feels the urge of repentance on beholding the sincere repentance of another penitent, one also feels the urge towards more ardent repentance by feeling his own sincere repentance. There is truly a vast difference in degree between the first repentance and the later one."

H. H. N., p. 28a.

62. DIFFERENCES

1. In Differing Versions

A Hasid said to the Tzortkover that his father, the Riziner, was accustomed to tell the same story in differing versions. The Rabbi replied: "The story of Zaddik is phrased in words, appropriate at the time of its telling to the need for imparting a particular lesson."

Margulies, p. 30.

2. Differences Among Men

Honest differences of opinion among men show that good sense has a place in their midst. Complete agreement on all issues oftentimes betrays a density of mind.

Dor Deah, p. 178.

63. DILIGENCE

1. Transforming the Diamond

Said the Dubner: "A king possessed a magnificent diamond which, unfortunately, received a deep scratch as a result of an accident. His diamond cutters gave him their judgment that no amount of polishing would entirely remove the flaw. An engraver who was present remarked: 'I can so transform this jewel that it will become more valuable than before.' The king gave him permission, and with great delicacy and skill he engraved on the diamond the petals of a rose, utilizing the deep scratch as the stem of the flower.

"From this we learn that diligence and skill can transform evil traits into virtues."

Dubner, i, 130.

2. The Borrowed Tools

Said the Dubner: "A man grew weary of lending tools to his neighbors. One day a carpenter requested from him the loan of a saw. The owner sent him to look for it in the cellar, but the carpenter could not find it. The owner then sent him to the garret, but the workman could not locate the saw there either. Finally the owner remarked: 'Here it is under the table.' 'Why did you send me to the cellar and to the garret, when you knew it was under the table all the time?' asked the astonished carpenter. The owner answered: 'Because many persons come to me to borrow tools for small jobs which could be done with their own tools, but which they will not look for in their own possessions. I wished to make sure that you really needed the saw.'

"From this we learn that persistence and diligence bring their own reward."

Dubner, i, 157-158.

64. DIPLOMACY

1. The Humble Man's Tact

The Dubner Maggid said: "A prince became ill and the foremost physicians were unable to discover the cause of his malady. The king thereupon proclaimed that anyone who believed he could assist the prince would be invited to see the patient. A doctor from a small town out of curiosity came to the palace and quickly diagnosed the sickness, recognizing it as one he had encountered before. The remedy was a very simple one, but he was aware that if he prescribed this simple remedy, the other physicians would ridicule him. He therefore declared: 'I have heard of a case like this, and have learned that these and these herbs proved effective as a cure. But I am merely a small-town doctor and I cannot know whether I prepare the medicine properly. Therefore I wish only to specify the ingredients, and the royal physicians, with their superior knowledge, will know how to make the medicine ready.' This diplomatic approach disarmed the royal doctors, and the prince was cured."

The Dubner drew the lesson, saying: "Ecclesiastes declared that the wisdom of a poor man is disdained, but if the lowly man adds tact to his wisdom, his wisdom will be accepted."

Dubner, i, 68-69.

2. How to Answer a Drunkard

Said the Dubner: "A rich man took a walk in the company of his son. A drunkard accosted them, seized hold of the father's coat and shouted: 'You stole my coat; give it back to me.' The man smiled and said: 'But you loaned it to me for today. I shall give it back to you tomorrow.' The drunkard walked away satisfied. The father remarked to his son: 'Had I denied that it was his coat, he would have flown into a rage and a fight would have ensued.'

"From this we learn: a friendly reply pacifies even a drunkard."

Dubner, i, 285-286.

65. DISCIPLINE

1. Maintaining Discipline

Ber Oppenheim pursued his studies under Rabbi Baruch of Leipnik. When he received a call to become Rabbi of a certain community, he besought his teacher to give him a certificate with his signature, declaring his fitness for the post. Rabbi Baruch presented him with a letter to the Chief Rabbi of Moravia, Mordecai Bennett, instructing him to ask the Chief Rabbi for a certificate. Rabbi Mordecai told him that he was to await a test. He waited patiently but no such test was given him. Several days elapsed and then Rabbi Mordecai called over Ber Oppenheim and said: "Surely the Leipniker Rabbi's letter has indicated to me that you deserve a certificate. Yet I have asked you to remain here for this

time, in order to demonstrate that in this province only the Chief
Rabbi may decide who is fit to be a Rabbi. Discipline and authority
must be maintained."

Eibeshitz, p. 42.

66. DISCRETION

1. *Know When to Halt*

At midnight the Hafetz Hayyim would order all his students to
go to bed. He said: "The study of the Torah is a task for a lifetime.
Conserve your strength aright and thus you will be able to fulfil your
lifelong duty."

Pupko, ii, 20.

67. DREAM

1. *A Bad Dream*

A woman came to the Hafetz Hayyim and told him she had had
a bad dream. She inquired from the Rabbi whether, according to
custom, she should fast for the day. The Rabbi replied: "Instead of
abstaining from food, I advise that you abstain from talk, except
the words needed to protect your children's well-being."

Pupko, p. 30.

68. EATING

1. *The Guests' Preference*

At a Bar Mitzvah banquet, the lad delivered a Talmudic discourse. Some of the guests paid no attention but proceeded to
gorge themselves with food. The Maggid, with a smile, remarked:
"Gentlemen, I perceive that you prefer the 'Shulhan Arukh' (The
Prepared Table), to the Gemara."

Dubner, i, 47.

69. ECSTASY

1. *Ecstasy of Prayer*

The Berditschever would devote his entire strength into his
prayers. He would pray in a very loud voice, and manifested extraordinary ecstasy amid his vigorous motions. His manner of praying would stir his hearers to repentance.

Guttman, p. 7.

70. EDUCATION

1. In New Scenes

During his youth Abraham Abish was dull-witted and unable to make progress in his studies. This was particularly disturbing to him, inasmuch as his father and brother were both outstanding scholars. The young man went into a field and lifted up his voice in prayer: "O Lord, if Thou wishest me to be a dolt, why hast Thou placed me in a family of scholars?" Thereupon he fell asleep, and, in his dream, an Angel appeared to him, saying: "Abraham, leave your home and go to a city far away; take up your studies there, and if you apply yourself with your whole heart, success will attend you." The youth did so, and soon was transformed into a scholar of remarkable profundity. It was then he began to sign his name: "Abram who became Abraham."

Michelson, p. 28.

2. The Over-Educated

The Lubliner Zaddik said: "The coming of our Redeemer is in great measure hindered by those Jews who are over-educated in Rabbinic legalism. Redemption demands complete repentance, and a person of lofty attainments finds it difficult to experience lowliness of spirit. Therefore he does not fully repent, and the Messiah is delayed."

Walden, p. 65.

3. "Uplift Your Mind"

Rabbi Baer of Leova, a son of Rabbi Israel of Rizin, grew weary of the calling of a Hasidic Rabbi and determined to devote himself to the field of education. This led him to associate with the educated Jews and non-Jews of his community. He declined to grant interviews to his Hasidim. When asked: "Is it not to be feared that conduct such as this will bring harm to Judaism?" he replied: "Not if you uplift your mind, for then there is nothing to fear."

Raker, p. 165.

4. Maintaining Interest

Said the Dubner: "A father once bought an excellent watch for his small son. Not wishing his son to lose interest in it, he began by teaching him how to tell the time. Later he showed to him that the longer hand indicated the minutes; then he pointed out the moving hand for the seconds. Finally he opened the lid and step by step he showed him the various works inside. In this way the lad continued to find the watch of engrossing interest.

"From this we learn that the Lord wished Israel to maintain interest in the Torah. He first had Israel instructed in the Written Law, then in the Oral Law, and finally in the interpretations and explanations which he learned step by step to discover."

Dubner, i, 125-126.

5. Training Children in Religion

Said the Hafetz Hayyim: "I once asked a father: 'why do you not require your sons to receive an adequate religious education?' The father replied: 'they will behold my own religious practices and will imitate me.' Thereupon I added the words: 'But are you sure they will remain with you throughout their entire life?' Those who have absorbed much Torah are like a flame. It can kindle others and remain fiery themselves. But your sons are like a vessel that is placed above a fire. As soon as it is removed, it becomes cool. Your untaught sons cannot kindle religious enthusiasm in others. They themselves have lost their heat, and their children in turn become as cold as ice towards religion."

Pupko, ii, 15.

71. EFFORT

1. Doing the Utmost

Said the Hafetz Hayyim: "It is the duty of a man to bear two yokes, one the yoke of the Kingdom of Heaven, the other the yoke of the Mitzvot. It behooves every one of us to learn the 613 Mitzvot and to observe as many as he can."

Pupko, p. 118.

72. EMANATION

1. The World of Emanation

Once when the Rabbi of Tzanz was studying intently the subject of Emanation (a term of the Kabbalah) he began to cough violently. His son brought him a cup of hot tea and urged his father to drink it. The old Rabbi exclaimed: "In the World of Emanation tea is not drunk." "True, father," replied the son, "but in the World of Emanation one does not cough."

Raker, p. 100.

73. EMINENCE

1. Obscure and Eminent Men

Said the Hafetz Hayyim: "The Bible demands of men that they be clean in the eyes of God and Israel. But the Sage in the *Ethics of the Fathers* merely teaches us not to be wicked in our own eyes. The difference in counsel can be explained as follows: an obscure man can be satisfied if he is right according to his own personal conscience, but a man of eminence must also satisfy persons in the community outside himself."

Pupko, p. 90.

74. EQUALITY

1. Everyone's Equal

The Dubner Maggid said: "A certain city stood in need of a preacher. A rich and learned man volunteered his service without emolument. His admonitions, however, to deal honestly with God and men, fell on unheeding ears. The small merchants declared: 'He, the wealthy merchant, can afford to be strictly honest, but we cannot survive without an occasional deviation from the path of integrity.' The wealthy preacher resigned his post, and a poor teacher was hired to preach. His words, too, went unheeded, inasmuch as the business people affirmed he did not understand business ways. Finally a retired merchant, who had previously conducted a business of moderate size, was chosen. He was regarded as the equal of both the larger and the smaller merchants, and therefore his counsel was taken to heart."

The Dubner drew the lesson, saying: "The Torah commands us to reprove those comrades who are our equals, our peers. Only then will the reproof avail."

Dubner, i, 63.

2. Are All People The Same?

Said the Dubner: "A man came to a dealer in woolen goods to buy material for a suit. The merchant asked him regarding the quality of fabric he wished. 'Oh, I imagine they are all alike,' answered the would-be customer. Thereupon the woolen merchant extinguished all the lights and asked the man to select a piece of cloth in the dark. 'But I cannot see,' exclaimed the customer. 'What need is there that you see the material since you maintain that all are alike. Select any quality and I will give you the shade you wish in it.' The customer, however, refused to do so.

"From this we learn: though Korah declared: 'All Israelites are equal; and all Israelites are holy', nevertheless we can inquire: what shall we say of the quality of a man's mind?"

Dubner, i, 154-155.

75. ETIQUETTE

1. The Sabbath of Good Manners

A question was placed to the Gerer Rabbi: "We name the Sabbath before Sukkot, the 'Sabbath of Repentance'; the Sabbath before Passover, 'the Great Sabbath.' What shall we call the Sabbath before Shavuot?" The Gerer replied: "We should call it: 'the Sabbath of *Derek Eretz*' ('Good Manners'). Have we not learned that *Derek Eretz* preceded the Torah?"

Zlotnik, p. 87.

76. EVIL IMPULSE

1. Standing Aside

Said the Hafetz Hayyim: "If you labor diligently to resist the persuasion of the Evil Impulse, God will come to your assistance. If you yourself do not struggle against the Evil Impulse within you, God will assuredly stand aside. It brings to mind the Mitzvah of giving aid in the loading or unloading of a beast. If the owner of the animal leaves all the work to be done by some one who voluntarily offers to assist, there is no such compulsion on such a volunteer to give aid."

Pupko, ii, 60.

2. The Unending Struggle

A man complained to the Hafetz Hayyim that the Evil Impulse was giving him no rest. The Rabbi said: "But that is exactly what life is. There is a constant struggle between the good and evil impulses within man. If the struggle stops, life stops. If you win the battle you will receive your reward in This-World and in the World-to-Come."

Pupko, p. 97.

77. EVIL TONGUE

1. An Evil Tongue

When the Rabbi of Tzanz heard that the Rabbi of Leova had returned from associates in Tzernovitz whom the Tzanzer regarded as impious and that he had been accepted again by the Sadigurer Zaddik as a Holy Rabbi, his anger was aroused and he declared all the sons of the Hasidim to be apostates. This pronouncement was shown to the Zaddik of Sadigura. The Rabbi said in a low tone: "Amazing! Amazing, indeed! The Sadigurer is a renowned Gaon

EXAMPLE   **45**

and a Holy Rabbi, yet he has accepted as true the accusations by those who possess an evil tongue!"

Raker, p. 186.

2. *Guarding Our Tongue*

Said the Hafetz Hayyim: "One of the most important things we can do is to beware of the evil tongue. The Lord insists that we obtain the forgiveness of the person of whom we have spoken. This is frequently impossible, for the person offended may have moved away or died."

Pupko, ii, 9.

3. *Disciplining the Tongue*

Said the Hafetz Hayyim: "Goods which are difficult to procure are highly estimated. The disciplining of the tongue is rare indeed, and therefore it is a matter of high value."

Pupko, p. 99.

4. *Informers Against Man*

Said the Hafetz Hayyim: "When evil tongues are released, they create Informers on High who enumerate every sin of a man at the Judgment Seat."

Pupko, p. 103.

5. *A Demanding Vocation*

Said the Hafetz Hayyim: "To guard your tongue is a vocation requiring study and long practice."

Pupko, p. 98.

78. EXAMPLE

1. *The Wrong Roads*

The Dubner Maggid related the following: "An important merchant went on a journey with several wagons, heavily loaded with merchandise. The snow had fallen to a depth of several inches. It was not long before he lost his way, taking a road which led him not to the city but into a forest. After considerable hardship, he found at last the right road and continued on his way to the city. As he went forward, the merchant gave a heavy sigh. 'Why are you so troubled?' inquired a driver of one of the wagons. 'I often miss the road and have to turn back.' 'Ah,' answered the merchant, 'it is different in your case. You drive only a single light wagon, and any trails made by its wheels are quickly obliterated by the wind. But my several heavily-laden wagons made deep and lasting trails in the snow. Who knows how many poor wretches will be misled by these false trails?' "

The Maggid drew the lesson, saying: "A learned man often breaks open a false trail for the unlearned to follow to their hurt."

Dubner, i, 76-77.

79. EXILES

1. Garments of Exile

Said the Dubner: "A prince became incensed at his son's conduct and exiled him to an unfriendly country. There he was persecuted as an alien and was granted no opportunity for a livelihood. An ambassador of the prince reported that his son's garments were in tatters, and the prince therefore sent him new garments befitting his status as a prince's son.

"The courtiers of the father then asked him: 'If you care enough for your son to send him new garments, why do you not send for him to return?' The prince replied: 'It is known to me that my son is still rebellious against my authority; therefore I cannot send for him as yet. But if I were indifferent to his need for new garments, some kind person might donate to him clothing of the style and pattern worn in the country of his exile. Then my son would become assimilated and forget that he is still in exile.'

"From this we learn that when we Jews forget we are a unique people and wish to assimilate, our Father causes events to occur which remind us we are still in Exile."

Dubner, i, 244-246.

2. The Two Exiles

Said the Leover: "In Lamentations 1:8 we read: 'Jerusalem hath grievously sinned; therefore she is become as one unclean.' This verse applies to the Babylonian Exile. The transgressors were aware of their sins, repented of them, and, after a lapse of seventy years, were returned to holiness. Lamentations 1:9 reads: 'Her filthiness was (hidden) in her skirts; she was not mindful of her end.' This verse applies to the present Exile. The latter Exile has been decreed by God as a penalty for our hatred, each of the other, a sin which we scarcely recognize as an offense. Therefore we do not repent ourselves of it, and the termination of our Exile remains, therefore, unknown." *

Guttman, p. 23.

---

* Interpretations of this kind were repeatedly made after the Destruction of the Commonwealth in the year 70 C.E. It remains to be seen whether similar explanations will henceforth be offered, now that the Third Hebrew Commonwealth has been established.

3. *The Prolonged Exile*

The Hafetz Hayyim felt profound sorrow at the length of the Exile. He said: "At the beginning there may have been good in the Exile, for when Israel was an agricultural people, research in the Torah was hindered, and many were ignorant of the Jewish law. In Exile, however, the Torah was clarified by the Mishnah, the Gemara, the Commentators and the Codifiers. But now that this task has been accomplished, there is no further need for the Exile. It is high time for the Redemption."

Pupko, p. 18.

80. EXPERIENCE

1. *Speaking from Experience*

Rabbi Abraham Sopher declared in a discourse: "In *Kiddushin*, 40 we learn that Rabbi Tarphon affirmed that doing is more important than learning. Rabbi Akiba, however, offered the opinion that learning is more important. All those who were present agreed with Rabbi Akiba. Why was this? Because Rabbi Akiba commenced his studies at the age of forty and by personal experience perceived that learning leads to doing. Rabbi Tarphon, however, had been privileged to engage in study from his childhood, and hence did not attach the importance to it which Rabbi Akiba felt."

Sopher, p. 95.

81. FALSITY

1. *Substitutes for Diamonds*

Said the Hafetz Hayyim: "A miner dug up precious diamonds from the earth, but a treacherous friend substituted worthless stones in their place. When the miner wished to sell them, he found, to his indignation, that he had been betrayed. Likewise a man performs good and pious deeds, but he allows evil thoughts to enter his mind. When he takes his place at the Judgment Seat, he becomes greatly distressed when shown that his piety is spurious."

Pupko, p. 101.

82. FAMILY

1. *Warning an American Brother*

The Hafetz Hayyim advised a man to write his brother in America in these words: "My brother, I am but a mortal. When

I shall die and my soul arrives at the Judgment Seat, it will be
asked: 'Why did you fail to reprove your brother?' Therefore, I
am proceeding to warn you to remain ever faithful to God and to
His commandments."

Pupko, p. 104.

83. FASTING

1. Who Can, and Who Wants?

The Apter Rabbi said: "Were it within my power, I would abolish all fast days except the 9th of Ab and Yom Kippur. The reason
is this: on Yom Kippur, who wants to eat, and on the 9th of Ab, who
can eat?"

Zlotnik, p. 95.

84. FIDELITY

1. A Test of Fidelity

The Vorker thus interpreted the verse in Exodus 16:14: "Behold,
I will cause it to rain bread from Heaven for you; and the people
shall go out and gather a day's portion every day, that I may prove
them, whether they will walk in My law, or not." He said: "Since
bread will rain from Heaven, namely, since man's sustenance is to
be provided for him, why should he be required to go out and
gather it? The answer is this: God wishes to prove and test him, in
order to discover whether he will walk in His law, even though he
may be laboring for his livelihood."

Zammlung, p. 104.

85. FIRMNESS

1. Making Firm Man's Steps

Said the Hafetz Hayyim: "One of the Blessings reads: 'Blessed
art Thou, O Lord our God, King of the Universe, who hast made
firm the steps of man.' (Singer, p. 6.) From this we learn that
every step a man takes is dependent upon God. It behooves us to
consecrate our steps to the performance of a good deed, or to the
conservation of our health. Another Blessing declares that it is God
who opens our eyes. Therefore, it behooves us to utilize our power
of vision to search out a worthy action."

Pupko, p. 115.

86. FOLLY AND FOOLS

1. *Wise Man and Fool*

Said the Riziner: "The house of Rabbi Baruch the Medzibozer is a wonderful place. There the wise man is able to acquire buckets-ful of the Fear of Heaven, but the foolish man, by the same token, only increases his folly there."

M. B., p. 34.

2. *Without Moderation*

Said Rabbi Ber of Leova: "We read in the Talmud: 'No one commits a sin until the spirit of folly has entered into him.' If we ask: 'How can a spirit of folly enter into a man who is sinless?', the answer is: 'even a good deed done without moderation brings on the spirit of folly which causes sin.'"

Guttman, p. 24.

3. *The Fool and His Desires*

Said the Strelisker: "Remember, oh man, that on each and every occasion you permit your desires to rule over you, you become a fool. A wise man, however, rules over his desires at all times."

I. K., p. 41.

4. *The Folly of the Wise*

Said the Hafetz Hayyim: "I have heard the proverb: 'every fool is wise with respect to himself.' I amend the saying as follows: 'Many wise men act like fools with respect to themselves.'"

Pupko, p. 51.

5. *"Old, Foolish Ruler"*

Said the Hafetz Hayyim: "In *Kohelet* the name given to the Evil Impulse is: 'old, foolish ruler.' Is, then, the Evil Impulse truly foolish? Nay, but it is the mission of the Evil Impulse through its persuasiveness to make others foolish. Therefore read: 'old fool-maker that rules over the weak and susceptible.'"

Pupko, ii, 62.

6. *Betraying His Folly*

The Dubner Maggid said: "A king sent his Crown Prince to a famous university in order to perfect himself in science and philosophy. The prince was something of a fool, and the king hoped that a thorough education might compensate for his lack of native ability. When the prince returned, a banquet was held at the palace. A nobleman asked the prince: 'Does your scientific knowledge enable you to describe the article which I hold in my palm?' The prince looked hard at the nobleman's palm and pronounced the object within it to be round with a hole in it. This proved to be an excellent description, for the object was a signet-ring. The nobleman was greatly astonished, and was curious to discover to what degree his scientific studies had improved the prince. Therefore he asked the prince to state specifically the nature of the object. The prince replied: 'To name the object is a task in which science cannot help me. I must use my own intelligence instead, and it leads me to believe it is a mechanic's tool.' "

The Dubner drew the lesson, saying: "Education is never an adequate substitute for common sense."

Dubner, i, 66-68.

87. FOOD

1. Eating to Live

The Tzanzer Rabbi inquired of a man at his table whether he had been served with food. The man replied: "I came here, not to eat, but to learn." The Rabbi replied: "The soul has been sent to earth to acquire spiritual riches, not to eat. But lack of food drives it away from this world."

Tzanzer Hasidut, p. 245.

88. FORGIVENESS

1. Forgiveness as a Gift

Rabbi David Mirapoler delivered this discourse on Rosh ha-Shanah: "We come unto Thee, O Lord, not with a request for Hesed, nor with an enumeration of our Mitzvot, our virtuous deeds. Like the poor and the destitute do we knock at Thy door. These words we find in the prayer petitioning the Almighty to pardon our sins. Why do we say: not with a request for Hesed? In the Holy Tongue Hesed means kindness, but in the folk-speech, the Yiddish, it indicates a loan extended without interest charge. Therefore we declare: 'We do not ask Thee for pardon as a loan on our promise to perform good deeds in the future. We ask it not as a reward for the Mitzvot we have performed. No, like lowly suppliants, we beg Thee to grant us forgiveness as an outright gift.' "

Kaufman, p. 147.

2. Forgiveness for Dishonesty

Before the closing Yom Kippur Services in 1916 the Hafetz Hay-yim called over his Disciples and counselled each one to devote a day in order to investigate any unfair deed he may have performed against a fellow-man. The Disciple was also enjoined to correct his misdeed. For in the *Neilah* Service we pray that we be forgiven any dishonesty. Such a resolution is certain to be accepted in Heaven.

Pupko, ii, 16.

89. FORTITUDE

1. Resistance for Faith

Said the Hafetz Hayyim: "Do you know the nature of true service to God? Oftentimes it brings about conflict between those who are Jews and those who do not share our views. Our adversaries erect many obstacles to prevent us from serving the Lord. Then it is our duty to stand firmly against them and to go forward in our service to the Almighty."

Pupko, p. 111.

90. FORTUNE

1. What Is Good Fortune?

Said the Hafetz Hayyim: "There is no greater good fortune for a man than his poverty; there is no greater misfortune for a man than his wealth."

Pupko, p. 114.

91. FREEDOM

1. The Capitol of the Realm

When Hungary granted civil emancipation to its Jews, Rabbi Moses Sopher remarked: "I see no genuine cause for thanksgiving. It is like a prince who has been banished by his father. After a time, the king sends an architect to build a palace for the prince at the place of his banishment. The prince exclaims: 'Why should my father build a palace for me here? If he were less angry with me, he would recall me to the capitol of the realm where he reigns.' By the same token, if the Lord truly wished to improve our lot, He would not do so in a land of exile. On the contrary He would recall us to His Holy Land."

Sopher, p. 44.

92. FREE WILL

1. The Reason for False Leaders

The Tzortkover heard a self-styled Zaddik whose behavior was unseemly. He declared: "When so many true Zaddikim appear simultaneously, Satan complains they will have so overwhelming an influence that free-will must disappear. The Lord thereupon says: 'You are right! I shall send to earth some Zaddikim who will serve thee, rather than Me. Then the Hasidim will be compelled to display their power of choice.'"

Margulies, p. 31.

2. God's Influence

God's influence is manifested in granting to men the primitive clay of life. Men may work it into manifold forms, and each man may sculpture it according to the particular design he chooses.

Berditschevky, p. 12.

The world is comparable to a music hall, replete with many instruments and many manuscripts of music. Each man may select and play upon the instrument of his choice, and each man may select and sing his own song. This gives pleasure to the Lord, his Maker.

Berditschevky, p. 15.

3. Honor for God

Said Rabbi Samuel Zevi of Alexander: "If two paths lie before you, it behooves you to reflect on the question: which will bring more honor to God? Then you are to choose this path."

Zammlung, p. 93.

4. God's Omnipresence

Hasidim teach that God is everywhere and in everything—even in sin. The Gaon of Wilna, however, declared: "If this be truly your teaching, the sinner will feel no repentance, for he will regard God as his partner in sin. You should phrase your teaching thus: God has endowed man with freedom of will, whereby he can choose to commit or to avoid sin."

Teitelbaum, i, 25.

5. An Act of Free Will

Said Rabbi Israel Isaac (Yerachmiel) of Alexander: "We read in Psalm 111:3: 'Great are the works of the Lord, sought out of all them that have delight therein.' I comment upon this verse as follows: 'Men of greatness are the works of God Who has endowed them with keen minds and with diligence. But those who seek after the delight which the love and fear of God can bring them include all who desire to embark upon such a quest. Everyone is able to do so by using his freedom of will.' "

Zammlung, p. 86.

6. Free Will and Prayer

Said the Bratzlaver: "I am often asked how the doctrine of free will can be reconciled with the prescribed prayers wherein we ask God's aid to attain repentance. I answer as follows: free will lies in the domain of man's reason. But there are countless sparks of holiness above reason, being dependent on faith. It is chiefly for this, namely, to have faith, that we petition God for aid. Our own free will cannot help us therein, but, on the contrary, the rational approach makes it difficult for us to have faith."

H. H. N., p. 41b.

93. FRIENDSHIP

1. Friend, not Master

Said the Leover: "The Zaddik who enacts the role of a friend in his prayers for another receives an earlier answer to his petitions than one who prays in the role of a Master."

Guttman, p. 27.

2. Your Closest Friend

Said the Bratzlaver: "God is your closest friend. Tell Him your troubles. Acquaint Him with your struggles. Open your heart to Him. Ask His aid."

H. H. N., p. 6a.

3. The Two Friends

Said the Dubner: "A storekeeper had two friends. One manifested his friendship by giving his patronage to his friend. The other displayed his friendship by advertising the storekeeper's goods and thereby inducing them to make purchases, though he himself had little need of any merchandise. Which friend did more?

"From this we learn that one man learns Torah himself out of the love of learning. The other person learns little himself but works hard to assure that Talmud Torahs and other institutions of learning exist. Who does more for the Torah, which both men love?"

Dubner, i, 272-273.

94. GAMBLING

1. Gambling a Public Vice

"The vice of gambling," said a Rabbi, "is indeed an evil one. Other sins may be committed in secret, but no one can gamble by himself alone."

Zlotnik, p. 62.

95. GEHENNA

1. Gehenna Is Preferable

The Rabbi of Ohel reprimanded his son-in-law, the Rabbi of Vishnitz, for his habit of tardiness in commencing the Morning Prayers. He wrote him: "Believe me when I say that he who transgresses a law of the *Shulhan Aruch* will inherit Gehenna." "This may be true," replied the Vishnitzer, "but you, my dear Rabbi, will have as your companions in Gan Eden (Paradise) the butcher, the teamster, and others like them. As for me, however, when I am in Gehenna, I will have as my companions all those who have at one time or another been tardy in the recital of the Morning Prayers. These include the Lubliner, the Koznitzer, the Lizensker, Rabbi Sussya, and my own Rabbi, the Ropshitzer. I greatly prefer the company of Zaddikim in Gehenna, if your dictum is correct, to the company of ordinary Jews in Gan Eden."

Raker, p. 148.

96. GENEROSITY

1. The Reward of Generosity

Said the Dubner: "A prince once was traveling with his royal entourage and he halted at a certain inn. The innkeeper furnished him with appropriate accommodations, to the full satisfaction of the royal guest. The next morning the prince asked for the bill and paid it. He gave no further thought to the innkeeper. At the next stopover the prince received an even finer welcome, but when he requested the bill, the second innkeeper said: 'I require no payment. The honor of welcoming a prince to my humble tavern is more than sufficient recompense.'

"The prince took his departure, but thought constantly of the good-hearted tavern-keeper. When he returned home, he dispatched to the generous man gifts worth fivefold the amount a payment for the service rendered would have entailed.

"From this we learn that your generous help to your fellow-man

without the expectation of a reward is returned to you later with
compound interest."

Dubner, i, 209-210.

97. GIFTS

1. Gifts to an Unrighteous Official

During the First World War, the students of the Yeshivah of the
Hafetz Hayyim moved to the town of Saulewitz. The Polish mayor
launched a persecution against the Jewish community, and declined
to be dissauded by any gifts. The Hafetz Hayyim advised the community's spokesmen to follow the example of the Patriarch Jacob in
his dealings with Esau, and to beg the official to accept the proferred
gifts. This plea was successful, and the mayor became a friend
of the Yeshivah and the community. The Rabbi explained: "I imitated the action of Rabbi Judah ha-Nasi. Let me add, however, it
is a sin to offer gifts to a righteous official who strives merely to
bring about obedience to the law. Non-Jews, like Jews, are instructed to obey the laws of the government, and we are guilty of
transgression if we seek to mislead them. But if an official is un-
righteous in his actions, bringing injury to innocent folk, we commit
no offense if we seek to prevent his misdeeds by gifts."

Pupko, p. 61.

2. Unaccepted Gifts

The Hafetz Hayyim spent much valuable time in the selling of
his books. A friend asked him: "Why do you not accept gifts and
therefore gain time for study?" The Rabbi replied: "Gifts are offered to me because the donor knows I will not accept them. If it
were known that I accept gifts, no one would offer them to me."

Pupko, p. 52.

3. Counterfeit

Said the Dubner: "A man distributed some silverware among his
servants. All the gifts were of pure silver but one servant received a
disk of plated silverware. This servant thanked his master and said:
'I do not care to receive a free gift. I therefore ask you to accept
from me this thaler.' The master looked at the coin and exclaimed:
'But it is counterfeit.' 'Yes,' answered the servant, 'And so is the
gift.'

"From this we learn that tact should accompany the telling of a
fact."

Dubner, i, 152.

4. Praise for Small Gifts?

Rabbi Baruch of Medziboz heard praise being given to a Rabbi because he accepted only small donations. He said: "When we come to the portals of a royal palace, those who are the important attendants receive large gifts, since they open the portals into the inmost sanctum. But those who merely open the side-doors receive small gifts. Shall we, therefore, praise the latter because of this?"

M. B., p. 15.

98. GOD'S OMNIPRESENCE; DIVINITY

1. In the Midst of Barter

It was the custom of Rabbi Leib Saras to make his appearance at every Fair in Poland. He would take his stand in the very center of the market and discuss Torah. Thus in the midst of barter God was not forgotten.

G. A., p. 11.

2. God Is Omnipresent

The Lubavitzer Rabbi declared: "God is within us, above us and all about us. No space, no place, no solid matter is free of His presence. His abode is everywhere."

Berditschevky, p. 56.

3. Divinity in Heaven and on Earth

Said the Tzernobiler: "The Holy 'Ari' uncovered the divinity resident in Heaven. The Besht, who was no less holy, uncovered the divinity resident on earth."

Twersky, p. 21.

4. Damaging the Image of God

Said Rabbi Zevi of Alexander: "In Exodus 20:3, we read: 'Thou shalt have no other gods over My countenance.' * We can interpret this verse as follows: 'Refrain from sin, for a sin damages the image of God He has granted you, and gives to your face the image of Satan, placed over God's countenance.'"

Zammlung, p. 96.

* The Hebrew is: *'al panay.*

5. Man Is Half-Divine

Said the Hafetz Hayyim: "A man should never forget that he is a semi-divine creature. His thoughts, his power of reason and his indwelling soul will return to Heaven, but his desires, his earthly pleasures and his body will remain behind."

Pupko, p. 115.

99. GOOD MANNERS

1. Moderation in Worldly Ways

The Ropshitzer, while a young man, once pushed and shoved his way through a crowd in order to come closer and hear better his Rabbi. An older Hasid protested: "you should show good manners, young man; you shouldn't push like this." The Ropshitzer retorted: "Don't you know that a knowledge of Torah is acquired through moderation in worldly manners?" (*Ethics of the Fathers* 6:6. The phrase is: *Be-miut sehorah.*)

Zlotnik, p. 29.

2. The Merit of Good Manners

Said Rabbi Yehiel of Alexander: "The Midrash declares that when Moses ascended to Heaven to receive the Torah, the angels began to exclaim: 'what is one born of a woman doing among us?' Thereupon God brought it about that Moses looked like the Patriarch Abraham, and thereby convinced the angels that mortal man, not angels, merited the gift of the Torah. How did God thus convince the angels? He said to them: 'My Torah may be given only to beings with good manners. Now when the three angels were sent to visit the Patriarch Abraham, he comported himself in an admirable manner, although he did not know they were angels. As for you, however, as soon as a mortal man visits you, you begin to shout against him. Tell Me, then, who possess better manners, mortals or angels?' "

Zammlung, p. 69.

100. GOODNESS

1. Testing With Goodness

Said Rabbi Feivel Gritzer: "We read in Psalm 23:6: 'Surely only goodness and mercy shall pursue me all the days of my life.' Why does the Psalmist use the verb 'pursue' (in the Hebrew)? It is because the Lord oftentimes tests a man with goodness and on other times with poverty. David therefore offers this petition: 'If I am to be tested, let it be by goodness and not by poverty, though it is often more difficult for the rich to remain pious than for the poor.' "

Zammlung, p. 33.

101. GRATITUDE

1. The Blind Man's Thanks

Said the Dubner: "Once at a banquet a man passed the platter to his neighbor who was almost blind. The latter thanked him profusely. His other neighbor, however, remarked to him: 'Instead of thanking so heartily the man who passed you the platter, you should reserve your gratitude for the giver of the repast. Your right hand neighbor not only gave you nothing of his own, but he took care to place the best portion on his own plate before passing the platter to you.'

"From this we learn: we should not be like the blind man and thank excessively the man who merely gives us out of his abundance that which he himself does not need. Rather should we express our gratitude to the Lord, our Supreme Provider."

Dubner, i, 303-304.

2. Accepting Honors Gracefully

When the Tzernobiler Maggid was inducted as Rabbi, many honors were showered upon him. He gave clear indication of his dislike for the ceremony and the accompanying tributes. Rabbi Baruch of Medziboz who was present at the occasion, remarked: "The Maggid believes that honors are incompatible with his sense of humility. I take a different view. I believe that God has decreed that honors should be granted you, and it is your duty to accept them gracefully and gratefully. Obedience to God's will is more meaningful than the cultivation of personal humility."

M. B., p. 13.

102. GREATNESS

1. Appreciating Greatness

Said the Dubner: "An illustrious scientist was forced for reasons of health to settle in a little village with an excellent climate. The inhabitants of the town, however, were persons without learning. The newcomer was asked his occupation and he replied that he was a veterinary. His wife asked him: 'Why haven't you disclosed your reputation as an authority in the fields of anatomy and physiology?' The scientist replied: 'Because, my dear, these people would not have understood my true occupation, but they do know what a veterinary is.'

"From this we learn that a great man can be appreciated aright only by those who have a measure of greatness themselves."

Dubner, i, 263-264.

2. Greatness After Death

A grandson of the Hafetz Hayyim asked him: "We read in *Erubin*, 13: 'Greatness escapes the man who pursues it, but greatness pursues the man who flees from it.' What is the difference, seeing that in both instances greatness and the man do not meet?" "This is true," replied the Rabbi, "but when greatness pursues a person who flees from it, it does overtake him after he has passed away."

Pupko, p. 89.

103. GREED

1. The Penalty

Said the Dubner: "A hospitable householder entertained several guests. He ordered his waiters to inquire from each guest the sort of food he liked. Those who preferred plain food were served at one table, and those who liked delicate foods at another table. One guest had asked for the delicate food and was served it. When, however, he noticed the plainer food, he took a fancy to it and requested a portion of it. The householder, however, overheard him and said: 'Please move over to the other table, and you will receive the food for which you have asked.'

"From this we learn: Some Israelites at first wished to reside in a holy land and were brought there. Later they cast covetous eyes at the profane pleasures to be enjoyed in other lands. Therefore they were exiled to these other countries."

Dubner, i, 230-231.

104. GRIEF

1. Mixed Joy

When Rabbi Isaac Ziditchover died, his Hasidim came in a group to the Tzanzer Rabbi. He remarked: "I recall visiting Rabbi Hirsch Ziditchover after the death of my Master, the Ropshitzer. Rabbi Hirsch said: 'My joy in your visit is mingled with grief. For is it not the consequence of a Zaddik's demise?' To you, my friends, I make the same statement."

Braver, p. 52.

2. Unending Guidance

When Rabbi Bunam died, the Vorker visited the chief mourner, Rabbi Abraham Moses. When Rabbi Abraham expressed his grief in losing his father's teaching, the Vorker replied: "I beg of you to feel no sense of loss. Is is not possible to believe that you have truly lost nothing. In place of teaching you in life, your father's spirit will now continue to teach you from on High."

Rokotz, ii, 13.

105. HABIT

1. *The Value of Habit*

Rabbi Israel of Pikov said: "We read in Psalm 15:3: 'That hath no slander upon his tongue, nor doeth evil to his fellow.' The Hebrew word: *Ragal*, translated here as 'slander' also has the meaning: 'habit.' If we use the second meaning of the word, we can paraphrase the verse thus: 'That hath no habit upon his tongue to say that he doeth no evil to his fellow.' We sometimes find some wretched persons complaining in this manner: 'Why are we despised? Are we doing any evil to our fellows?' They fail to understand that a man is required to do good unto others, not merely to abstain from doing evil. Positive goodness, not negative, is desired."

Guttman, p. 35.

106. HANUKAH

1. *Hanukah Thoughts of the Gerer*

Said the Gerer:

"1. The Hanukah Menorah brings out the Light of the Torah. We read: 'The Mitzvah is a lamp, and the Torah is a light.' Therefore it behooves us to study the Torah immediately after kindling the Hanukah Lamp, and all obscure passages will become luminously clear to you.

"2. On Hanukah it is our duty to recite the Hallel. Our obedience truly brings us the gift of more abundant life. For we read in Psalm 115:17: 'The dead praise not the Lord.'

"3. The story of Hanukah tells that 'all the oils,' namely, all branches of learning in Israel became unclean. Only one tiny portion of oil, sealed up within the breasts of the Jews, remained pure, uncontaminated by the influence of the pagan world. This was the belief in monotheism, and this sufficed to rescue Israel.

"4. The name: 'Hanukah' meaning dedication, indicates that the commencement of service must be undertaken by pure and holy men. The service may then be continued by those who are impure. Hence the dedication or inauguration of a service is the holier portion in our worship of the Almighty.

"5. The Sages did not ordain any special festive meal for Hanukah, inasmuch as it would have had value only in the case of the minority who are able to appreciate aright the martyrdom displayed by the Jews in Maccabean days."

Rokotz, ii, 46-50.

2. Hanukah in the Pentateuch?

It was asked: Is there a suggestion in the Pentateuch pointing to the Festival of Hanukah? An affirmative reply was given. We find it written in the Book of Leviticus, following Chapter 23 which deals with the Festival in the first verse of the next Chapter: "Command the children of Israel that they bring unto thee pure olive oil beaten for the light, to cause a lamp to burn continually." From this we learn that the Feast of Lights is also a Festival, inasmuch as these words occur so close to the Chapter on the Festivals mentioned in the Pentateuch.

Mahzor Vitry, p. 198.

3. Eight Days of Hanukah

The Mirapoler Rabbi said: "The institution of eight days of Hanukah teaches us that not merely the supernatural, but also the natural, partakes of a miracle. One day's supply of oil was available, yet the Menorah of the Maccabees burned for seven days by virtue of a miracle. Yet the celebration was ordained for eight days."

Kaufman, p. 50.

107. HAPPINESS

1. Where Light Enters

Said the Riziner: "He who wishes happiness must bear with patience a measure of unhappiness. Light can enter only where darkness has been."

Margulies, p. 23.

108. HASID

1. The Nature of the Hasid

"1. The Hasid is above place and time, above his surroundings and circumstances.

"2. The Hasid always looks upon the world with fresh eyes and with human interest.

"3. The Mitnagedim are afraid that they may transform holiness into matters profane. The Hasid is confident that he can turn matters profane into matters holy.

"4. Through enthusiasm the Hasid enlarges himself, and by virtue of it he aspires to a higher status.

"5. By cleaving unto holiness, the Hasid erases his own self, striving to become no longer what he has been.

"6. By cleaving to holiness, the Hasid becomes the type of person to which his capacity entitles him—a man of purity, cleanness of spirit and holiness."

Berditschevsky, p. 10.

109. HEALING AND CURES

1. *Do Not Despair*

Rabbi Isaac of Ziditchov said to a Hasid who despairingly told him that the physician of a kinsman had given up hope for his recovery: "A doctor has the duty of curing his patient, but he is not embounded to give up hope. To abandon hope is not within his province." To another Hasid whom thieves had despoiled of all his possessions, and who already had expressed his despair over recovering them: "It is a rule of Jewish law that if an owner despairs of his lost property he no longer has any claim upon it. Why is this? Because he should not lose hope, but should pray for the recovery of his lost goods."

Braver, p. 72.

2. *Bitter Medicine*

Said the Hafetz Hayyim: "Oftentimes an ill person is ordered to drink bitter medicine as a remedy. Tribulations and sufferings can act as a medicine to cure your soul."

Pupko, p. 97.

3. *Feeling No Pain*

A physician visited a patient. On inquiring whether he felt any pain or discomfort, the patient replied: "No, I do not." "If this is the case," replied the physician, "why are you in bed?" "Thus it is in spiritual matters," said the Hafetz Hayyim: "If you lay claim to spiritual perfection, why do you lack love of God and reverence for Him?"

Pupko, p. 98.

4. *Torah as a Cure*

A grandson of Rabbi Isaac of Ziditchov became very ill. His grandfather said: "Once I read in a Communal Record of Lvov that Rabbi David, author of the legal commentary, *Turei Zahav*, was implored to offer prayer for a sick person. He replied: 'I offer to him who is ill the gift of the new comment I have inscribed today in my manuscript. May the merit of the Torah heal him.' I, too, present to him who is ill a new interpretation of Torah I have written down." The patient recovered.

Braver, p. 37.

5. *A True Healing*

Rabbi Isaac of Ziditchov learned much of the art of healing during the many years of his 'wandering' in the earlier period of his life. When his grandson fell sick, the lad's father implored Rabbi Isaac to do something to aid him. Rabbi Isaac was buried in thought and did not utter a single word in response. The sick boy became steadily worse. A second grandson, Judah Zevi was sent upstairs to the room of Rabbi Isaac. At the door he coughed, and when he was allowed to enter, he said: "Grandfather, Joshua Heshel has improved a little. Can't you hasten his recovery?" Rabbi Isaac went over to a cupboard, took out a container of herbs and said: "Have these brewed at once and let the sick boy drink the brew." This remedy brought about the patient's complete recovery. The Rabbi thereupon made this explanation to the boy's father: "You, my son, disturbed my thoughts with your dire report about your sick boy. In my anxiety I found it impossible to collect my thoughts and forgot the remedy at hand. But when Judah Zevi came to me with encouraging news, my fears were allayed, and I was able to think aright."

Braver, p. 41.

6. *The Lord's Promise*

A weeping woman besought Rabbi Isaac of Ziditchov to save her dying son. The Rabbi offered this prayer: "O Lord, long have I resisted accepting the role of a Rebbe. But Thou hast so arranged it that my resistance has been broken down. Wilt Thou permit me to fail in my work?" He entered the reception hall and announced: "I have God's promise that my prayer has been accepted." The woman's son recovered.

Braver, p. 41.

7. *The Rabbi's Need*

A Hasid came to Rabbi Isaac of Ziditchov intending to test his wisdom. He sent in a petition on which were written the words: "for a healing." The Hasid had in mind not a healing of the body, but of the spirit. The Rabbi read the petition and exclaimed: "Such a healing, I myself need."

Braver, p. 47.

8. *Hurrying the Redemption*

Rabbi Abraham Stretiner quarrelled with his friend, Rabbi Isaac Ziditchover. Unfortunately he became very ill. A Hasid remarked:

"Why not apologize to the Ziditchover Rabbi and beseech him to pray for you?" The Stretiner replied: "Our quarrel occurred because he refused to aid me in hastening the coming of Redemption. How, then, is it possible for me to recede from my position?"

Braver, p. 55.

9. Twofold Advice

Rabbi Hirsch of Ziditchov said: "Whenever a person comes to me seeking aid for his bodily needs, I hear at the same time, between the lines of his tale, the account of his spiritual needs. Therefore, my advice to him is twofold: advice to benefit his body and advice to strengthen his weakening spirit."

Braver, p. 69.

10. Learning Obedience

Said the Dubner: "A nobleman's son became seriously ill. The town's physicians were summoned and prescribed a regimen of diet and conduct. The son refused to obey these instructions, and as a consequence, his malady became worse, and prospect for a cure grew less. The nobleman made inquiry and located a sanitarium where the discipline was strict, and where the high birth of the patient would not avail him in the slightest. There the young man learned obedience to the regulations, and in time began to recover.

"From this we learn: When Israel was afflicted with moral illness and disobeyed the Prophets, physicians were sent to effect a cure. They, too, were disobeyed. Israel's Father in Heaven thereupon exiled Israel among heartless peoples, where the harsh treatment Israel received, gradually purified his spirit."

Dubner, i, 286-287.

11. The Spiritually Ill

Said the Dubner: "A father complained to a neighbor that his son was ill, and would not eat his meals. The neighbor visited the boy and offered him a pleasing toy if he would eat a meal in his home. He was successful in having the boy consume a goodly portion of food. When the neighbor met the father, he told him of his stratagem. 'What you tell me only confirms my anxiety for my son's health', commented the father. 'If he were really healthy, he would eat to satisfy his appetite, not because he was eager for a toy.'

"From this we learn: he who becomes a man of charity and good deeds only by reason of expecting rewards in the World-to-Come is spiritually ill."

Dubner, i, 268-269.

12. *The Sugar on the Pill*

Said the Dubner: "A physician prescribed for a boy patient some pills coated with sugar. The patient failed to show any improvement, and the physician resolved to investigate the cause. By carefully watching the boy the doctor noticed that the foolish lad licked off the sweet coating with his tongue but spat out the pill itself. He then took the proper measures to remedy this unsatisfactory situation.

"From this we learn: many a member of an audience in a synagogue will swallow appreciatively the stories and ancedotes, but will refuse to heed the bitter truths which the preacher seeks to impress upon the congregation."

Dubner, i, 188.

13. *The Unwanted Visit*

Said the Dubner: " A prime minister of the realm was visited by the king during his illness. The official's wife remarked: 'Isn't it a great honor that the king has come to our very home?' The prime minister replied: 'It may be an honor, but I really would not have desired it. It would have been far better if I were in good health and were able to visit the king in his palace.'

"From this we learn: it is true that God visits us even though we are in Exile, but it would be better if we were a healthy nation in our own land, and visited Him in His Beth ha-Mikdash (His Sanctuary)."

Dubner, i, 275.

14. *"A Peculiar Treasure"*

The "Yud" commented on Exodus 19:5: "Ye shall be unto Me a peculiar treasure." He said: "The word 'Segulah' used in this verse later received the meaning of 'remedy.' Neither the one who administers the remedy, nor the sick person who receives it, understands the virtue of the remedy, namely, the reason why it achieves a cure. This is how the Lord wishes us to be in our cleaving unto Him: we should be in primitive ignorance, without reasoning why we act as we do, and we should cleave unto Him in a spontaneous outburst of feeling."

H. Hak., p. 127.

15. *A Genuine Cure*

Said the Dubner: "A rich man's son loved the cup that cheers all too well. His father besought a physician to cure him of his addiction to drink. Eventually the physician assured the father that his son was totally cured. The father wished to test the effectiveness of the cure. He instructed his son to purchase a quart of the best wine. When the proprietor of the wine-shop went down into the cellar for the wine, the son felt an uncontrollable urge to smash the bottles of wine on the shelves. With his cane he began the work of demolition. The wineshop owner returned from the cellar, drove the youth away, and sent a bill of considerable size for the damage done. The father gladly paid the amount asked, inasmuch as he perceived that his son had developed intense revulsion at the very sight of wine.

"From this we learn the following: when the Children of Israel (according to Numbers 31) imitated the immoral conduct of the Midianites and then repented of their behavior, the Lord desired to test their penitence. He therefore sent an Israelite army into the land of Midian. When the Children of Israel no longer imitated the vices of the Midianites, but made war on them, the Lord knew that Israel was truly cured."

Dubner, i, 137-138.

16. *Pray Like a Child*

When the Bratzlaver fell ill, his daughter's child, a boy of four, entered the room. The Bratzlaver asked the lad to pray for his recovery. The boy replied: "Give me your watch and I will pray for you." The Rabbi smiled and said: "See, he is already a 'good Jew'. He wishes to be paid for his prayer." The Bratzlaver handed his watch to the boy, and the child exclaimed: "Dear God, dear God, let grandpapa become well!" The Bratzlaver commented: "This is the real way to offer prayer. Any other way is futile."

H. H. N., p. 22b.

17. *The Healer of the Soul's Diseases*

Said the Bratzlaver: "No physician can heal unless he is well acquainted with the physiology and anatomy of the body. In the same way no healer of those sick in soul can cure them unless he thoroughly understands what particular spiritual remedy will furnish solace and comfort to every particular disease of the soul. He must know what the soul lacks before he can cure it. One man may be cured by reading ethical books; another by practicing more hospitality; a third by the reading of Psalms; a fourth by engaging in profound learning; a fifth by performing deeds of kindness; a sixth by doing communal work."

H. H. N., p. 48b.

18. Why He Wept

Rabbi David Lelever's son was once very ill. Scores of persons came to visit him, each one bringing a gift of food or wine to strengthen him. When the youth had recovered, the Rabbi commenced to weep. "Why do you shed tears?" he was asked. "Because my heart is filled with sorrow at the thought that you fail to show such helpful sympathy in the case of other persons who are sick. Every ill person should receive equal consideration," said the Rabbi.

H. Hak., p. 17.

19. "I Will Be Feverish Tomorrow"

The Hafetz Hayyim remarked: "Frequently preachers rebuke us for our unsatisfactory service to the Lord. Is there truth in this? Are there not days when we serve Him with great zeal? In this we are reminded of a man who, when asked how he was feeling, replied: 'I am feverish.' The questioner looked at him in surprise and said: 'But you look the picture of health.' 'I know I do,' said the other man, 'but tomorrow I am sure I will have a high fever.' Thus is it with us. Today we may pray in a satisfactory way, but inasmuch as we not do so tomorrow, our service is inadequate."

Pupko, p. 76.

20. Her Own Credit

The wife of Rabbi Bunam once went to visit her husband's great Disciple, Rabbi Jacob Aryeh of Radzimin. Rain poured down in torrents and darkness enveloped the town. The woman beheld a light in a house and knocked at the door. On entering it she was told that a child lay dangerously ill in a room of the house, and therefore it was not possible for her to remain there overnight. The woman, however, promised she would ask the Radziminer Zaddik to pray for the child's recovery if permission were granted her to remain. The next morning, after the storm had cleared, she went to the Rabbi's home where she was received with great respect. She told him of the sick child and said: "Forgive me, but I promised recovery to the child on your credit." Rabbi Jacob Aryeh replied: "There was no need to call on my credit. Your own credit is more than sufficient." The woman offered her prayers and the child recovered its health.

Zammlung, p. 49.

21. For All Purposes

Said the Bratzlaver: "The Psalmist says: 'The Lord is good for all.' (Psalm 145:9) * This may be interpreted to mean: 'The Lord is good . . . for all purposes, namely, to cure the sick, to furnish a livelihood, to bring us forth from all tribulations. Therefore, we are in duty bound to pray unto him.'"

H. H. N., p. 4b.

* The Hebrew word: *La-Kol* means "for all" or "to all."

22. God, The Great Physician

A Hasid fell ill and complained to the Rabbi of Neshkiz that the physician in his home town did not know the cure for his malady. The Rabbi declared: "Go to Hanipol and visit the local doctor there." When the Hasid reached Hanipol, he discovered that no doctor resided there, and in great distress returned home. He went to the Rabbi again and informed him that his journey had been useless. The Rabbi asked the Hasid: "What, then, does a resident of Hanipol do when he falls sick?" The Hasid replied: "He prays for his recovery." The Rabbi continued: "It is for this very reason that I sent you to Hanipol, namely, to learn that if a mortal doctor fails you, do as the sick folk of Hanipol do; they pray to God, the Great Physician."

Twersky, p. 54.

23. The Best Cure

The wife of the Hafetz Hayyim instructed her son to the effect that she never summoned a physician when a son became ill. She would distribute forty pounds of bread to the poor, and her husband, the Rabbi, would ascend into the attic and offer prayer. She was convinced this served as the best cure.

Pupko, p. 12.

24. Demanding a Miracle

A man of wealth, stricken with paralysis, was brought to hear Aryeh ben Pinhas when he preached his first sermon in his new position, on healing and faith. The Rabbi spoke of reconciliation with the inevitable, contentment and peace of spirit. But the afflicted magnate, visiting the Rabbi after the Services, exclaimed: "This is cold comfort. I thought you would have some secret, mystic word, some miraculous knowledge which would give me back the use of my legs. But you offer me in your preaching only what they all have told me. I want something that will make me walk again!" The Rabbi replied: "If it is possible for God to restore you to full health, He will surely do so. But if He cannot, seeing that nature has decreed otherwise, are you any the happier because you remain so bitter?"

Selected.

25. Sympathy With The Sick

A wealthy Jewess visited the Leipniker Rav to see his son to whom she wished to marry her daughter. She observed that the Rav was greatly upset and inquired the reason. The Rav answered: "A child in town is dangerously ill." "Why should you worry about a strange child?" exclaimed the woman. On hearing this the Rav declined to allow his son to marry into the family of a woman so callous and unsympathetic.

Eibeschitz, p. 12.

26. The Rabbi's Promise

A man, not a Hasid, came to Rabbi Dov of Biale, beseeching the Rabbi to promise him that a member of his family, lying seriously ill, would recover, even though the physicians had given up hope. The Rabbi consoled him by giving the solemn promise thus asked. An intimate of the Rabbi asked him with surprise: "How can the Rabbi give a solemn promise such as this, especially to a non-Hasid? He may damage the Rabbi's reputation for veracity." Rabbi Dov replied: "It is my custom to promise good tidings to anyone who comes to me. Afterwards I plead with the Lord, saying: 'O Lord, wilt thou make of me a falsifier?'" The patient recovered.

Selected.

27. Avoiding Insincerity

Rabbi Mendel Kotzker visited the Lubliner Zaddik only once. Soon after he fell ill, and the "Yud" advised him to appease the Lubliner whom he had offended. The Kotzker replied: "Shall I visit him again, even though I cannot accept the system he teaches? Nay, I dislike mind-reading and fortune-telling even by means of the Holy Spirit. There is more to Hasidism than that."

Walden, p. 34.

28. Medicine and Food

Said the Hafetz Hayyim: "The study of ethics is like medicine for the soul. It behooves you to take the medicine, but then you must turn to substantial food, namely, the study of Torah. Too much medicine is injurious."

Pupko, p. 42.

29. The Physician and The World

In his last illness, Rabbi Baruch of Medziboz, knowing that the end was imminent, refused to have the attention of a physician. He said: "Man is a microcosm. What there is in man is found in the world in larger form. If a physician cannot understand and cure

the afflictions of the world, how can he understand and cure the
afflictions of man?"

M. B., p. 34.

30. *The Seventh Person*

A new student was accepted in the Yeshivah of Rabbi Moses
Sopher. He displayed great diligence in his studies and quickly
gained a reputation for learning. But he overtaxed himself and fell
ill. Rabbi Moses entered the room where the youth lay ill, bent
over him, and asked: "Dost thou see?" "Yes," replied the youth.
This was repeated several times, whereupon the patient began to
recover. Rabbi Moses invited him to explain what he had seen.
The lad replied: "I seem to have seen six holy men. Three of them
told me that I would die; three said I would recover. Then a
seventh person appeared and said: 'A great man is praying for your
recovery.' Immediately the other persons disappeared, and I felt
myself recovering my strength."

Sopher, p. 15.

31. *A Cure for Melancholy*

Rabbi Eliezer Komarner said: "When a Zaddik's heart breaks
into a thousand fragments, and he fears he will become obsessed
with melancholy, he indulges in self-praise as a preventative. But
when he feels pride and satisfaction are about to overwhelm him, he
turns to self-belittlement as a cure."

Braver, p. 35.

32. *Light and Healing*

Said the Bratzlaver: "A word from the Zaddik can illumine the
dark recesses of your mind." Said the Leover: "A word from the
Zaddik may prove to be the very word of healing which your
atrophied mind may require."

Guttman, p. 18.

110. HEALTH

1. *Study and Health*

Said the Hafetz Hayyim: "While it is a man's duty to increase
the amount of time he devotes to study, yet if he perceives that
such an increase is injurious to his health, he should take care to
study only as much as his strength permits. For if he should fall
ill from over-study, he will be compelled to study even less."

Pupko, p. 96.

111. HEART

1. Space in The Heart

Rabbi Nahman of Bratzlav said: "How is it that you have the heart to trouble me with worldly matters? Do you not know that it is my mission to clear a space within your hearts so that the Shekinah may find a dwelling-place therein?"

Guttman, p. 7.

112. HEBREW

1. A Wise Transition

The Berditschever was accustomed to speak the Holy Tongue exclusively on the Sabbath. At the conclusion of the Service, at the time of Havdalah, he would offer a prayer in which Hebrew and the folk-speech, Yiddish, were commingled. He explained that the descent from Hebrew into Yiddish at one moment would be too abrupt. Mingling the languages created a bridge between them.

Guttman, p. 8.

113. HELP

1. Sources of Help

Said the Strelisker: "Melancholy men can draw consolation from the enthusiasm of David. Feeble men can draw strength from the courage of Samson. David was able to compose the Psalms. I, however, am able to recite them."

I. K., p. 30.

2. Help in Good Time

The Dubner said: "Two brothers inherited equal portions from their father. One prospered in his business, but the other was unsuccessful. The unfortunate brother besought the other to assist him with a small sum of money so that he might be able to pay part of his most pressing debts, thus avoiding the collapse of his business. The prosperous brother refused, saying: 'You had the same amount of money left you as I. Get along the best way you can. If you are in real want, then I will aid you.' The creditors seized all the assets of the unfortunate brother, and he had nothing whatsoever left. The prosperous brother at last took pity on him and reestablished him in business, but at a cost many times higher than the amount previously requested."

The Dubner drew the lesson, saying: "It is always less expensive to preserve for a needy man his means of livelihood, than to help him make a fresh start because, through your indifference, he has lost everything."

Dubner, i, 55-56.

114. HERESY

1. Matching Heresy With Orthodoxy

The Hafetz Hayyim refused to inscribe or speak curses against heretics and unbelievers. He was convinced that such a course would do more harm than good. His strategy, however, was expressed as follows: "As they progress in their unbelief and heresy, I shall progress in my Orthodoxy."

Pupko, p. 73.

2. Purifying The Community

A question was placed before Rabbi Simon Sopher of Cracow: "Why does the Talmud speak critically of the *Minim*, or sectarian heretics?" He gave the answer: "Because the *Minim* profess to be Jews, yet they ridicule Jewish traditions. When they finally separate themselves from Jewry by their own choice, the Jewish community is purified of its dross."

Sopher, p. 101.

3. Heresy Regardless

The Talmud relates that Moses was about to write down the words: "Let us make man in our own image." He hesitated for a moment and inquired of God: "Why must I write thus? Will these words not give to the heretics a text to deny Thy Unity?" The Lord responded: "These words can teach persons in power to consult men lower than themselves. In the same way I have consulted with My angels. As for the heretics, I am certain that they will preach heresy no matter what is written in the Torah."

Kaufman, p. 12.

4. Injuring Non-Combatants

The son of the Hafetz Hayyim settled in Warsaw and went about selling the works of his father in other Polish communities. The synagogues of the Hasidim bought many books from him, declaring that the volume: *Mishnah Berurah* was as nourishing to them as bread. But in every place he set foot, the son of the Hafetz Hayyim was compelled to listen to abuse of the great Rabbis. When the Hafetz Hayyim came to Warsaw and heard of this from his son, he remarked: "We Mitnagedim are timid and conceal ourselves in our holes. The Hasidim, however, do battle with the heretics; they show no fear and oftentimes they are victorious. Never forget that oftentimes when soldiers engage in a just battle, they cannot help doing some injury to non-combatants."

Pupko, p. 17.

115. HOLIDAYS; HOLY DAYS

1. The Winter Holidays

Said the Hafetz Hayyim: "During the winter months we have two holidays: Hanukah and Purim. These commemorate our liberation from the imposition upon us of idolatry and from danger to our life. In our present Diaspora we are similarly compelled on many occasion not only to abandon our religion but also to forfeit our life. Passover is the symbol of redemption from both perils."

Pupko, ii, 49.

2. Prayer and The Awesome Days

Said the Bratzlaver: "The chief purpose of our worship during the Holydays of Tishri is to build up the sacred edifice of prayer which during the remainder of the year is greatly neglected and tends to crumble into ruins. This building up is achieved chiefly by reason of the fact that during these Holydays we do not pray for our own material welfare. Rather are our prayers directed almost exclusively towards the goal of increasing holiness, attaining greater knowledge of God, and the universal acknowledgment of his rulership. A prayer for our own welfare is an inferior prayer, secondary to the learning of the Torah, even though we offer such a prayer in order that we may be enabled to learn and to fulfil the Torah. But a prayer for the increase of holiness within us is as great as the Torah, for the objective of the Torah is also the acquisition of holiness. In order to increase holiness we must first fulfil all the commandments of the Torah; moreover, we must meditate daily in solitude upon our shortcomings and upon the mercies of God. We find that the Psalmist was accustomed to contemplation in solitude; he composed the Psalms as prayers in order that he might achieve merit by fulfilling the Torah and the Mitzvot. Thus he was able to subdue his evil impulses, those impulses which the Psalmist declares to be his enemies."

H. H. N., pp. 47a-48b.

116. HOLINESS

1. Ascending in Holiness

Said the Hafetz Hayyim: "If a man who possesses the capacity to ascend a degree in holiness, but fails to utilize this ability, he is not serving God. For serving God lies in this very achievement: to ascend in holiness the very moment a man is able to do so."

Pupko, p. 95.

2. Boring a Hole

Said the Bratzlaver: "If you feel a lack of holiness in your heart, keep on praying and addressing the Lord, so that eventually He may supply you with abundant holiness. If after many days you still feel no improvement in your heart, keep on praying nonetheless. Remember the dripping raindrops which bore a hole in a rock, and then you can rest assured that your prayers will in the end bore through and through your flinty heart."

H. H. N., p. 21b.

117. HOLY AND PROFANE

1. The Other Person is Holy

The Vorker observed that at a gathering some persons in the audience leaned against other persons. He proclaimed that such an act is unlawful. Why? Because it is unlawful to place a profane book on top of a sacred book. And each Jew must consider himself profane and every other Jew as a holy person.

Walden, p. 7.

118. HONESTY

1. Encouraging Honesty

The wife of the Hafetz Hayyim once kept a store. The Rabbi counselled her: "Beware lest you purchase from a non-Jewish woman things that belong to her husband, such as grain or wheat. You may buy eggs, fowl and home-made linen cloth, since these ordinarily belong to a housewife. It is a rule of the Christian religion that one may not steal, and the fact that the woman makes her sales in secret may be evidence that she has taken the goods without the consent of her husband. This is equivalent to theft, and we are enjoined never to encourage evil."

Pupko, p. 23.

119. HONORS

1. Honors Transformed Into Prayers

Rabbi Isaac of Ziditchov said: "My Masters taught me to read carefully in letters addressed to me the list of honors they ascribed to me. I was not to skip over them lightly, but I was enjoined to take them for use as a prayer. I learned to say: may it be the will of the Lord that I merit becoming a true Zaddik, a holy man, an eminent leader and a benefactor unto my Disciples. Then I will live up to the terms of praise they write regarding me."

Braver, p. 60.

2. "Go Up to Heaven"

When Rabbi Abish became Rabbi of Frankfort, the most desirable Rabbinical post at the time, he was informed that a minority of congregants were opposed to his selection. He invited the members of the opposition to his home, and addressed them as follows: "Gentlemen, you may ask me three questions: 'How has it transpired that so lowly a Rav as myself should presume to accept so lofty a post? How did such a superior community come to elect me? Why was it the will of Heaven that I should become Rav of Frankfort?' My answer to the first question is as follows: I was elected, and therefore I accepted the call. My answer to the second question is: the community elected me because it was the Will of Heaven. The third question I answer thus: In order to know why it was the Will of Heaven that I be elected Rabbi of Frankfort, go to Heaven and ask them there."

Michelson, p. 41.

3. An Honor Declined

Rabbi Koppel was an innkeeper in a small town. His learning was so remarkable that his fame reached as far as the community of Amsterdam. Its leaders sent a delegation with a call to become Amsterdam's foremost Rabbi. Rabbi Koppel, however, declined the honor. He explained: "In this village I can acquire my livelihood without difficulty, and am, therefore, able to devote time to study and self-improvement. In the big city, however, my communal duties will rob me of all leisure, and prevent me from devoting myself to duties which seem to me personally to be important."

Walden, p. 5.

4. Kotzker Hasidism

The Kotzker Rabbi was accustomed to say: "Hasidism and the quest for honors are two opposites. True Hasidism requires a man to consider himself as insignificant."

The Sachatzover Rabbi remarked: "That which was accounted as pure Hasidism in Parsischa was regarded in Kotzk as still commingled with impurity. The Kotzker always used a fine-grained sieve wherewith to obtain pure Hasidism."

H. Hak., p. 50.

5. For Whose Honor?

The Dubner Maggid said: "A rich man had two sons who lived at a great distance from him, one being wealthy and the other moderately affluent. The rich son received an invitation from his father to attend the wedding of his youngest sister. The father wrote: 'Come, my son, and we shall rejoice together. Bring with you your brother, also. I guarantee that I shall repay you all the expenses which you will have incurred for the sake of honoring me.'

"The rich son bought expensive clothing for himself and his family, sparing no expense in adorning himself. When he was ready to depart, he sent for his poorer brother, and ordered him to climb into the coach just as he stood. The brother remonstrated that he could not go because he lacked suitable wardrobe. The richer brother refused to listen and insisted that he accompany him.

"When the coach arrived, the richly-dressed son descended with his family, and were welcomed by the rich father's guests. The poorly-dressed brother descended quietly and unobtrusively and was unnoticed.

"Two weeks later the rich son said to his father: 'I am a merchant and cannot afford to remain away any longer from my business.' The father answered: 'Well, if you must go, I will not detain you.' Thereupon the son took out a paper and showed his father that he had bought new clothing and incurred other expenses for the journey. The father said calmly: 'May you wear your new garments in good health!'

" 'But father,' exclaimed the rich son; 'Did you not promise to repay my expenses?'

" 'Certainly not,' replied the father.

" 'But here is your letter,' exclaimed the son.

" 'Read it again, my son,' continued the father. 'I promised to repay you whatever you would spend for the sake of honoring me. Had you cared to honor me, you would have given your poorer brother the means to prepare himself with a suitable wardrobe.

Then in truth, I would have felt myself honored. But whatever
you have spent was spent with your own honor in mind. Come,
now, did I promise to reimburse you for that?' "

The Dubner drew the lesson, saying: "The Lord promises man
to reward him for whatever he expends for His sake. If a man aids
his poorer brother, thereby enabling him to live like a good Jew,
this brings honor and pleasure to God. But if a man spends his
wealth only for himself, what reward is he entitled to receive?"

Dubner, i, 51-54.

120. HOSPITALITY

1. Hospitality to the Poor

Said the Hafetz Hayyim: "The Tanna tells us: 'do not excuse
thyself from giving hospitability to a poor man by saying: "I had
no time to prepare for it." Consider them rather as members of thy
family, and give them as much as you are prepared to offer.' A
second meaning can be found as follows: 'Say not: "the people are
not pious enough; they do not wash their hands; they do not recite
the benediction, etc." ' It is for you to remember that if a member
of your family had failed in these things, you would nevertheless
have given him food."

Pupko, p. 49.

2. A Couch for a Guest

The Hafetz Hayyim was once occupied with the preparation
of a couch for a guest. Bystanders began to insist that the old
Rabbi designate one of their number to perform the task. The
Rabbi declined, however, saying: "Would you insist upon relieving
me of the duty to don the Tefillin on the ground that it would
make me weary?"

Pupko, p. 86.

3. True Hospitality

Said Rabbi Leib Saras: "Forget not that persons who are well-
known have little need of your hospitality. Rather is it the poor,
those unknown to thee, the tired, the famished and troubled
wanderers who merit thy welcome. Be not like Lot who welcomed
angels, but rather like Abraham who was eager to show hospitality to those who appeared as dust-covered Bedouins."

G. A., p. 11.

4. An Identical Welcome

The Maggid of Radislav visited the Lubliner Zaddik and received
a hearty welcome. The Maggid, a Mitnaged, expressed his surprise.

The Lubliner replied: "We are taught in *Ethics of the Fathers,* i, 15, to receive all men with a friendly countenance. I must admit my heart would welcome you more warmly if you were my Hasid, but my countenance expresses an identical welcome for Hasid and Mitnaged alike."

Walden, p. 84.

5. A Wide Open House

A jester remarked: "We read in the *Ethics of the Fathers,* i, 5, 'Let thy house be wide open; let the poor be members of thy household.' This teaches us that he who keeps a wide open house and lives above his means will soon discover that the members of his household will become poor."

Zlotnik, p. 27.

121. HUMANITY

1. Men

1. The world is a pasture. Men are the shepherds; therefore let us seek food.
2. The world is a chandelier. Men are the candles; therefore let us give light.
3. The world is a body. Men are its eyes; therefore let us see.
4. The world is a skull. Men are its brains; therefore let us think.
5. Only men know their Creator.
6. Only men are responsible for their actions.
7. Only men live in two worlds: the material and the spiritual.

Berditschevsky, p. 5.

2. For All Humanity

Said the Hafetz Hayyim: "A man should pray, not for himself alone, but for all humanity."

Pupko, p. 107.

122. HUMILITY

1. The Humble Visitor

Rabbi Ber Alesker paid a call upon the Lubliner. To the surprise of the Hasidim, the visitor addressed the Master in these words: "By right, O Master, it was your duty to make the first call." Noting their surprise, Rabbi Ber explained: "The Zohar says that the Zaddik should seek out the sinner in order to save him."

Walden, p. 112.

2. The Shekinah in the "Yud"

A Rabbi said: "We have learned that the Shekinah, God's In-dwelling Presence, resides within the number Ten. Usually it is understood to refer to a quorum of ten men. I wish to offer a second interpretation. Ten is the numerical value of the letter: 'Yud.' The Skekinah dwells within the person who considers himself to be lowly and small, even as the 'Yud' is the lowliest and smallest letter."

M. B., p. 19.

3. The Ashes of Humility

The Mezeritzer Maggid overheard a conversation between two women. Said the first: "The fire in my grate has gone out. How can I prevent this?" The second replied: "I place ashes over the burning coals and thus I keep the fire going underneath." The Maggid turned to his Disciples and said: "Learn from this woman that you can preserve the fire of your enthusiasm in serving God only if you cover the flame with ashes, the ashes of humility."

Migdal David, p. 84.

4. Remembering God

Said the Lubliner: "If a man forgets God, in that moment he is spiritually dead. If a man remembers God, he fulfils that for which he was created. But he must feel no pride therein, because a worm also fulfils that for which he was created."

Walden, p. 55.

5. The Meekness of Moses

The Tzortkover Rabbi commented on the assertion in the Torah that Moses was more meek than anyone else. "How is it possible," asked the Rabbi, "that a man who spoke with God, face to face, should feel meeker than all others?" "The answer is this: 'Moses thought in his heart: I have lost the desires of the body and am able to abstain from food for forty days, and for yet another forty days; therefore it is no cause for wonder that I should be able to serve the Lord aright. But another person who is captive to his bodily demands, and yet tears himself away from them, and at times serves the Lord, is truly greater than I am.'"

Margulies, p. 25.

6. The High-Placed and the Lowly

The Hafetz Hayyim once narrated to his son a story which proved useful at a later time. The Czar, Nicholas I, once attended army maneuvers near Vilna. He arrived earlier than anticipated,

and the commanding general had not yet made his appearance.
The Czar called for a volunteer to take charge of the maneuvers.
A soldier of the Jewish faith volunteered and conducted the maneuvers with a skill seemingly born of experience. When the General
finally arrived, the Czar ordered him to remove his uniform so that
the private soldier might put it on. The Czar said: "General, you
receive a handsome salary, whereas this private soldier receives
only a few pennies a day. Yet you have given an exhibition of
indolence, whereas he has given us complete satisfaction."

In the year 1921 a famine occurred in many parts of Russia. A
large number of sick and starving Jews migrated to Kharkov where
the famine had not yet reached. The son of the Hafetz Hayyim
accepted the responsibility of gathering food, at first with success,
but later with difficulty when after a few months the donors ceased
their contributions. Hundreds of the starving clamored for food, but
none was made available to them. Finally a kinsman of one of the
Rabbi's co-workers arrived in the city and gave him a sum of money
as a loan. A few days later when the Rabbi encountered a group of
the wealthy Jews in the community, he recited to them the exact
words which the Czar had used in expressing to the General his
opinion of him.

Pupko, p. 64.

7. The Meekness of Moses

Said the Hafetz Hayyim: "We are told that Moses was the
meekest man on earth. How can this possibly be said regarding
this illustrious man? The answer is as follows: every man is
obligated to serve God according to his own understanding. Moses
felt in his heart that he was not rendering service commensurate
with the understanding granted him. Therefore he considered himself a man, less in worth, than other persons who gave service
to God according to their individual understanding, however small."

Pupko, ii, 47.

8. The Rabbi's Humility

Rabbi Akiba Eger visited the city of Warsaw, and his fame
drew to him a multitude of visitors. One them besought the Rabbi
for his blessing, but the Rabbi declined to pronounce it, pleading
unworthiness. The visitor quoted the Talmudic saying, by a slip
of the tongue, "Let not the blessing of the layman seem cheap in
your eyes." Immediately he perceived the error he had made and
corrected himself, saying: "Let not the blessing to a layman seem
cheap in your eyes." Rabbi Akiba smiled and said: "You need

not correct yourself. Let the words you have spoken stand without any change."

Sopher, p. 74.

9. Pseudo-Humility

Said the Tzernobiler: "Oftentimes you will encounter a man famed far and wide for his humility. If one should dare to ridicule this man's humility in his presence, however, he will become enormously enraged. Needless to say, such alleged humility is not a virtue."

Twersky, p. 16.

10. Giving Way

The Hafetz Hayyim was walking on a narrow sidewalk, and an officer approached from the opposite direction. The Rabbi, to the officer's surprise, stepped down from the sidewalk. "Why did you step down, Rabbi?" he asked. The Rabbi replied: "It is my custom to give way." The officer responded: "Such a custom should assure you a life of happiness."

Pupko, p. 36.

11. The Value of Water

The Pulnoer Rabbi visited the Besht, and the latter invited him to be his companion on a journey he was making. When the time came to recite the Afternoon Prayer, both men were in a field. Inasmuch as the Besht was scrupulously careful to wash his hands before offering prayer, he asked the Pulnoer to search for some water, but none was found. The Besht thereupon began to entreat the Lord, saying: "O Lord, my whole life long, I have never neglected the pious act of washing before praying. If no water is at hand, please take away my soul, so that I may not be forced to alter my custom." Soon after a small quantity of water was discovered. At a later time, the Pulnoer remarked: "Surely a person who would rather die than transgress a small rule of piety is worthy to be my Rabbi." The Besht, on learning this, remarked: "I know a Rav who once forgot to prepare his sermon for Shabbat ha-Gadol, the Great Sabbath. He locked himself in an attic room in order to prepare it. Time passed swiftly, and he found himself to be terribly thirsty. Seeking a water-carrier on the street below, he cried out to him: 'I beg of you, bring me a little water to save my life.' The water-carrier replied: 'I ask you; how can I do this? You are so high, and I am so low, yet you wish water from me!'" The Pulnoer recognized the story as applicable to himself, and hence no longer felt himself to be higher than the Besht.*

Zammlung, p. 103.

* Water is oftentimes construed as a symbol of learning.

12. *The Power of Humility*

It is related of the Mezeritzer that there came to him a man who became his disciple because the Maggid's ways pleased him. But, lo, though he attached himself to the Maggid as an adherent, he grew poorer and poorer each day. "Why am I thus afflicted?" the disciple asked his master. The Maggid gave this reply: "Doubtless you remember the saying of the Talmud: 'He who desires to be wealthy should turn his face towards the north, when reciting the *Amidah* prayer: he who desires wisdom should turn towards the south. But if he desires both wealth and wisdom, in what direction should he turn?" The disciple was at a loss for an answer. The Maggid continued: "Let him transform himself by humility and the renunciation of self-pride; thus he will become a spiritual being and the spirit knows no horizon." The man abandoned his pride, and, in due time, became wealthy again.

Szlamovitz, p. 50.

13. *True Humility*

Rabbi Baruch of Leipnik heard that a Rav in the neighborhood professed to be a greater scholar than himself. The Rabbi smiled and said: "I do not doubt at all that there exists in the world a person greater than I am. Does it matter to me if this particular Rav believes himself to be that greater man?"

Eibeshitz, p. 39.

14. *"His" or "Naught"*

Said the Medzibozer: "In Psalm 100:3, the word *Lo (Lamed Alef)* is to be found; but the *Keri* of Tradition gives as an alternative reading *Lo (Lamed Holem)*. The first *Lo (Lamed Alef)* means "naught," but the second reading of *Lo (Lamed Holem)* means "His." This can mean that if we consider ourselves to be as "naught," God will consider us to be "His." But if we consider ourselves already to be "His," God will regard us as "naught."

BDH., p. 64.

15. *The Two Reminders*

The Dubner Maggid said: "A rich man met a handsome and learned young man at an inn in a small town. He took a great fancy to the youth, who was the innkeeper's son, and desired that he might become his son-in-law. He therefore brought his daughter and his wife to meet him, and both were enthusiastic in their approval. The father proposed that the marriage should take place at once. The innkeeper protested that he required a little more time to prepare an appropriate wedding meal, but the rich man insisted there should be no delay. He presented the bridegroom with a new suit of clothes and gave whispered instructions to his servant to remove quietly the cheap garments he was wearing and to make a bundle of them. The bridegroom, however, observed this, and, on his part, wrapped some of the black bread of the meal in a napkin and hid it on his person.

"Some time later the father-in-law and the young man had an argument. The father-in-law opened the bundle containing the old rough suit he had worn, and said to his son-in-law: 'You have already forgotten your lowly descent, and the sort of clothing you wore when I took you as my son-in-law; otherwise you would not argue so stubbornly.' The young man in his turn unwrapped the black bread, and pointing to it, replied: 'It is true I was poor when I was married to your daughter. But let this recall to you how eager you were to get me, not allowing my father to prepare anything better than this black bread.'

The Dubner drew the lesson, saying: "At the Seder meal we eat bitter herbs to remind us of our low estate when God took us as His Chosen People. But we also eat Matzah as a reminder of the Lord's haste to get us for his daughter, the Torah. We, therefore, have good reason to be proud."

Dubner, i, 56-58.

16. Reminders of our Lowliness

A wealthy Jew became a widower with small children. He determined not to marry a rich widow or a girl from a rich family. Instead he resolved to take unto himself a wife who had been one of his servants, with whose ways he was acquainted and who was a favorite of his children. Before leading her to the canopy, he said to her: "Do not think that your duties will be lighter because I have chosen you from among the servants of my house to be my wife and to be their mistress. No, your duties will become greater and more numerous. When you were a servant, one duty only confronted you, namely, that to which you were assigned. But when you become a mistress over all the servants and nursemaids, it will be necessary to supervise their work, and to answer to me for the negligence of any one of them."

"If you inquire what advantage you will gain from marrying me, I give you this answer: as long as you are humble in spirit and give close attention to your duties, I will forget that you were once my servant and you will continue to have my love and respect. But if you grow proud and neglect your duties, I shall take the occasion to remind you of your former state."

The Dubner drew the lesson from this story, saying: "A poor man must perform only a single duty, namely, to provide for his family's sustenance. When he becomes rich, however, his duties increase many times, and he must assist others to gain their livelihood. If he proves to be a man of charity, his wealth will remain with him, and he will merit the respect and admiration of his fellows. But if he should refuse to aid others, he will be reminded by the Lord that once he was a poor man, and will thereupon forfeit the respect of people."

Dubner, i, 58-60.

17. Inferior in a Dream

Rabbi Levi Isaac, later known as the Berditschever, took unto wife the daughter of Rabbi Israel Peretz, and resided at his father-in-law's home. Rabbi Israel urged his son-in-law to pursue his studies at home, and not to go to a Yeshivah in another town. Levi Isaac, however, had heard many tales of the remarkable teachings of Rabbi Schmelke, then Rabbi of a near-by community, and his soul yearned to study under his tutelage. As a consequence he became melancholy and depressed. Rabbi Israel asked him whether he had dreamed a disturbing dream. Levi Isaac replied: "I was under the impression that I had learned sufficiently at the Yeshivah here, and could now continue my studies at home. But I have dreamed that I know but little, and that I will remain half-ignorant if I do not become a pupil of Rabbi Schmelke. Is it not a bad and disturbing dream if it makes me feel inferior?" Rabbi Israel sent Levi Isaac to Rabbi Schmelke, who in turn recommended him as a pupil to the Mezeritzer Maggid.

Guttman, p. 3.

123. IDLENESS

1. The Dangers of Indolence

Said the Dubner: "A wealthy business man permitted his son to become accustomed to idleness. The youth was sickly and weak of body, and, as a consequence of his idleness, grew nervous and melancholy. Thereupon the father took his son into business with him, and the responsibilities of business activity drove out the youth's ailments and built up his strength.

"When Adam was idle in the Garden of Eden, he possessed no strength of character and could not resist any persuasion. Therefore the Lord made him till the soil, and his character as a result became firmer."

Dubner, i, 92-93.

2. The Open Bible

When the Hafetz Hayyim who lived from 1839 to 1934 was far advanced in years, his eyesight was almost completely impaired. Yet he asked that the Bible always be open before him. "It would be unseemly conduct on my part," he said, "in fact, a profanation of God's Name, were a visitor to find me sitting idle."

Pupko, p. 86.

124. IMITATING GOD

1. Opposing God's Will

Rabbi Jonathan of Hamburg said: "In *Nedarim*, 50 we read: 'Bar Kappara looked upon the opulence of Rabbi Judah ha-Nasi and remarked: "If God gives such riches to those who oppose His Will, how much more will He grant to those who conform to His Will?"' What is the meaning of this statement? How could Bar Kappara include Rabbi Judah ha-Nasi among those who oppose God's Will? The explanation can be found in this: that the true Zaddik does not conform to God's Will when God intends to do justice, but always entreats the Almighty to change justice into compassion. In this respect the Zaddik opposes God's Will."

Michelson, p. 36.

125. IMMORTALITY

1. Accomplishments in "This-World"

Said the Hafetz Hayyim: "In 'This-World' a man is near to God and may offer prayer to Him, beseeching His favor. In the 'World-to-Come,' however, a man may be far from the Almighty, for there are myriads of barriers separating a man from Divinity. Your status in Heaven is measured according to your accomplishments in 'This-World.' You cannot add anything to your spiritual merit in the 'World-to-Come.' It is too late." *

Pupko, ii, 57.

* It has been pointed out, however, that some theologians believe that the admirable conduct of a man's sons or the benefits arising from the charitable donations of the departed add to the spiritual merits of those in the "World-to-Come."

2. Removing The Garment

Before his death the Bratzlaver exclaimed: "I will gladly take off this garment (the body). I cannot remain in the same position of holiness, and I feel that I cannot ascend higher in life."

H. H. N., p. 8b.

3. The Rewards in The After-Life

Said the Hafetz Hayyim: "The man who has studied Holy Writ will be granted eternal life; for other virtues, however, he will merely receive his reward in the World-Above. And those women who lead their sons to school for their studies at the Talmud Torah, and those who greet their husbands when they return from the synagogue, will be granted eternal life. Others, however, will receive their reward in the World-Above."

Pupko, p. 116.

4. Because He Desired It

The Emperor Ferdinand of Austria paid a visit to Rabbi Mordecai Bennett at Nikolsburg. He spoke with him on various subjects and then asked: "Will the Holy Rabbi assure me of a share in the World-to-Come?" "Your Majesty," replied the Rabbi, "I give you such a promise." After the Emperor had departed, the Rabbi was asked how he could assure the monarch a share in the *Olam ha-Bah*. The Rabbi answered: "I did so, because the Emperor believed in the World-to-Come, and desired a share therein so earnestly that he asked me to make this promise. Surely for the sincerity he merits a share in the After-Life."

Walden, Y. A., p. 34.

5. Eternal Necessities

Said the Hafetz Hayyim: "Most people worry because they lack the necessities of life. But I ask: 'Have they the necessities for the After-Life?'"

Pupko, ii, 42.

6. The Coming Resurrection

Said the Hafetz Hayyim: "In Isaiah 58:7 we read: 'Hide not thyself from thine own flesh.' In other words, if you believe in Resurrection, do not mar your body by dissipation, but make it worthy for the After-Life."

Pupko, ii, 50.

7. The Privileges of 'This-World'

Said the Hafetz Hayyim: "A man has privileges in 'This-World' which are not granted him in the 'World-to-Come.' On earth we lead our life as if in a wedding hall. We enter it, and if we sincerely beg for good things, we shall receive them in abundance. In the 'World-to-Come,' however, we can acquire good deeds no longer. Only the privileged few are permitted to offer praises to God after

their demise. The majority must depend on what they have
acquired while alive."

Selected.

126. IMPERFECTION

1. Long-lasting Blemishes

Said the Hafetz Hayyim: "If you find a blemish on a garment,
you inform the seller that the garment is worth only half the price.
Why? Because a defective garment is regarded as a blot on your
personality which may last a long time. Remember this, also, with
respect to the good deeds which are the garment of your soul. Do
not compel your soul to wear defective or imperfect garments for
a long time."

Pupko, p. 93.

2. Satisfied With Imperfections

Said the Hafetz Hayyim: "In Tanna de-be Eliyahu, Zuta, 2, the
qualities of God are enumerated. One quality is satisfaction with
His lot. Rabbi Hayyim inquired of the Vilna Gaon the meaning of
this statement. The Gaon replied: "The statement means that the
Lord is satisfied with His people, Israel, no matter in what estate
He finds them. God still loves us, even though our state of holiness
is far below that of our fathers."

Pupko, p. 47.

3. Knowing The Defect

Said the Dubner: "A nobleman sent his servant to purchase an
antique vase of which he had heard. The dealer showed the servant an imperfection in the vase, but despite this knowledge, the
servant purchased it for his master. The nobleman, however, on
perceiving the defect, expressed his unwillingness to keep it. The
servant endeavored to return it to the seller for the money expended,
but the dealer reminded him that he had pointed out the imperfection before the purchase.

"From this we learn that when man sins and the Angel of Justice
pleads for his punishment, the Lord declares: 'I knew before I
created man that he was imperfect. I must, therefore, hold fast
to my bargain.'"

Dubner, i, 166-168.

127. IMPUDENCE

1. Three Instances of Impudence

Once while the Dubner Maggid was travelling in a stage-coach, he was ridiculed by a young man who lacked religious feeling. The Maggid remarked: "There are three impudent animals. One is the he-goat; he is quite useless, but he impudently jumps about and breaks up the possessions of his master. The second is the rooster. He likewise is quite without profit, but he arouses his owner from sweet slumber. The third is the dog; he frequently barks at the moon and disturbs his master. Nevertheless the he-goat has some reason for being: he has a beard. Moreover, the rooster awakens his master so that he may study. But you, sir, are like the dog who has no beard and does not arouse anyone to study. Where, pray, do you acquire the right to engage in impudent barking?"

Dubner, i, 45-46.

128. IMPURITY

1. Washing Away Impurities

Said the Hafetz Hayyim: "It is necessary that we wash away all impurities before we can clothe ourselves in the garments of holiness. We must remember that before we don our Sabbath garments, we must thoroughly cleanse ourselves."

Pupko, p. 112.

129. INDIVIDUAL

1. Nation or Individual?

The Hafetz Hayyim disliked personal honors intensely. His son asked him: "Do we not pray for a life of wealth and honor?" The Rabbi replied: "This is true, but the words apply to our nation and not to any individual."

Pupko, p. 20.

2. Rising or Descending?

Said the Hafetz Hayyim: "In his dream Jacob beheld a vision of those who were ascending and those who were descending. It rests with the individual whether he will ascend or descend on the ladder of holiness."

Pupko, p. 113.

130. INHERITANCE

1. His Own Heritage

Said the Dubner: "A man inherited a large apartment house which he rented out to tenants. He himself took up his residence in a small rented house. A fire threatened to raze the houses in the neighborhood. The man kept sprinkling water on his rented house. A friend, however, said: 'Why are you wasting your efforts to save a stranger's house, while you are failing to preserve your own heritage?'

"From this we learn that many a Jew becomes a member of non-Jewish organizations in his neighborhood, but refuses to become a member of Jewish organizations located, perhaps, at a distance. He neglects and forgets his own inheritance."

Dubner, i, 205.

2. Inheriting Good Deeds

Said the Hafetz Hayyim: "If a man abuses you, and you remain silent, you will inherit the slanderer's good deeds, whatever they may be, and you will receive whatever reward was contemplated for him."

Pupko, p. 104.

131. INITIATIVE

1. Begin Today

Said the Hafetz Hayyim: "A man who decides to obey the Words of God should begin his good deeds today, not tomorrow."

Pupko, p. 99.

132. INSTRUCTION

1. Teaching The New Generation

Said the Hafetz Hayyim: "An assessor was informed that he was to be succeeded by a younger man. He was also told that he must teach his successor the regulations concerning his work. Naturally the older man was depressed by the situation. So is it with all of us. The new generation rises up to take our places. All that remains to us is to continue in This-World for a time in order to instruct our successors in the ways of the world."

Pupko, ii, 2.

133. INTENTION

1. According to Intention

Rabbi Abish once spent a night at a tavern where he was unknown. The wife of the tavern-keeper was distressed to discover that eighty thalers were missing, and she accused the guest of taking them. The Rabbi was searched, and, by a coincidence, exactly eighty thalers were found on him. The tavern-keeper beat him severely and took the money away from him. A few months later the tavern-keeper's wife found the money she had mislaid. Her husband searched out his guest, was told his identity, returned the money and tearfully implored the Rabbi's forgiveness. Rabbi Abish replied: "There is really nothing which I need forgive. It was your intention to punish a thief, not an honest man."

Michelson, p. 21.

2. Without Conscious Intent

In Zheshov, there lived a Jew who disliked the Hasidim so intensely that he did not hesitate to denounce the Zaddikim to Austrian officials, accusing the Rabbis of many offenses. On one occasion a Hasid told the Rabbi of Dzikov that the denouncer had left at the office of the Lemberg Stadthalter an accusation against the Rabbi. The Dzikover sent a messenger to the Tzanzer Rabbi, petitioning the Rabbi that no harm come to him. The Tzanzer replied by saying there was no cause to fear the false accuser. He finished his letter with the words: "I am under the impression that your accuser is dead." And, lo, when the accuser entered the Stadthalter's office, he dropped dead on the instant. When the Dzikover learned this, he exclaimed: "What a clear manifestation of the Holy Spirit!" But when the Tzanzer heard it, he declared: "Believe me, the words came from my pen without any conscious intention on my part."

Raker, p. 144.

134. INTERCESSION

1. Fashioning an Angel

Said the Bratzlaver: "Not a single word of your prayer is ever lost. In the measure that you are whole-hearted and sincere, every word of prayer uttered by you fashions in your behalf an Angel of Intercession. When your unceasing phrases of devotion have completed the creation of your Angel, he will bring your wants before the Lord, and you will be answered. Do not become discouraged if you behold no sign that your prayers have been accepted. It may be that, because of the lesser quality of your particular prayer, only a small portion of it has been utilized to fashion your Angel. Eventually your Angel of Intercession will be completed and you will of a surety behold God's Mercy." *

H. H. N., pp. 24a-24b.

* In the Hebrew the word is "Holiness," not "Angel." The theme, however, remains the same, if the concept of "Building Holiness" is substituted for "Fashioning the Angel of Intercession."

135. INVENTIVENESS

1. Learn from the Inventors

Said the Hafetz Hayyim: "It behooves you to imitate the inventors of mechanical implements. They give to their task steady and strenuous thought; they labor untiringly on the improvement of our material life. Their example should inspire you to devote your conscientious thinking and unceasing labor to the improvement of your spiritual life."

Pupko, p. 116.

136. INWARDNESS

1. On Inwardness (Kavvanah)

Inwardness *(Kavvanah)*, say the Disciples of the Besht, gives life to the words of our prayers and vitalizes the performance of a Mitzvah.

Moreover, inwardness, concentration, full intention, true *Kavvanah,* gives a glow, a light and an extra pleasure to the Shekinah.

Teitelbaum, i, 5.

137. ISRAEL

1. Joseph as a Symbol

Said the Hafetz Hayyim: "The story of Joseph in Holy Scripture is a symbol of the story of the people of Israel. As in the case of Joseph, all endeavors to humiliate us will prove to be fruitless. They will serve merely as the means of restoring our greatness in the days to come."

Pupko, ii, 47.

2. Israel Like The Stars

Said the Tzanzer Rabbi: "God said to Abraham: 'Look now towards heaven, and count the stars . . . so shall thy seed be.' (Genesis 15:5) By this the Lord indicated that just as the stars when viewed from earth seem small in size, but are vast and majestic in the heavens, so, too, shall Israel be accounted."

Tzanzer Hasidut, p. 237.

138. JEALOUSY; ENVY

1. *Higher Than Jealousy*

When Rabbi Abraham of Tzechinov fell ill, he sent for his son, the Bialer. Later the venerable Rabbi improved. The Hasidim who admired the Bialer's conduct assembled in the old Rabbi's synagogue and made merry. A Hasid with a fine voice was invited to lead the singing. The Tzechinover's younger son, Zeev, was vexed by this voice, and made no secret of his envy. His father, however, told him to join in the merriment, for merriment takes precedence above all else.

Zammlung, p. 56.

139. JEWELS

1. *Gathering Pearls*

Said the Hafetz Hayyim: "Be like the vessel which the pearl-fishers used to gather up pearls. Thou, too, hast been sent down from heaven to gather pearls, namely, the learning of Torah and the performance of Mitzvot."

Pupko, p. 104.

140. JEWISH LIFE

1. *Living as a True Jew*

Said the Hafetz Hayyim: "Every man should remember that God is able to provide him with sustenance wherever his domicile may be. It behooves you to refrain from moving to a place where you cannot conduct yourself as a true Jew, and lead the true Jewish life."

Pupko, p. 116.

141. JEWISH PEOPLE

1. *"We Have No Rights"*

Rabbi Ber Meizels of Cracow was elected in 1848 as a deputy in the Austrian Parliament. He took his seat among the Leftists. When the Speaker asked him: "Why does an Orthodox Rabbi sit on the Left?", the Rabbi promptly replied: "Because we have no rights."

Raker, p. 205.

142. JOY

1. Holy Sadness

The Rabbi of Rozwadow was accustomed to deliver a short discourse daily. One morning he said: "Holy feelings of joy come to me, together with holy feelings of sadness. I feel joy in the knowledge that I have achieved much holy comprehension. I feel sadness in the realization that there is so much in holiness that I do not yet understand. A Zaddik's soul never has rest. It always aspires to more understanding."

Raker, p. 149.

2. The Power of Joy

Said the Tzortkover Rabbi: "The feeling of fear must be probed to determine whether it arises out of melancholy. But the feeling of joy is welcome, whatever its source. Joy is a sign of faith and trust in God. In an hour of tribulation joy may bring release and salvation. The Besht was accustomed to say: 'What I cannot accomplish by severe labor in the service of God, my Hasidim accomplish through joy.'"

Margulies, p. 27.

3. A Merry Heart

A Hasid was walking on the road to Lublin. The rain was coming down heavily, but the Hasid was singing quite merrily. When asked the reason for his good humor, the Hasid replied: "When the Temple was standing, pilgrims on their way to observe the Festivals would laugh at any discomfort because of their joyous anticipation of sojourning in Jerusalem, the Holy City. I, too, sing with merriment in anticipation of my sojourn in Lublin, near my Holy Rabbi, the Lubliner."

Walden, p. 67.

4. The Rejoicing Islands

Said the Hafetz Hayyim: "In Psalm 97, 1 we read: 'The Lord reigneth, let the earth be glad; let the islands rejoice.' This text teaches us that under the reign of a mortal monarch, no land or island is secure from seizure. But when God will truly reign, peace and security will prevail, thereby gladdening the earth."

Pupko, ii, 41.

5. Saying of the Lelever

Said the Lelever:
1. "A joyful countenance is evidence of intimacy with the Lord."

2. "An Israelite is a member of a peculiar nation; even if he sins grievously, his Jewishness still remains in his soul."

3. "An angel fears to tread where ten Jews came together, for the Shekinah abides there."

4. "Neither an individual nor a nation engrossed in self-satisfaction can attain redemption."

5. "In the Messianic Age the Lord will beseech the Zaddikim to forgive Him for their sufferings in This-World."

H. Hak., p. 20.

6. A Reason for Joy

The Lelever's son once complained to his father that a storekeeper next door was underselling him. The Lelever commented: "You should feel joy in the knowledge that a fellow-Jew is thus able to support his wife and children."

H. Hak., p. 17.

7. "God Reigneth"

Said the Hafetz Hayyim: "The Heavens rejoice and the earth is gladdened when it is said among the nations: 'God reigneth.'"

Pupko, p. 100.

143. JUDAISM

1. A Bulwark for Judaism

Said the Hafetz Hayyim: "In this generation of unbelief when many persons feel ashamed to perform Mitzvot, the Hasidim, despite all their faults, stand as a bulwark for Judaism. It is they who display enthusiastic adherence to the Law of Israel; it is they who instruct their offspring to follow in their ways."

Pupko, p. 16.

144. KABBALAH

1. Studying Kabbalah

The Hafetz Hayyim evinced great interest in the teachings of the Kabbalah. He said: "Without mysticism we could never comprehend the connection of the universe and God. Without mysticism we would be doomed to walk in darkness." Yet he was able to spare for the study of Kabbalah only the late night hours.

Pupko, p. 20.

2. Secret and Revealed Torah

Said Rabbi Moses Sopher: "A person who openly confesses that he has no respect for the Secret Torah, the Kabbalah, is certain to lack within himself respect for the Revealed Torah, the Talmud and the Jewish Codes."

Sopher, p. 44.

3. Two Forms of Kabbalah

Before the advent of the Besht, the Kabbalah concerned itself with things spiritually divine, with objects in the higher spheres.

The Kabbalah of the Besht, however, concerned itself with things materially divine, with objects in the lower strata.

The Kabbalah before the Besht found God above us; the Kabbalah of the Besht found God within and about us.

The Besht taught that the divine light descends directly into men's heart. This is called in the Kabbalah: "The Inner Light."

Teitelbaum, i, 4.

145. KADDISH

1. Kaddish for a Saintly Father

Rabbi Solomon Strelisker declined to say Kaddish when his father, Rabbi Uri, died. He explained: "Kaddish is said in order to exalt the soul of a departed parent. But my parent was a holy Seraph. Is it possible to upraise a soul any higher than an angel?" He added: "What son can long outlive such a father?" He died a few months later in 1827.

I. K., p. 28.

146. KASHRUT

1. Doubtful Kashrut

On the day before Yom Kippur, many women came to Rabbi Abish for a decision as to Kashrut. In every instance he pronounced the food Kasher. A Dayyan asked him: "Is it not fitting that we be more strict than usual on the eve of Yom Kippur?" Rabbi Abish replied: "On the contrary. If I should pronounce Tereifah a fowl of doubtful Kashrut, I would be guilty of a sin against men, and deprive them of their meal before the Fast. And a sin against men is not forgiven on Yom Kippur. But when I pronounce the fowl Kasher, even though there may be doubt involved, I sin only against God. And we are taught that Yom Kippur brings forgiveness of sins against God."

Michelson, p. 13.

147. KINDNESS

1. A Small Gift

A leather merchant visited the Hafetz Hayyim, and was asked by the Rabbi how he fared in his dealings with the army officers. The merchant replied: "With each delivery of goods, I find I must make a gift to those who accept them; otherwise they would turn back most of my leather, and in war time, I can do nothing with material rejected in this way." The Rabbi commented: "The precepts which are our offering to Heaven are closely examined, to determine whether they have been followed in reverence for God and in love for Him; they, too, are scrutinized to see whether they are mingled with slander and evil speech. A small portion of our deeds are accepted without question. Therefore if we make a gift of a kind deed, that which we bring of Mitzvot as an offering is deemed acceptable. Always be ready to devote time to perform a kind deed or two. They can prove of great help."

Pupko, ii, 24.

2. Love and Kindness

Said the Hafetz Hayyim: "Kindness must be accompanied by love to have merit. For thus it becomes lovingkindness."

Pupko, p. 113.

148. KNOWLEDGE

1. Depths Below The Surface

Said the Hafetz Hayyim: "The prophet foresaw that 'the earth shall be full of the knowledge of the Lord, as the waters cover the sea.' It is known that while the surface of the ocean is the same everywhere, the ocean floor varies in depth according to the particular spot. Likewise it can be said that though on the surface there seem to be no variations in knowledge among men, the depths are different according to the learning of each individual."

Pupko, ii, 39.

149. KOL NIDREI

1. Eating on Kol Nidrei

Two pious Jews came before a Rabbinical Court, offering to swear that they had seen Rabbi Bunam eat cake and coffee on Yom Kippur. The accusation was investigated, and it was found that Rabbi Bunam's daughter-in-law had given birth to a son on Yom

Kippur Eve. According to the Jewish law, food was offered to her, even though it was Yom Kippur Eve. The new mother, however, refused to accept the food unless the Rabbi himself brought it to her. The two would-be witnesses chanced to pass the house at the moment, and they saw the Rabbi holding in his hands cake and coffee. In their folly they suspected the Rabbi of a breach of piety and sought to accuse him.

Zammlung, p. 102.

150. LAUGHTER

1. A Neutral Observer

Said the Bratzlaver: "Oftentimes I feel a desire to be transplanted to another planet, so that from this vantage point I could look at the earth in the role of a neutral observer and laugh at the world."

Guttman, p. 16.

151. LEADERS; LEADERSHIP

1. The Leader and His Generation

Rabbi Solomon Sopher said: "Each generation is the clay from which the leader moulds a form. But not every leader can mould the material he finds at hand. Therefore the Lord designates for each generation its fitting leader. The Sages declare that we must obey an unlearned leader like Jephthah in his generation, in the same way that we obey a holy leader like Samuel in his particular generation. I go further and say: 'Jephthah was the leader fitted for his own generation, and this generation would have refused to be led by Samuel. In the same way Samuel's generation would have refused the leadership of Jephthah.'"

Sopher, p. 31.

2. Rav versus Zaddik

Rabbi Isaac of Ziditchov did not aspire to be a Hasidic Rebbe, but sought to become a learned Rav. He learned of a vacancy and besought Rabbi Meir of Premislan to give him a recommendation on behalf of the post. Rabbi Meir replied: "I interpret the passage in *Ethics* 1:10: 'Love work, hate lordship, and seek no intimacy with the ruling power,' to signify the following: 'Love the labor of the Zaddik whereby he turns hearts to God, but hate a position as a teacher of the Jewish law.'" Rabbi Isaac replied: "I, for my part, understand the saying in *Baba Batra*, 110, to mean: 'Decide whether a slaughtered animal is kasher in accordance with the law, but do not say that you are a Zaddik, a Leader.'"

Braver, p. 19.

3. A True Leader

Rabbi Isaac of Ziditchov gave this interpretation of the remark of Rabbi Jose in *Ethics*, 2:17: "Let the property of thy friend be as dear to thee as thine own; qualify thyself for the study of the Torah, since the knowledge of it is not an inheritance of thine." He said: "The Tanna speaks to a leader in Israel: 'An authentic leader is the man who is willing to see another person possess the property, while he qualifies himself to inherit a knowledge of the Torah.'"

Braver, p. 63.

4. Moses, The Shepherd

Said a Hasid: "We read: 'And Moses was a shepherd.' Moses was Moses because, being a shepherd, he removed himself from cities and from multitudes of men. He dwelt in solitude, in communion with nature, and thus he was near to God while preparing for his labors for Israel."

Berditschevsky, p. 20.

5. Forever "Aus"

Professor Ignaz Goldziher was Secretary of the Jewish community of Budapest for many years. Eventually he received notice of his election as Secretary-Emeritus, making unnecessary any further activity on his part. A group of Jews who had affairs to discuss with the community paid him a visit at his home. The Professor raised his voice and said: "I wish you to know that 'between me and the children of Israel it is forever "Aus"'" (a play upon a quotation from Exodus 31:17)."

Zlotnik, p. 20.

6. A Congenial Valet

In his youth Rabbi Isaac of Ziditchov desired to visit the Rabbi of Apt but had no money for the fare. He therefore hired himself out as a valet to a certain Rabbi who was contemplating a visit to the Apter. After both had left, the Apter Rabbi remarked: "Is it not strange? The valet pleased me more than his master."

Braver, p. 11.

7. The Danger of Authority

Baron Rothschild of Vienna proposed to Rabbi Moses Sopher that he be allowed to invite the government to appoint him as Chief Rabbi of Hungary with full authority in Jewish affairs. The Rabbi declined, saying: "The appointment may be beneficial in many respects. But after my demise, it may be given to an unworthy man, and great harm to Judaism may result."

Sopher, p. 32.

8. *Rebuking The Leaders*

Rabbi Moses Sopher went to the mineral springs near Pressburg in order to take the cure. A wealthy Jew of little learning offered the Rabbi a wing of his house in which to reside during his stay. The offer was accepted. On Saturday afternoon, the Rabbi overheard his host, saying: "The Pressburg Rabbi is really not a pious Jew." He called the magnate to him and asked what he had done wrongly. The host replied: "I perceived that you did not recite verses of the Kiddush over the wine at your noonday meal." The Rabbi explained: "I attend the early Services and recite the Kiddush before breakfast." When the host had left, Rabbi Moses turned to his Disciples and said: "God be praised that persons like our host are among us. They tenaciously adhere to the customs of Judaism and do not hesitate to criticise an old Rabbi for seeming to abandon them. It is a clear sign of the fact that if some Jewish leaders some day seek to lead the Jews astray, there will be Jews who will disobey and will have the courage to rebuke such leaders."

Sopher, p. 42.

9. *The Chameleon*

Rabbi Moses Sopher said: "We must not condemn a public leader if he seems to change his countenance like a chameleon that changes the color of its skin. To different people the leader must know how to speak in different ways."

Sopher, p. 42.

10. *A New Leader In Piety*

Said Rabbi Israel Salanter: "The book: *Hafetz Hayyim* manifests the advent of a new leader in piety among our generation."

Pupko, iii, 16.

11. *Reading Our Soul*

The true spiritual leader need not read the souls of his adherents. He should instruct them so that they can read their own souls and thus can eject all that is spurious.

Yehudi ha-Kadosh, p. 94.

12. *The Lesser Officials*

At the Vienna Conference in 1923, the Hafetz Hayyim said: "I am told that when the Austrian Emperor would go on a journey, his cabinet ministers accompanied him a short distance in order to look

out for their Sovereign's safety and comfort. The governor of the
province and staff then took their place, while the royal carriage
was in the capital city. Then the city mayor and later the local
official in a village would care for the ruler's security and comfort.
I believe the same situation prevails with the Lord. In early times
His affairs were conducted by eminent personages, such as Moses,
the Prophets, and the Scribes; later the Talmudists and still later the
Geonim. Today, however, it is the duty of ourselves, the lesser officials of the Almighty to preserve His commandments and to guard
against any breaches."

Pupko, p. 79.

152. LEARNING

1. Lessons From Everything

Said the Sadigurer Rabbi: "We may learn some good trait from
everything. Thus the punctuality of the railroad train teaches us
that every minute counts. A moment's delay in performing a hu-
mane deed may mean the loss of everything. The telegraph teaches
us that we must account for every word. The telephone teaches
us that a word spoken here is heard elsewhere."

Nissanzohn, R. H., p. 284.

2. God Learns from Man

Rabbi Abraham Moses explained the verse: "And all thy children
shall be taught of the Lord" Isaiah 54:13, as follows: "God will be
taught how to act towards a man by a knowledge of this man's
actions towards his fellow-men. If the man forgives a person who
has offended him, and goes out of his way to aid him, God will do
the same in his behalf. This is what the Torah means by the verse
(Leviticus 19:18): 'Thou shalt not take vengeance, nor bear any
grudge against the children of thy people, but thou shalt love thy
neighbor as thyself: I am the Lord.' The meaning is: 'Thou shalt
love thy neighbor. As thyself, I am, the Lord,' namely, 'I, the Lord,
will deal with thee, as thou dealest with thy neighbor.' "

Zammlung, p. 13.

153. LEISURE

1. The Use of Leisure

A merchant informed the Hafetz Hayyim that his competitors
wished to buy him out and to pay him annually a sum equal to his
yearly earnings. He declared, however, that he hesitated out of
fear that he would not know what to do with his leisure. The

Rabbi smiled and commented: "A man who has been granted the boon of leisure can find an abundance of charitable enterprises for which to care, and a wealth of moral studies in which to engage."

Pupko, p. 74.

154. LIFE

1. Life is Precious

Said the Hafetz Hayyim: "How very precious is life! The most powerful millionaire cannot lengthen life a single hour even if he expend all his possessions on the effort. To be sure, in order to gain our livelihood we must waste a part of our life, but it is an act of folly to devote all of our time to this task. Why exchange life which is so precious for accumulations which are valueless? The proper way to use life is to achieve spiritual gains."

Pupko, p. 23.

2. Prayers for Life

Said the Hafetz Hayyim: "During the Penitential Period we pray: 'Remember us for life, O King, who desireth life. Inscribe us in the Book of Life, for Thy sake, O Living God.' From this we learn that we beg to be granted life, so that we may remedy our shortcomings of previous years. Thus only can we pay that which we owe to God."

Pupko, p. 105.

3. Life for the Sake of God

Said the Hafetz Hayyim: "We beg for life so that we may use it for the sake of the Living God. We promise to accomplish good deeds for the sake of His honor." (Singer, p. 44).

Pupko, ii, p. 4.

4. Wherefore Life?

When the Hafetz Hayyim heard that the Russian authorities forbade the observance of religion, he sighed deeply and said: "Were I there, I would cry unto the Lord in these words: 'O Lord, why grant us life when we do not wish it? If we cannot obey the injunctions of our Torah, wherefore should we desire life?'"

Pupko, p. 112.

155. LIGHT

1. Light and Wisdom

The Berditschever Rabbi explained the comparison of light and wisdom contained in Ecclesiastes 2:13: "Then I saw that wisdom ex-

celleth folly, as far as light excelleth darkness." He remarked:
"Light can signify either daylight or moonlight, and can apply to
either the day or night. Darkness, on the other hand, can signify
only lack of light, or night. Likewise, the wise man may imitate the
fool, if it is required, but the fool can never appear to be genuinely
wise."

Guttman, p. 27.

2. The Borrowed Light

A Rabbi poured out his heart to the Riziner, saying: "When I
study a subject of the Torah, I feel myself to be encompassed by
holy light. But when I halt my studies, I feel myself chilled and
surrounded by darkness." The Riziner commented: "Whenever
you are not occupied with study of the Torah, occupy yourself with
the practice of a Mitzvah, and then the light will not fail you." He
continued: "The light which you feel round about you during your
studies is a light borrowed from the souls of the Sages. A light,
however, derived from your performance of Mitzvot is your own
light."

Margulies, p. 44.

156. LINEAGE

1. A Broken Toy

Said Rabbi Abraham Sopher: "In my eyes noble lineage is like
a chronometer. If every jewel within it and every piece of mechanism is functioning correctly, it is a possession of which to be proud.
But if something goes wrong inside it, it becomes like a broken toy.
And why boast of a broken toy?"

Sopher, p. 103.

2. Ancient and New Lineage

Said the Dubner: "Two boys were quarreling. One exclaimed:
'you should show me respect, for I am a member of an old aristocratic family.' 'My father also is a peer,' retorted his rival. To this
the first lad made the rejoinder: 'But your father's peerage was
recently created because of your father's war service, whereas ours
was established a long, long time ago.'

"From this we learn: Israel's greatness was established in an-
tiquity, whereas modern nations became great through their victo-
ries in recent wars."

157. LIQUOR

1. *Without Intoxication*

When Rabbi Yechiel visited in Tzechinov, a Hasid, Yekel Rades, partook freely of spirits, and then hurled himself in front of the horses drawing the Rabbi's wagon. The Hasid exclaimed: "The Rabbi may not leave the town unless he prays for the recovery of a Hasid, a friend of mine." The Rabbi answered: "Your action is commendable when you insist that a favor be done to your friend. But why should this be achieved under the influence of spirits?"

Ẓammlung, p. 61.

2. *"Sleep It Off"*

A Rav and a Shohet came to Rabbi Dov Bialer for judgment in a dispute. The Bialer remarked: "Listen to me closely, Rav. This dispute displays your inexperience in dealing with human nature. When my Father, the Tzechinover Rabbi, perceived that his Shohet was drunk, he would engage in no argument with him, but would instruct him to sleep off his drunkenness, and then come to him."

Ẓammlung, p. 55.

3. *Sufficient Punishment*

The Tzanzer told the story of a certain priest in a village who was vigorously opposed to the use of liquor. He let it be known that he would flog anyone whom he found drunk. Once a drunkard was brought to him, and to excuse himself, pleaded that the pleasure he found in liquor was irresistible. The priest thereupon decided to test the liquor to discover whether it gave him pleasure, and he drank a swallow or two. But the fiery liquid revolted him and he instantly spat it out. He then remarked: "To me the taste of liquor is an abomination, and hence it should be sufficient punishment for anyone." The Tzanzer drew a lesson from this incident, saying: "Just as the liquor by its abominable taste caused distress which served as sufficient punishment, so every transgression by the sense of distaste and distress it causes should carry in itself sufficient punishment for us."

Tzanzer Hasidut, p. 245.

158. LIVELIHOOD

1. *Lacking for Necessities*

A poverty-stricken Hasid complained to the Lubliner that he believed it wrong on his part to pronounce every morning the Benediction stating that God supplied all his wants. He knew this was not the fact. The Rabbi replied: "Perhaps God knows that if you possessed all you believe yourself to lack, you would no longer seek the truth in the words of your prayer."

Walden, p. 89.

2. *The Blind Son*

When Rabbi Hayyim of Tzanz was advanced in years, he asked that his third son, Rabbi Aaron, become his successor as the Tzanzer Zaddik. He was asked the reason, and responded with a parable: "A blind beggar accumulated considerable wealth, and on his death-bed he willed all his possessions to his seeing sons. To his one blind son, however, he left nothing. When his friends inquired the reason for this strange action, the beggar replied: 'My blind son will have the same opportunity that I had; it is therefore to my seeing sons that I must leave my property.' " (Doubtless, the meaning of the Tzanzer's request was that his son, Aaron, had common sense; his brothers, on the contrary, sought to act as if they were wiser than their father and criticized his actions frequently. Because of these shortcomings, the Rabbi therefore established a livelihood for them by a bequest other than the role of his successor as Zaddik.)

Raker, p. 70.

3. *"In Abundance"?*

A Hasid besought the Hafetz Hayyim to confer upon him the blessing for sustenance. When he received the blessing, the Hasid asked: "Will you not add the words: 'in abundance'?" The Rabbi replied: "Would you say that in these days and lands of exile, the glory of the Lord is in abundance?"

Pupko, p. 18.

4. *Fair Play*

The wife of the Hafetz Hayyim complained to him that the family lacked money for the very necessities of life. "Observe," she remarked, "the family next door consists of unlearned people, but they are blessed with riches. We have learning, but we live in poverty." The Rabbi answered: "God is fair in all His dealings. To the family next door he has denied learning, but has compensated for the lack by granting them wealth. Could you expect God to be so unfair as to give us both learning and riches, whereas the family next door would have nothing?"

Pupko, p. 54.

5. An Equal Share

The Hafetz Hayyim was asked: "Inasmuch as all Israelites shall have a share in the World-to-Come, wherein lies the difference between those who observe and those who do not observe the injunctions of the Torah?" The Rabbi replied by means of a parable: "In Kiev there lived a millionaire, by name Israel Brodsky. The magnate was kind-hearted and donated a monthly stipend to every poor relative in his family. Once Brodsky paid a visit at one of his factories. He inquired of each person as to the nature of his work. Finally he came to a man whom he asked: 'what is it you are working on?' The man answered: 'I am not doing any work; I am one of your poor relations.' Everyone round about who heard the remark burst into loud laughter." The Kabbalists had a name for such a stipend. They called it: "The Bread of Shame."

Pupko, p. 56.

6. Beyond Your Means

Said the Hafetz Hayyim: "Do not become accustomed to expensive living, even if you can afford it at the time. In later years your business affairs may not be so prosperous, and you will find yourself compelled to borrow money which you cannot repay. Then, if you are weak, you will be led into thievery."

Pupko, ii, 41.

7. What the "Seer" Foresaw

A Hasid came to the Lubliner and told him: "Rabbi, you knew me before this as a man of wealth; now, however, I have lost my entire fortune and am destitute." The Rabbi, whom his Hasidim called the "Seer," replied: "Your many acts of dishonesty and sin make your loss well-deserved. However, it is true that God sometimes turns away from justice and inclines towards mercy. I perceive in my fore-view that your fortune will be restored to you in a brief time."

The Hasid accepted a post as a porter in order to earn a few pennies. A few weeks after his visit to the Rabbi, a nobleman accosted him and handed him a heavy metal box to be taken to the inn. The owner said he would meet the porter at the inn, and reclaim the box. But the nobleman failed to appear, and, after a considerable interval, the innkeeper demanded that he remove the box. While carrying it to his home, the porter accidentally dropped it. Gold coins poured out of the box, to the exact amount which the porter-Hasid had formerly possessed. After due formalities, he was permitted to retain the money, and his prosperity henceforth was assured.

Walden, p. 114.

8. Reinforcing the Covenant

Said the Hafetz Hayyim: "Those who revere the Lord are at times obliged to travel for their livelihood. Thus they gain opportunities to spread a knowledge of our covenant with God to obey the Torah, and to reinforce its influence in places with little knowledge."

Pupko, ii, 44.

9. It May Be Harmful

The Hafetz Hayyim once overheard a man's reply to the query addressed to him: "How are things with you?" The man said: "Not bad, but it would not harm me if they were better." The Rabbi commented: "How do you know it would not harm you, if things were better with you?"

Pupko, p. 61.

10. It Does Not Pay

Said the Dubner: "A beadle was dissatisfied with his small salary in a small community. He induced a wealthy relative to secure a position for him in a larger town with double the salary. When he arrived there, he was delighted for a time with the change he had made, but he soon discovered that his expenses were likewise doubled, and therefore he had gained nothing whatsoever.

"From this we learn: a learned man may be glad that he is regarded as more important than an unlearned man. But he soon finds out that he is held accountable for his actions far more than the unlearned man."

Dubner, i, 222-223.

11. Men of Enterprise

Rabbi Isaac of Ziditchov said: "Frequently we come across the expression in books: 'Hasidim and men of enterprise.' I interpret this to mean: the 'men of enterprise' are not only enterprising in gathering good deeds, but also in earning a livelihood. A Hasid should strive to avoid dependence upon charity."

Braver, p. 82.

12. Not by Bread Alone

Said the Hafetz Hayyim: "Man prays for a livelihood. But was he born merely to eat?"

Pupko, p. 107.

159. LOSS

1. Recovering a Loss

Rabbi Shalom Guttman said: "Just as an energetic man who has lost his fortune feels a sense of joy while laboring to regain it, even though a little sadness at his loss still remains in his heart, so the Zaddikim experience joy in their labor to recover their holiness, at the same time that they feel a little sadness at its loss."

Guttman, p. 21.

160. LOVE AND FEAR

1. Love and Fear

Said the Medzibozer Rabbi: "Some Zaddikim serve the Lord through love and others serve him through fear. In Proverbs 8:21, we read: 'That I may cause those that love Me to inherit "yesh."' * This means that the Zaddikim who serve out of love will also inherit the faculty of fearing God. For 'yesh' has the initials of 'Yir'at Shamayim' (Fear of Heaven)."

I. T., p. 48.

* Translated to mean "substance."

2. Returning Love for Love

Said Rabbi Akiba Eger: "In the Sh'ma we are commanded to love the Lord. Why is there this command? Should the matter not be left to our own free will? This is the answer: we read at the end of the prayer which precedes the Sh'ma: 'Who hast chosen Thy people Israel in love.' Hence we can say that we are commanded merely to understand that it is our duty to return love for love."

Sopher, p. 62.

3. The Value of Love

Said Rabbi Menachem, son of the Turisker Maggid: "The verse in Leviticus 19:18 reads: 'And thou shalt love thy neighbor as thyself: I am the Lord.' We know that the word: *Ahavah*, or 'love' has a numerical value of thirteen. When one loves his fellow-man, the combined value of two loves, or of reciprocal love, amounts to twenty-six. This is the exact numerical value of the Holy Name of God: *YHWH*, which we pronounce *Adonai*."

Twersky, p. 73.

4. Among the Many

A visiting Zaddik, on leaving the Gerer, offered a prayer that love might always obtain between them. Rabbi Leib commented: "I suggest that you add in your prayer a supplication that between the rank and file of our Hasidim there may also obtain good will and love."

Rokotz, ii, 64.

5. Intimacy and Fear

The Strelisker Rabbi said: "The poet who composed the hymn: 'Adoration and Loyalty Belong to the Everlasting God' included a verse, reading: 'Intimacy and fear belong to the Everlasting.' The poet was correct, inasmuch as these combined traits appertain only to God. In an earthly court persons who are more intimate with royalty have less fear of their ruler than the less intimate. The reverse is true in the Divine Court."

I. K., p. 2.

6. Advice on Fear

Said the Hafetz Hayyim: "We read in Psalm 111:10: 'The fear of the Lord is the beginning of wisdom; a good understanding have all they that do thereafter.' A man does not need to be a philosopher in order to fear the Lord; this is within the reach of anyone who possesses only the beginning of wisdom. Does not man fear someone who is more powerful? And does not man observe the power of God Who sustains him and vouchsafes to him the use of his mortal endowment? But to do right and to live wisely in truth demands a good understanding."

Pupko, ii, 61.

7. Disliking and Loving Sinners

Said the Lentzner: "My Teachers, the Lelever and the 'Yud' have taught me that I may feel dislike towards a sinner only during the duration of his offense. I must, however, love him when he has ceased to offend. A Jew, even though he be the greatest of sinners, deserves my deepest love when he is not engaged in an act of sin."

H. Hak., p. 23.

161. LOYALTY

1. Resistance or Ridicule

The Besht narrated this parable: "A king desired to put the loyalty of a certain city to the test. He summoned one of his generals, and instructed him: 'go to this city and try to persuade its inhabitants to join you in a rebellion against me. If they imprison you, it will demonstrate their loyalty. But if they ridicule you and send you away, it will reveal their sagacity, in understanding that your effort is intended to trick them.' In the same fashion the Satan seeks to persuade us to rebel against God. Some of us take him seriously and combat him openly. The wiser ones among us merely laugh at him, and he takes his departure. Thus they manifest their knowledge that he has been sent to test their loyalty to God."

Srebrak, p. 5.

2. A New Garb

A Hasid sighed as he remarked in the presence of the Tzortkover Rabbi: "Even the Hasidim have changed. They wear modern garments, a thing decried in my younger days." The Rabbi replied: "The Lord is concerned only with the Jewish feeling within a person's heart. He is now testing Israel's loyalty to Him in a new garb."

Margulies, p. 26.

162. MAGIC

1. Overcoming Witchcraft

The Hafetz Hayyim said: "In an age when multitudes believed in the power of witchcraft, Rabbi Hanina exclaimed: 'Do your worst, O sorceress; the Lord is mightier than you are.' Rabbi Hanina held so firm a belief in the power of God over all things that he was convinced witchcraft could not prevail over the will of the Almighty. With this belief he overpowered every resort to magic."

Pupko, p. 94.

2. An Amulet and Its Efficacy

Said Rabbi Ber of Leova: "An amulet confers a benefit only upon him whose spirit is submissive to the will of God. But such a man has no need of an amulet."

Guttman, p. 23.

3. Nothing Supernatural

A Hasid begged the Tzortkover to offer prayer in his behalf, saying: "I can be helped only by supernatural means." The Rabbi replied: "God can help you only by natural means. For in God's economy there is nothing supernatural."

Margulies, p. 2.

163. MAN

1. "This is Man"

Said the Hafetz Hayyim: "We read in Ecclesiastes 12:13: 'Fear God,' namely, observe all His prohibitions; these are 365 in number, equalling the number of arteries in the human body; 'and keep His commandments,' namely, to do them; these are 248 in number, equalling the number of limbs in the human body. 'For this is the whole man,' namely, the whole of man's duty in the world."

Pupko, p. 93.

2. Man and Bee

Said the Hafetz Hayyim: "The bee is indeed a frail insect, yet it produces wax and honey. In the same way, man is flesh and blood, yet he is able to produce words and ideas of Torah."

Pupko, p. 95.

3. Utilize the Present

Said the Hafetz Hayyim: "A man may be compared to a soldier who has been stationed at a certain spot and is expected to stand there. If your soul has been sent to earth at the present moment, stand guard now and utter no complaint. To do so would be foolish."

Pupko, p. 95.

164. MARRIAGE

1. A Harried Husband

A Hasid complained bitterly to the Lubliner that his wife ruled him with an iron hand. The Zaddik said: "We read in Genesis 3:16: 'Thy love shall be unto thy husband and he shall rule over thee.' Perhaps if you, the husband, do not show so much love to your wife, you will be able to rule her."

Walden, p. 87.

2. A Man, not an Angel

After the death of the Lubliner's wife, his friends wished to persuade the Rav of the city, who was a Mitnaged, to give his daughter in marriage to the Zaddik. The Rav replied: "The Bible enjoins a father to give his daughter in marriage to a man. But your Rabbi, you call an Angel."

Walden, p. 76.

3. Two Tribulations

A man came to Rabbi Israel Isaac of Alexander to invite his advice about the betrothal of his son to the daughter of a tanner. "The tanner has two daughters and therefore a son-in-law will be welcome," continued the man. The Rabbi responded: "Since you have asked me, I must call your attention to the following: the Sages have said: 'Woe to him whose trade is that of a tanner,' and they have also said: 'woe is the father whose offspring are only daughters.' In all honesty, I must caution you against pushing in amidst two tribulations."

Zammlung, p. 74.

4. When Divorce is Necessary

Although the Hafetz Hayyim strove at all times to make peace between litigants, at times there were exceptions. Once a man and his wife came to the Rabbi, and told him they were completely incompatible. The Rabbi advised the husband to grant his wife a divorce. A bystander expressed his surprise, but the Rabbi said: "If it were always possible to bring about peace between a husband and a wife, our Torah would not have countenanced divorce. There are times when divorce is the only pathway to peace for both parties."

Pupko, p. 44.

5. The Returning Husbands

The Dubner told the following story: "Two women had been deserted by their husbands. One was very poor and left for another town in the hope of earning a livelihood. The second husband was rich and had left his home because of the nagging and quarrelsome nature of his wife. After a time a merchant came to the towns of the two women and sent for them. He informed them that he had received letters from their respective husbands which, unfortunately, he had left at the bottom of his trunk. He asked them to call again the next morning. The rich wife at once took her departure, but the poor wife refused to go away, saying she would wait until the trunk had been unpacked. The merchant inquired: "Why are you more anxious than the other woman?" The wife replied: "She is rich, and since she knows her husband has decided to communicate with her again and return home, she is satisfied. I, however, am in great financial distress. It is good to know that my husband is coming home, but I should like to know also whether he has been successful in earning a livelihood for his family and himself."

"In other words," said the Maggid, "love must be accompanied by favorable economic circumstances."

Dubner, i, 74-75.

6. Not For Our Sake

Said the Dubner: "A poor man received from his wealthy brother a dowry for his daughter. He spent most of it for clothing and for repairs on his home, in order to make a good appearance when the bridegroom arrived. A friend advised him not to ask his brother a second time for money towards the dowry, but to celebrate the wedding ceremony first; then he could come to his brother and say: 'I do not ask this gift for my sake, but for the sake of your reputation. It will be a family disgrace if I am to be sued for the money by my son-in-law.'

"From this we learn: we ask the Lord to help us not for our sake, since the Lord has done enough for us. We seek the Lord's aid for His sake, for the sake of His reputation."

Dubner, i, 149-150.

7. The Father's Opinion

Said the Dubner: "A very pious man who was accustomed to spend most of the day in the Beth ha-Midrash wished to see for himself the family of the girl whom the marriage-broker had recommended as a wife for his son. He therefore visited the family, and found both the bride and her family greatly to his liking. He gave his consent to the marriage and returned home. There he first mentioned the good qualities of the father and mother, and then he described the girl as a vertible jewel, a diamond beyond compare. On hearing this, the son began to weep. 'Why are you troubled?' asked his mother. The son replied: 'I am sure that the girl must be ugly of countenance, if my father, who never looks at a woman, praises her so highly.'

"When the Children of Israel heard from Moses that God had praised so highly the Land of Israel, they were convinced that it must be a land where spiritual riches abounded, but where material wants would be difficult to supply. They could not believe that the Lord's idea of material resources would correspond with theirs."

Dubner, i, 84-86.

8. Preparing for the Wedding

Said the Hafetz Hayyim: "The Prophet exclaims: 'And as the bridegroom rejoiceth over the bride, so shall thy God rejoice over thee.' (Isaiah 62:5). Since it is the rule always to make preparations for a wedding, it is proper to prepare at least a little knowledge of Holy Scriptures so that God may rejoice over you."

Pupko, p. 120.

9. *Advice before Marriage*

Rabbi Solomon Eger presented to his son, on the eve of his marriage, a number of words of advice:

"1. Obey your wife's father and mother.

"2. Do not laugh at any one, even though he may deserve derision.

"3. Always speak gently to your wife.

"4. Love your children tenderly, but do not spoil them.

"5. Honor all your teachers.

"6. Be sure to associate with those from whom you can learn goodness.

"7. Give up any habit of complaining against those who speak loudly and harshly.

"8. If you have guests, do not impose extra burdens on your wife by asking her to prepare special dishes.

"9. Every day devote yourself to learning a passage in the Pentateuch, the Prophets, the Holy Writings, the Mishnah, the Gemara, and the Codes. But never forget to study also a work on ethics."

Sopher, p. 77.

10. *The Business Woman*

Said the Dubner: "A man fell in love with a business woman. He proposed marriage but stipulated that she should give up her business and pay off her creditors. His proposal was accepted. The transaction, however, dragged on at too slow a pace for the suitor, since the business woman, by force of habit, could not resist making fresh purchases which she believed would be profitable. The suitor thereupon spread a rumor that the woman intended to go into bankruptcy. As a consequence the wholesalers refused to grant her credit. She went to her suitor and complained sharply of his behavior. He replied, however: 'What I did was dictated solely by my great love for you.'

"From this we learn that God Himself corrects those whom He loves."

Dubner, i, 135-137.

11. *The Two Questions*

Said the Dubner: "A widower had re-married, but to his dismay he observed that his son and his second wife were continually quarreling. When the son grew up, the father was recommended to a fine matrimonial prospect for his son. The girl and her family met his highest expectations. As soon as he returned home he arranged that his son should journey with him to visit the prospective bride. After a couple of hours of traveling had elapsed, the young man asked the coachman how far they had traveled. Later the father inquired of the coachman how near they were to their destination. The son asked: 'Father, why are our questions dissimilar?' The father replied: 'You have not seen the beautiful girl and the excellent family of which she is a member. Therefore you are concerned only with the distance we have traveled from the home where you have not been happy. I, however, look forward with enthusiasm to the home where it is certain you will find happiness.'

"From this we learn that the Children of Israel did not appreciate how pleasant a home the land of Palestine would be for them; hence they merely thought of the distance they had placed behind them after leaving Egypt. Moses, however, was aware of the beauty of Palestine, and his gaze was directed not on the land they had left, but to the land which was the goal of their journey."

Dubner, i, 107-109.

12. Bridegroom of the Torah

The Rabbi of Tzanz, though he had reached the age of seventy, wished to marry again. His son, Baruch of Rudnik, remarked: "I have heard, father, that the Rabbi of Ziditchov declined to remarry, because, he said: 'I am already married—to the Torah.'" "If this be the case," replied the Tzanzer, "I cannot marry the Torah, since I would not wish to make her guilty of bigamy."

Raker, p. 100.

13. A Change of Mind

Said the Dubner: "A professional matchmaker proposed two matches to a wealthy man for his daughter. One was a match with the son of the Rabbi, the other with the unlearned son of a rich merchant. The wealthy man preferred the Rabbi's son, but when he discovered that the Rabbi would not pay any portion of the wedding expenses and would not give any presents to the bride because of his poverty, he notified the Rabbi that the match was off. A friend of his, however, persuaded him to rescind his decision, asking the Rabbi to permit the match. The Rabbi refused, saying: 'Formerly I was agreeable, inasmuch as I believed that you appreciated my son's scholarship above any money he might or might not have. But since your change of mind demonstrated to me your lack of proper appreciation, I do not care to have my son marry into your family.'"

"From this we learn: when the Israelites showed a lack of appre-

ciation of the desirability of obtaining for themselves the land of
Palestine, the cradle of their nation, God refused to heed their repentance, and caused them to end their span of life in the Wilder-
ness."

Dubner, i, 224-226.

14. The Duty of Matrimony

On Yom Kippur Night, immediately after Services, the Hafetz
Hayyim called over to him the older students of his Yeshivah, and
persuaded them to arrange matters so that they might be able to
enter into holy matrimony before the next Yom Kippur. Such a
duty was incumbent upon mature youths on Yom Kippur and on the
15th of Av in midsummer during the days before the Exile.

Pupko, 83.

165. MEDITATION

1. Deep Meditation

On the Second Day of a New Year, the Hafetz Hayyim walked
in a field on the outskirts of the town; sat down on a stone, and fell
into deep meditation. A Disciple approached him, and the Rabbi
told him: "I have been exploring my heart, in order to discover
therein the reverence and the love I owe my Creator."

Pupko, p. 85.

166. MEEK

1. Shielding the Meek

Said the Hafetz Hayyim: "It is strictly forbidden to speak evil
even if it be known that the person affected does not mind the
affront. Miriam was punished for speaking ill of Moses who was renowned for his meekness."

Pupko, p. 99.

167. MELANCHOLY

1. Broken-heartedness versus Melancholy

The Bratzlaver offered this explanation: "He who is obsessed by
melancholy is constantly complaining of the harsh treatment he has
received from the Lord. He is always dissatisfied with God. But
he who is broken-hearted is like a son who tries to conciliate his
father who has become cold towards him. Broken-heartedness is
followed by joy."

H. H. N., p. 19a.

2. The Melancholy Zaddik

Rabbi Ber of Leova said to his Hasidim: "Why do you come to me? You seek light from me, when I myself am in darkness. You look to me for the secret of happiness, when I myself am unhappy."

Guttman, p. 17.

168. MERCY

1. Mildness in Censure

Said Rabbi Ber of Leova: "He who insists that the other person obey every statute strictly will be judged strictly in Heaven. But he who is merciful in judgment will be judged with mercy in Heaven."

Guttman, p. 22.

2. The Merciful Hebrews

Said the Tzanzer: "When Pharaoh's daughter beheld in the river the child Moses, 'she had compassion on him, and said "This is one of the Hebrews' children."'" (Exodus 2:6). When the summons of compassion filled the heart of an Egyptian princess, she understood that this must have been due to a child of the Hebrews, renowned for their mercy, and thereupon her heart was moved to mercy."

Tzanzer Hasidut, p. 238.

3. Compassion for a Weakling

Aryeh ben Pinhas tells of the magnate who pointed out to his companion a man who was passing by on the other side of the street. "Once," he said, "we were freinds, closer than brothers. But we became estranged, and, in his weakness, he tried hard to injure me whenever and wherever he could. May God forgive me that man's sins against me!"

Selected.

169. MERIT

1. An Outstanding Deed

Before his death, the Ziditchover Rabbi remarked: "I have carefully scrutinized and searched out my deeds, and have found nothing extraordinary. Perhaps one deed, however, may be accounted as such. Whenever I gave in marriage a child or a grandchild of mine, I helped bring about the marriage of an orphan at the

same time, and I settled on this orphan the same amount as I did
on my child or grandchild."

Szlamovitz, p. 16.

2. Assessing the Value

Said the Hafetz Hayyim: "Do you wish to know the estimate in
Heaven of your value? You are measured by the value you place
on worship of the Lord. Do you wish to know the estimate of the
value of your Mitzvot? The value in Heaven is the same as the
value you associate with them. If you are ready to abandon the performance of a Mitzvah for the sake of earning ten zlotes, the value
you thus place upon the Mitzvah is the exact value it receives
in Heaven."

Pupko, ii, 35.

170. MESSIAH

1. The Gullible Hasidim

It was said that the mother of the Riziner Zaddik informed her
son that she had lost in a fire her husband's genealogical tree, which
traced his descent from King David. Those Hasidim who beheld
the splendor of the Riziner's mansion believed that in truth he was
the Messiah. The Hasidim inquired from the Zaddik why he seldom
spoke of the Anointed Redeemer. The Rabbi answered: "When
a marriage is contemplated, the parents discuss it at length but the
bridegroom remains silent." The gullible Hasidim commented:
"These words are a hint to the effect that other Hasidic Rabbis may
assist in the coming of the Messiah, but the Riziner Zaddik is
veritably the Messiah himself."

Raker, p. 131.

2. The Messiah's Shofar

On Rosh ha-Shanah in the year 1851 the Rabbi of Rizin declared:
"I have heard the blast of the Messiah's Shofar, but not in This
World." The Hasidim explained this as follows: the Riziner was
summoned back to Heaven because his generation did not merit
the revelation that he was the promised Messiah. In fact, the
Rabbi passed away soon after this remark.

Raker, p. 141.

3. Blaming the Rabbi Only

Many Zaddikim and their Hasidim expected the advent of the
Messiah in the year 1860, for this year seemed to be indicated by
many portents. Rabbi Eliezer of Dzikov, son of the Rabbi of

Ropshitz, solemnly declared: "I swear to you that the Messiah will of a surety *not* come this year." No one dared to place questions to the Rabbi, but all were crestfallen. Finally, Meyer, the Rabbi's son, dared to inquire why his father had made so definite an assertion. The sagacious Rabbi replied: "Many Hasidim, and many persons by no means so pious, have become fully convinced that the Messiah will come this year. If they are disappointed, the danger of their apostasy will become great. Now, however, if the Messiah does not appear this year, the whole blame will be directed at me, but the faith of the confident will not be harmed."

Raker, p. 143.

4. When the Messiah Calls

Said the Hafetz Hayyim: "When Pharaoh called for Joseph, he was speedily released from prison. In the same way when the Messiah summons us, we shall be speeded like a swiftly-flying cloud from the imprisonment of our Exile."

Pupko, ii, 65.

5. Forefather of the Messiah

Rabbi Bunam said: "A passage in *Bereshit Rabbah,* commenting on the Sedrah *Wayyeshev* reads: 'After Joseph was sold into slavery, Reuben donned sackcloth, and fasted, but Judah separated himself from his brethren and married. The Lord who has insight into our minds, labored to create the Messiah.' This passage can be explained as follows: 'Judah blamed himself exceedingly for not using his authority with his brothers to bring Joseph back to Jacob. Through this grave sin, he felt that he had lost all the Mitzvot and spiritual assets he had previously acquired. He was convinced it was necessary for him to start afresh in order to accumulate a store of Mitzvot. Hence he commenced with the first Biblical commandment: 'be fruitful and multiply.' The Lord was pleased with this indication of Judah's sincere repentance, and brought it to pass that Judah begat Perez, the forefather of the Messiah.' "

Zammlung, p. 6.

6. "The Messiah Has Come"

The "Yud," though a disciple of the Lubliner, originated a different system in Hasidism, based upon profound learning and profound piety. The Lubliner still held to the more democratic system of the Mezeritzer and preached that superficial piety and little learning can also be regarded as acceptable Hasidism, if sincerely undertaken. He did not believe that the requirement of profundity in learning should exclude the simple folk from Hasidism. It might be thought that the Lubliner's way would attract a greater number of the populace than the "Yud's"; in point of fact, however, the reverse was true. The Lubliner was chagrinned to see that most of his Hasidim deserted him to go over to the "Yud." This brought about a serious misunderstanding between the two Rabbis. The Lubliner felt that the Mezeritzer's democratic, folk-Hasidism was essential. He believed that this democracy provided the justification for the very existence of Hasidism, inasmuch as Mitnagedut (the views of the Opponents) also preached profundity in learning and piety, and held aloof from the common people. He also believed that the essence of Hasidism, namely, unlimited love for every Israelite, was being endangered, by instituting an aristocracy in Hasidism, namely, an aristocracy of deeper learning and deeper piety. The "Yud," however, found that this aristocracy existed in fact; that it would also be a sin against the concept of love of Israel, to compel Jews of deeper and higher insight to lower their intelligence to the standards of the commoners. If these commoners admired the teacher of the aristocrats more than the teacher of their own class of Jews, it was unforeseen, and, by no means, desired by the "Yud." Heartily he wished that only the higher minds would come to him, and that the multitudes would remain with the Lubliner. The misunderstanding between the two Zaddikim grew, and strife abounded between the disciples of the Lubliner and those of the "Yud." The "Yud" resolved to travel to the Rimanover, a friend of the Lubliner from the days of their early youth, and to induce him to act as arbitrator. The entire itinerary became a triumphal procession. The whole populace of every town and village would walk out to greet the "Yud," to gaze at him and admire him. Several kilometers before the entrance into Rimanov, the roads were filled with coaches and wagons. Thousands ran breathlessly to catch a glimpse of the "Holy Jew." The youngest grandson of the Rimanover, a child of six, ran to his father and exclaimed: "Grandfather! The Messiah has come!"

H. Hak., pp. 112-115.

171. MIRACLES

1. Working a Miracle

An innkeeper was threatened with eviction by his landlord. The poor Jew came from his village to the Rabbi of Tzanz for assistance. The Rabbi sent him to a famous inn where many Polish noblemen often lodged. When the innkeeper arrived there, he discovered that the very landlord who was demanding his eviction, had become confused in a severe storm, and had found his way after much hardship to the inn. The owner of the inn gave the landlord a room with a warm bath together with a change of clothing. When the Polish landlord wished to make a handsome payment to the inn-keeper, the latter refused to accept it. Instead, he interceded for his friend, the village innkeeper, of whose plight he had been told, and he urged the nobleman to rescind the eviction order. This was done, and the village innkeeper returned to his home rejoicing. Thus the Zaddik's wisdom in sending the distressed innkeeper to the famous tavern of his friend had brought about a veritable miracle.

Raker, p. 85.

2. Miracles for the Many

Said the Gerer: "To witness a miracle one must be exceptionally pious and deserving. We are told that many miracles performed by Elijah, Elisha, Rabbi Phineas ben Yair and Rabbi Haninah ben Dosa were equal to the miracle of the Division of the Waters of the Red Sea and to the marvels in Maccabean days. Why, then, do we not celebrate the former in the same way that we commemorate the latter? Is it not because, in the case of individuals, it is not rare for them to be worthy; but at the Red Sea and in Maccabean days, it was necessary for many to be worthy. Only when the multitudes were worthy it was possible for them to witness the miracles. Needless to say the worthiness of multitudes is an occasion which deserves a celebration."

Rokotz, ii, 47.

3. Miracles Unnecessary for the Believer

Said the Riziner: "We read in Exodus 20:15: 'And all the people perceived the ... mountain smoking ... and stood afar off.' Miracles are valuable only for those whose belief is incomplete and remote. A truly pious man does not need to be convinced of the Unity and Power of God by means of miracles. Therefore when the people beheld the miracles at the mountain, 'they trembled,' for it was proof that their faith was remote from perfect belief and confidence."

Nissanzohn, Royal Hasidut, p. 272.

4. The Miracle of Nature

Said the Bratzlaver: "Most of the occurrences which are hailed as miracles are not supernatural but natural in character." The Leover said: "The greatest miracle is not super-nature, but nature itself."

Guttman, p. 18.

172. MITZVOT

1. The Mitzvah Today

Said the Hafetz Hayyim: "The word: 'Today' in the Bible makes it imperative for every man to bear in mind that he has only today for living. Hence when he encounters an opportunity to perform a Mitzvah, he must regard it as the last Mitzvah he may be able to perform, and proceed at once to do it."

Pupko, p. 69.

2. A Strong or Weak Advocate

Said the Hafetz Hayyim: "If you are the defendant in a court of justice, much depends upon your advocate's ability. When you are before the Judgment Seat every Mitzvah you have performed becomes your advocate. If you have performed it well, it becomes an able advocate in your behalf. If you have performed it weakly, your advocate will be weak."

Pupko, p. 123.

3. No Interest Accepted

A merchant visited Rabbi Moses Sopher and informed him in strict confidence that he was supposed to go to the Leipzig Fair, but that he could not, because his money was tied up and unavailable. The Rabbi loaned him one hundred guldens. The merchant fortunately made an excellent profit at the Fair and on his return both repaid the loan to the Rabbi and made him a handsome gift. The Rabbi admired the gift but thereupon gave it back to the merchant, saying: "I cannot accept this gift since it would appear to be a form of interest on my loan to you." His son inquired of the Rabbi why he had shown so much admiration for the costly gift. The Rabbi smiled and answered: "It is indeed a rare thing that a Rabbi has the opportunity to obey the law which forbids the taking of interest. Therefore when I held the gift in my hand, I felt the joy that comes from performing a rare Mitzvah."

Sopher, p. 45.

4. What Tidings?

Said the Hafetz Hayyim: "We read in Ecclesiastes 12:13: 'The end of the matter, all having been heard: fear God and keep His commandments; for this is the whole man.' What reply is given today when the question is asked: 'what tidings are there?' The answer is usually in terms of political alliances and wars. In the future, however, the answer will be different. It will concern itself with the fear of God, and with the keeping of his Mitzvot, as it is written: 'For then will I turn to the peoples a pure language, that they may all call upon the name of the Lord, to serve Him with one consent.' (Zephaniah 3:9)."

Pupko, ii, 68.

173. MODERATION

1. The Path of Moderation

Said the Hafetz Hayyim: "There are Jews today taking the right hand road which is too warm; these are the Hasidim. Others decide to take the left hand road, which is too frigid.* It is best to take the middle pathway, according to the custom of the Sages."

Pupko, p. 14.

* By this is meant: "the over-educated."

174. MODESTY

1. Only at the Commencement

Said Rabbi Ber of Leova: "The Torah commences with the words: 'In the beginning.' This gives us the suggestion that a man should always regard himself as being merely at the commencement of the performance of his moral and religious duties. He who has the feeling that he has advanced far in his service to God is, on the contrary, very remote from God."

Guttman, p. 22.

2. A Cold Stone

The Lubliner saw in his synagogue a Hasid who lived far away and seldom visited him. The Zaddik introduced the Hasid to some of his new adherents and gave him high praise. The Hasid's face visibly reddened at the Zaddik's words. The Rabbi remarked: "You have not yet learned the lesson of true meekness. Were you truly meek, you would have felt the praises I uttered no more than a cold stone."

Walden, p. 54.

3. In Their Own Estimation

The Strelisker recalled to his Hasidim the saying of Rabbi Simeon ben Yohai to the effect that he had looked about him and had observed that superior persons are small in number. Said the Rabbi: "How could he identify the superior persons? He did so by discovering those who were small in their own estimation."

I. K., p. 39.

175. MONEY

1. Untainted Money

Rabbi Leib Saras visited two Rabbis, who welcomed him profusely. One Rabbi suggested that he among them who had in his possession clean and untainted money should treat the others with wine. The first Rabbi said: "I believe that my money is clean. I was called upon to decide a civil suit, involving financial matters, and I received payment for my trouble." The second Rabbi retorted: "There is no certainty whatsoever that the money is clean, inasmuch as the loser did not give it with his whole heart. But the money I have is clean. I prayed for a sick man, and when he recovered, he gave me a gift."

Rabbi Leib Saras responded: "Yours is not clean or untainted money either. For the sick man was led to believe it was your prayer and not his own which availed with the Lord. In truth it may have been his own petition that was acceptable to the Supreme Healer. It is the money in my keeping, however, which is clean and pure beyond doubt. I have in the community a good friend who often lends me money. With his whole heart he is convinced that I will repay him soon, even as I have done many times before. I shall borrow the necessary sum from him, and with it I shall order the wine."

G. A., p. 12.

2. The Strength of the Thaler

A Rav sent a book he had written to the Leipniker and wrote him: "My work may not meet with your approval, but I am greatly in need of the thalers it is bringing." The Leipniker sent him the price of the book and wrote: "To the one who delighteth in the strength of the thalers."

Eibeshitz, p. 8.

3. "Any Manner of Loan"

Said the Hafetz Hayyim: "The words: 'any manner of loan' in Deuteronomy 24:10 indicate that all worldly values are of no worth. For the word: Meumah means not only 'any manner,' but also 'naught.'"

Pupko, p. 45.

4. The Many Children of the Poor

Said a wit: "After the conclusion of the Sabbath, the hymn: Ha-Mavdil is chanted, of which the first verse ends with the words:

777

'May He who makes a distinction between holy and profane, pardon our sins; our offspring and our possessions may He multiply as the sand, and as the stars in the night.' (Singer, p. 311 of 1934 edition). Now the poor man chants this hymn shortly before nightfall, being in a hurry to go to his work. Money cannot be granted to him for it is still the Sabbath; hence he is granted offspring. The rich man, however, chants the hymn after nightfall, and since the children have already been granted to the poor worshiper, the rich man obtains the money."

Zlotnik, p. 32.

5. Money for Swamps

The town of Turisk had considerable swampy land which it was necessary to dry out at considerable expense. When Rabbi Abraham took up his residence there, a friend asked him why he had chosen Turisk. The Rabbi replied: "Two kinds of money are received by me. The donations of religious Jews I utilize in order to build my House of Learning. But the gifts of the impious, who boast they keep me in affluence, I utilize to dry out the swamps."

Twersky, p. 55.

6. Accounting for Every Penny

Rabbi Mordecai Kozmirer, a son of the Turisker Maggid, once meditated with considerable distress of spirit: "I accept money from those who place their faith in me, and I know I shall be called before the Heavenly Tribunal to render an account for every penny." In a few moments, however, his countenance cleared, and he said: "I know I do not deceive or mislead a single donor of mine. I simply promise to offer prayer for those who come to me for counsel and help, and I am faithful in keeping this promise. My hope is that these prayers I offer may be accepted by the Lord."

Twersky, p. 75.

176. MOTHERS

1. Overzealous Advice

The mother of Rabbi Moses Sopher invited her son, the principal of the great Pressburg Yeshivah, to visit her in Frankfort. Inasmuch as many difficulties interposed at the time, the Rabbi sent an inquiry to the Rabbinate of Frankfort, explaining the circumstances. He asked: "What is more important, honoring one's mother or teaching Torah to multitudes?" The Rabbinate rendered the reply: "Teaching is more important." Rabbi Sopher sent the reply to his mother, who was satisfied that for the time being her son delayed his visit.

Sopher, p. 30.

177. MURDER

1. The Instinct to Murder

Said the Hafetz Hayyim: "In 1916 many Jewish fathers told me with distress that their sons had been conscripted. I gave them my blessing with the prayer that their sons would return in complete safety. But to myself I said: 'In ancient days many Jews were slain and by the sacrifice of their life they sanctified the Name of God. Once again Jews are being forced to face death. For what? Many will return crippled. Who will be the gainer? As far as I can see, only the instinct to murder is the beneficiary.'"

Pupko, ii, 29.

178. MUSIC

1. Fasting or Music?

At a time of severe distress, the Rabbi of Apt proclaimed a fast. Rabbi Israel of Rizin, however, disregarded the announcement, and ordered the members of his choir to sing. When report of this came to the ears of the old Rabbi of Apt, he declared: "With the Riziner, it appears that music avails more before the Lord than fasting. Therein he imitates the Torah which says: when an oppressor comes, 'then shall ye give sound with your trumpets, and ye shall be remembered before the Lord your God, and ye shall be saved from your enemies.'" (Numbers 10:9.)

Raker, p. 121.

2. A New Zest

Said the Besht: "A king enjoyed immensely the playing by a certain musician, and he invited him to play before him daily. After a time, however, the king observed that the musician had wearied of playing before the same listener constantly. Therefore the astute king invited fresh guests daily to listen with him. The musician responded by displaying his skill with a new zest. In the same way, God enjoys hearing new interpretations in theology offered by a Sage. But He sends to the interpreter new disciples in order to awaken a new zest in him in giving form to the fruit of his intellect."

Srebrak, p. 9.

3. The Power of Music

Said the Bratzlaver: "There is one reason why the Levites were ordered to sing in the Temple; why music is always played at weddings; why Psalms are chanted before Services; why hymns are in-

cluded in divine worship. The reason is that music serves to unite
minds that are in conflict; music breaks down enmities; music in-
stills courage; music awakens an unworthy mind to the realization
of its unworthiness; music creates in man a yearning for a higher
spiritual state."

H. H. N., pp. 45a-45b.

4. The Musical Zaddik

Rabbi Leib Saras once heard a Jewish shepherd lad singing with
extraordinary beauty snatches from some Hebrew hymns. "Such
a talent should be saved for service to God," thought the Rabbi. He
took the lad to the school of Rabbi Schmelke. Later the singing
shepherd became the renowned Rabbi Isaac Taub of Kalev. The
Kalever Rabbi asserted that persons dedicated to holiness are blessed
with joy and music, whereas those who concern themselves with
impurity are obsessed by sadness and melancholy. He believed
that holy sparks of music fell into the domain of mundane minds,
and that it is a good deed for a Zaddik to strive to restore them to
their Holy Source."

G. A., p. 13.

179. MYSTICISM

1. The Additional Soul

When Rabbi Leib Saras became Bar Mitzvah he was taken by
his father to the Mezeritzer Maggid to receive the latter's blessing.
The Maggid blessed him and said: "I have given thee this day a
benediction of prime merit." The boy did not comprehend the
Zaddik's meaning at the time, but later he understood. He had in
truth received the gift of an additional soul—the soul of a mystic.

G. A., p. 6.

2. Both Are Needed

The Rabbi of Apt said: "It would be possible for me to convert
the Leipniker Rav to Hasidism, but I do not wish to do so. The
nature of some persons includes a feeling for mysticism and its
secrets; the nature of others inclines towards the Law of Judaism
and its exposition. Both natures are needed among us."

Eibeshitz, p. 9.

180. NATURE

1. Sun and Shield

The Tzortkover explained the verse in Psalm 84:12: "For the
Lord is a sun and a shield" as follows: "To see the sun we need a

cloudy glass as a shield for our eyes. Likewise to see God we must observe nature which is the shield of His effulgence."

2. Revelation in Nature

Said the Ladier: "The study of the works and laws of nature enables man to comprehend God's handiwork. Only through the study of matter can one gain an insight into Divine Revelation in the universe. For divinity is made manifest in its active aspect within the universe. And sound reason is required to observe this revelation in nature."

Teitelbaum, i, 17.

181. NEIGHBORS

1. Loving They Neighbor

Rabbi Israel Baal Shem Tov interpreted the commandment: "Love thy neighbor as thyself," in the following manner: "Love thy neighbor despite all his shortcomings and displeasing habits in the same way that thou lovest thyself with all thine own shortcomings and undesirable ways."

Dor Deah, p. 35.

182. NERVES

1. Controlling Our Nerves

Rabbi Baruch of Leipnik visited his brother and encountered there a tutor who later became renowned as the "Yud." He was greatly impressed by the astute young man, and when an inquiry elicited the fact that the tutor often visited the "Seer" of Lublin, Rabbi Baruch asked: "But what can he teach you? In all likelihood you know more about Torah than he does." The "Yud" replied: "One thing above all others I have learned from the 'Seer.' He has taught me to have perfect control over my nerves. As a result of my visits to him, the moment I lie down to rest, I fall asleep."

Eibeshitz, p. 63.

183. NEWS

1. "No News"

A visitor at the home of the Hafetz Hayyim was asked by the Rabbi if he had any news to impart. The visitor replied in the negative. "You are right," remarked the Hafetz Hayyim. "The only news that would be important is the proclamation that 'God reigneth.'"

Pupko, ii, 37.

184. NINTH OF AB

1. Let Him Take It Back

A Rabbi visited the Koznitzer Maggid on the 9th of Ab and commented upon the apparent lack of the spirit of mourning in the Maggid's synagogue. The Koznitzer replied: "If the Lord dislikes the spirit with which we observe the 9th of Ab, let Him take the Day away from us."

Zlotnik, p. 96.

2. Only Half-Pious

Hershel Ostropoler, a well-known wit, entered a restaurant on the 9th of Ab and commenced to eat whatever was placed before him. A Jew, convalescing from an illness, was also eating at the restaurant. Seeing the Ostropoler, he remarked: "Hershel, why don't you at least wash your hands before eating your bread?" The witty Hershel answered: "Don't you know that it is forbidden to wash the hands on the 9th of Ab?"

Zlotnik, p. 99.

3. A Walk Together

A poor Jew was taking a walk with his wife on the 9th of Ab. He was asked: "Why this frivolity on a Day of Mourning?"

"Let me explain," answered the Jew. "My wife and I are never able to take a walk together because we own only one pair of shoes between us. Today, however, when, according to Jewish custom, we must go barefoot, we are able to indulge in a walk together."

Zlotnik, p. 99.

4. A Table for the Sinful

The Rabbi of Tzanz completed the study of a volume of the Talmud during the Nine Days prior to the Ninth of Ab. He therefore ordered a celebration in honor of the achievement, and had a table set with wine and meat. Inasmuch as the Mitnagedim (the Opponents) do not eat in this fashion during the Nine Days, a Rabbi from Hungary entered the room and vehemently expressed his displeasure. The Tzanzer Rabbi called him over and remarked: "Let me explain. The Gemara declares that after the loss of the Altar of the Holy Temple in Jerusalem, the table of each man serves as an altar, where sins are forgiven. You, our Opponents, are without sin and therefore require no forgiveness. Hence you have no elaborate table set during the Nine Days. We Hasidim, however, are filled with sin, and for this reason we must have the table set in this way even during the Nine Days."

Raker, p. 95.

185. NON-JEWS

1. Pretense Breeds Fear

Said the Medzibozer: "Jacob exclaimed: 'I have great fear of my brother, Esau.' Why did Jacob fear Esau so much? It was due to his feeling of guilt over the fact that he had pretended to be Esau when he came into the presence of his father, Isaac. The same is true of all those Jews who pretend to have abandoned their identity with the Jewish people, though they profess to adhere to the Mosaic religion. They soon feel fear of the non-Jews among whom they live."

BDH., p. 54.

2. Caring for His Servants

A sleep-loving priest resided next door to the home of a pious Jew. Being a light sleeper, the priest would be awakened early in the morning when the Jew left his home to attend Services. In anger the priest during the night dug a deep pit, hoping the Jew would tumble into it on his way to synagogue before daylight. Fortunately for the Jew, however, he was entertaining a guest with whom he discoursed until late in the night passages of the Torah. As a consequence he overslept and escaped the trap set for him. On seeing the failure of his plan, the priest praised God for the care He gave His servants.

Walden, p. 123.

3. The Compassionate Priest

One day a Jew observd two packages drop from a mail wagon, on one of which were stamped the words: "Contains thirty thousand florins." The temptation was too strong for him and instead of placing the package with the money where it belonged in the wagon, he took from it the money. Later he was arrested on suspicion of theft. His wife, who was shocked at her husband's act, induced him to disclose the hiding place of the package of florins, and then threw the money into the house of the Leipniker Rav, hoping thus to save her husband. The Rav thought the matter over, and realized that if he declared he was unaware of the identity of the person returning the money, he, as a Rabbi, would not be believed. There-

fore he went to a friendly priest, who, he knew, would not be required to disclose the identity of the person who had returned the
florins. The compassionate priest restored the money to the postal
authorities, and the Jew was released.

Eibeshitz, p. 21.

4. A Daily Convert

Rabbi Aryeh Leib of Ger has written in his work *Sefat Emet*
that the "Yud" would attain daily a measure of understanding concerning service to the Lord still higher than the day before. In comparison with yesterday's comprehension, today's was so much loftier
that it would seem to him as if yesterday he had been like an uninformed non-Jew. In this way he was daily converted from being
an uninformed non-Jew into a Jew, into a "Yud."

H. Hak., pp. 47-48.

5. The Cross on the Tombstone

Said the Hafetz Hayyim: "On Judgment Day a cross on a grave
will be evidence that a faith has been followed which the Household of Israel does not accept."

Pupko, p. 98.

186. NON-RESISTANCE

1. Harm No Living Creature

The Tzortkover Zaddik declared that on his seventh birthday he
made a vow never to harm any living creature. A Hasid put the
question: "Suppose an evil non-Jew attacks an innocent Jew, what
would your reaction be?" The Rabbi replied: "Earnestly would I
pray that the Jew be saved from harm, and I am convinced that
such a prayer would be heard in Heaven. As for the assailant, I
have no business with him."

Margulies, p. 7.

187. NOURISHMENT

1. Feeding the Soul

Said the Hafetz Hayyim: "A teamster feeds his horses even when
they do not work. Likewise we feed our body even if the soul within
it has not earned the nourishment. If the body is healthy, it may
yield to the soul an opportunity to bring about the performance of
meritorious deeds."

Pupko, p. 90.

188. NOVELTY

1. The Needed Receptacle

Said the Hafetz Hayyim: "New interpretations of the Torah require a proper receptacle. If you have learned a little Torah, you can utilize it as a receptacle into which you can pour clearer interpretations of what you have already learned. But if you have learned no Torah at all, you cannot acquire any clarifications of it, and the receptacle remains empty."

Pupko, p. 101.

189. NUMBERS

1. The Number: Forty-Five

When the Berditschever Zaddik was installed as Rabbi in Berditschev, he said: "There is a sequence of references to the number: forty-five in this occasion. The Hebrew year is 5545 (1785) which contains 45; my age is 45 years; and today's number in Counting the Omer is 45." Hasidim explained this statement as a reference to humility. The word: *"Mah"* in the phrase: "And what are we?" (Exodus 16:7) has the number value of 45.

Guttman, p. 1.

190. OBEDIENCE

1. The King's Imports

Said the Hafetz Hayyim: "It is incumbent upon us to perform the Mitzvot and achieve the merit of good deeds not for our own sake, but for the sake of the Lord. This brings to mind a custom house. A batch of goods intended for our own personal benefit is strictly examined by the officials. But the imports intended for the King will not be so closely scrutinized. In the same way, if we perform a good deed, in the hope that we will derive reward from it, its value will be carefully investigated. But if it has been done with the intention of obedience to the Lord, the examination will by no means be so thorough."

Pupko, ii, 1.

2. Still Less Worthy

After the demise of the Gerer Rabbi, one of the Gerer Hasidim paid a visit to Rabbi Leib Eger. The latter asked his visitor to repeat to him some counsel he had heard from his late Rabbi. The Hasid said: "I heard the Gerer say: 'Because you have refused to listen to the Prophets of old, you are now compelled to listen to a person as lowly as myself. Let your prayer, however, be that you be spared the necessity of listening to a person more lowly and more unworthy than I am.'" Rabbi Leib Eger absorbed these words, and then gave a deep sigh.

Rokotz, ii, 29.

191. OBSTACLES

1. The Locked Boxes

Said the Besht: "A king distributed gifts among his courtiers in the form of locked boxes. Some of the recipients secured keys which fitted the locks and easily opened the boxes. Others, however, could find no such suitable keys, and hence broke open the boxes. By the same token, it is for us to understand that God has endowed us with potentialities whereby we can acquire excellent character traits with which we can perform good deeds. Some of us find the performance of such good deeds to be an easy matter; others, however, must break through and overcome obstacles to achieve goodness. Of what importance, however, are these hindrances, considering the value of the possessions to be acquired by breaking through all obstacles?"

Srebrak, p. 5.

2. Angels or Men?

Rabbi Akiba Eger, the illustrious Rabbi of Posen, explained the Talmudic saying: "If the Former Teachers (Rishonim) were angels, we are men; if, however, they were men, we are donkeys." He said: "If we consider the words of the Former Sages as words of angels who cannot err, then we are men, and we labor to comprehend them. But if we consider the Former Sages to be mere men, liable to error, we ourselves behave like donkeys. Everytime we find a difficulty in their words, we remark: it is an error, and we do not labor to clarify the matter."

Sopher, p. 60.

192. OFFERINGS

1. Offerings of Higher Quality

Said the Hafetz Hayyim: "Sometimes a man has the feeling within that his power to learn and to pray is far from perfection. He may excuse himself on the ground that other people are even less endowed, but this is an unsatisfactory excuse. He may possess an admirable intelligence, whereas others have far less intellectual

competence. According to the Torah, a rich man's offering must
be of a quality higher than that of a poor man."

Pupko, ii, 43.

2. Each Thoughtful Offering

Said the Hafetz Hayyim: "In the Book of Exodus the offerings
of the chiefs of the tribes are mentioned in only a few words, but
in the Book of Numbers, many words are employed to describe each
offering of the chiefs, although they were all identical. Why is
this so? Because in the prior instance, the chieftains thought: 'let
us wait until the common people complete their giving, and then we
will make our gifts.' Thereby they manifested their indolence. In
the latter instance, however, each chieftain took care to imitate with
exactness the offering of the other chieftains, in order to avoid show-
ing any superiority over a colleague. The Lord therefore made
much of each thoughtful offering."

Pupko, p. 48.

3. Repeating the Offering

Said Rabbi Samuel Zevi of Alexander: "In the hymn *Lekhah
Dodi* we read: 'And He will have compassion upon thee in mercy.'
How can we explain the repetition of the theme of pity? The
answer is as follows: each Jew receives his share of mercy from
Heaven. If he is unable to accept his share because of his impious
conduct, the share of mercy cannot return to Heaven, inasmuch as
Heaven confers a gift, but does not accept it back. The poet prays
that God may make each person deserving of mercy, for thus the
Lord can show His compassion upon the mercy which has found
no place for itself."

Zammlung, p. 90.

193. OPINIONS

1. Contradictory Opinions

Rabbi Feivel Gritzer visited the Lubliner "Seer." He wrote out
a "Qittel" (a plea) for himself and for his friend, Rabbi Zussa
Plotzker. When the Lubliner read the plea, he began to speak of
the Plotzker in derogatory terms and pronounced him an unworthy
person. A few hours later he summoned Rabbi Feivel to his Study
and began to speak words of high praise for the Plotzker Rabbi.
When Rabbi Feivel later encountered Rabbi Zussa Plotzker, he told
him of the contradictory opinions the Lubliner had expressed regarding his character. Rabbi Zussa said: "In truth the Lubliner is
a 'Seer.' In the morning a poor Rav came to me and implored me

to collect a dowry for his daughter from a wealthy friend in Warsaw. I declined to do so, since I knew the task was too difficult for me. The Rav then told me of a new Torah interpretation, and I declared that it was not according to the Law. Thus the Rav left my presence without any money and without any credit for a new Torah comment. After his departure I though the whole matter over. I sought out the Rav and informed him I had been in error regarding his Torah comment, and I praised him for it as a notable suggestion. Moreover, I went to the home of my wealthy friend, and very soon, I had collected the dowry for the Rav's daughter. Thus it is possible to explain the 'Seer's' contradictory opinions regarding me."

Zammlung, p. 31.

194. OPPONENTS

1. Praying for Opponents

The Rabbi of Medziboz was heard praying thus: "O Lord! Mayest Thou keep all my opponents healthy and prosperous amid their families! Thou knowest it is repugnant to me that anyone should be punished because he opposes me."

M. B., p. 20.

195. ORIGINALITY

1. Original Study

Said the Mezeritzer Maggid: "In the *Ethics of the Fathers,* 2:17 Rabbi Jose says: 'Qualify thyself to learn Torah since the knowledge of it is not an inheritance of thine.' By these words he means: 'Learn new, fresh Torah, which you discover by your own processes of thought; not merely the Torah which you have received from books and from teachers.'"

BDH, p. 72.

196. PAIN

1. Feeling the Pain

Rabbi Mordecai Neshkizer said to his son, Rabbi Leib of Kovel: "Would you know who is truly a good Jew? He is one who feels in himself the pain suffered by each and every Jew who is ill, as if he were the actual sufferer. Moreover, he strives to aid the afflicted man by his earnest prayer and by every other means at his command."

Kolbiel, p. 6.

197. PARABLES

1. Parables

The Gaon of Wilna once asked the Dubner Maggid: "Does it take you long to create a parable?"

"No time at all," replied tthe Maggid. "Just show me a verse in the Prayer Book, and I shall put a question and give an answer, illustrating both by parables."

The Gaon opened the Siddur and pointed out a verse: "Answer me, O Lord, as Thou hast answered our father, Abraham, at Mount Moriah." The Maggid immediately launched into a question by means of a parable:

"A storekeeper had two steady customers, one wealthy and the other poor. The rich customer invited the merchant to his son's wedding, and the merchant brought a valuable gift, worth fifty thalers. The following year the poor man married off his daughter, and the storekeeper, on receiving an invitation, brought a small gift, worth only two thalers. The poor man complained about the inequality of the presents. The merchant, however, replied: 'Do I not sell to the rich man many times what I sell to you? How can you compare yourself to him?'

"In the same way, I say, how can we compare ourselves to Abraham? Abraham brought to God many sincere and good deeds of charity, but we, what do we bring to Him? An insincere prayer; a donation given because of our pride?

"Now let me answer the question, as follows:

"A very rich but unlearned man wished to gain a higher social status, and he sent his son to an Academy. The boy was a brilliant student and soon became renowned as the Academy's best scholar. Soon after the Head of the Academy died, and the young scholar was being considered for the post. Certain persons objected on the ground that the young man's father was an unlearned man. The father thereupon donated 25,000 thalers to the Academy, and his son received the appointment. Later, the son's son became a distinguished scholar, and upon his death was being considered as his successor. Some older men recalled the donation of 25,000 thalers because the new scholar's father had been appointed Head. The response was made: 'Ah, yes, but this scholar has an eminent father, whereas his father had an unlearned father. Therefore we cannot request a monetary gift as a condition of his appointment.'

"Likewise, we may say: Abraham's father was a pagan; therefore he had to bring to God a rich contribution. But we have an

illustrious father, Abraham; therefore God may answer our entreaties, even though our contribution is indeed a poor one."

Dubner, i, 27-29.

2. A *Parable on the Parable*

The Dubner Maggid was once asked: "Why does the parable
possess such great influence?"

The Maggid replied: "I will explain this by a parable." He proceeded to narrate the following:

"Truth was accustomed to walk about as naked as he was born.
No one allowed him to enter a home, and everyone who encountered
him ran away in fright.

"Truth felt greatly embittered and could find no resting place.
One day he beheld Parable attired in colorful, expensive garments.
Parable inquired: 'Why are you so dejected, my friend?' Truth replied: 'I am in a bad situation. I am old, very old, and no one
cares to have anything to do with me.' 'Nay,' retorted Parable, 'it
is not because of your age that you are disliked by people. Look,
I am as old as you are, and the older I grow, the more do I seem to
be beloved. Let me disclose to you the secret of my apparent popularity. People enjoy seeing everything dressed up and somewhat
disguised. Let me lend to you my garments, and you will see that
people will like you as well.' Truth followed this counsel and
dressed himself in the garments of Parable. Ever since then Truth
and Parable walk hand in hand, and men love both of them."

Dubner, i, 25-26.

3. *The Marksman*

The Gaon of Wilna asked his friend, the Dubner Maggid: "How
do you find a parable suitable to any particular subject?"

The Maggid, in accordance with his custom, responded with
a parable:

"A student at a military academy was returning home after
graduation. He stopped over at a village inn in order to give his
horses a rest. In the barn he noticed that circles had been chalked
on the walls, with a bullet hole in the very center of each circle.
He was astonished at such an exhibition of marksmanship and asked
to see the marksman. A little, barefoot boy came over to him and
introduced himself as the person responsible. 'Where in the world
did you learn to shoot so accurately?' inquired the military student.
'Nowhere,' was the boy's reply. 'I simply shoot at the wall and then
encircle the hole.'

"It is the same with me," continued the Maggid. "When I hear

or think out a good parable, I retain it in my memory. Then I strive
to fit it to an appropriate subject."

Dubner, i, 31-32.

4. The Small Coin

Said the Dubner: "A man hoarded his gold under the boards of
a floor in his house. One day he died, leaving the impression that
he was exceedingly poor. The heir chanced to drop a small coin
on the floor and it rolled between the cracks of the boards. There
to his astonishment on lifting the loose boards, he found a hidden
treasure. Needless to say, he preserved the small coin as a token of
good fortune.

"From this we learn: a man may glance in a book and find a
story, a fable or a parable. In so doing, however, he continues to
read deeply, and thus he gradually acquires solid and worthwhile
learning. The student then holds in high estimation the lighter
matter which introduced him to the heavier. It was through the
initial glance that he eventually became a scholar."

Dubner, i, 173-174.

198. PARENTS; CHILDREN

1. A Father's Reply

Said the Dubner: "A son greatly displeased his father by his
behaviour and was forced to leave the house. The son, on his own,
was able to find only a little work to support himself, and he lacked
the means to buy winter clothing. A neighbor asked the father to
take pity on his son and to buy him the warm garments he needed.
The father refused, however, saying: 'Why do you come to me?
Why do you not rather admonish the youth to improve his ways, so
that he may be reconciled with me?'

"From this we learn that the Zaddik would do better to admonish
his fellow-Jews to improve their conduct than that he should entreat the Lord to have mercy upon them."

Dubner, i, 129-130.

2. The Beloved Son

Said the Hafetz Hayyim: "We read in Jeremiah 31:20: 'Is
Ephraim a darling son unto me? . . . For as often as I speak of him, I
do earnestly remember him still; therefore My heart yearneth for
him.' When is a man a darling son of God? When he hearkens to
God whenever God speaks of him, and when he learns the words of
God and the verses of the Torah. Then God's heart yearns for him,
and God encompasses him with His mercies."

Pupko, p. 119.

3. *An Infant's Recognition*

Said the Hafetz Hayyim: "I have intense dislike for those philosophers who are constantly striving to produce proof of God's existence. God gives us life, health and sustenance. Need we, if we
are in our right senses, doubt His existence until we receive the
proofs furnished by philosophy? Even an infant child recognizes its
father? If he does not, it is complete evidence that his father bears
no love for him, or he for his father."

Pupko, ii, 18.

4. *The Little Girl and the Satan*

The Rav of Luna was disturbed while in his Study by the entrance of his little daughter. He asked her to play in the yard, but
in a few moments she returned and said: "The other children don't
want to play with me." The Hafetz Hayyim said to the Rav who
was with him: "What a difference there is between the actions of a
little girl and those of the Satan. In the Talmud the Satan is compared to a fly which persists in annoying a person even though it
is driven away again and again. Yet even a little child refuses to
play with comrades who show her no good-will and do not care for
her company."

Pupko, p. 71.

5. *"What Did You Bring Home?"*

The Sassover, becoming a Hasidic Rabbi, was once persuaded
by a merchant to take a bale of goods to the market, and to try his
hand in business. Instead, however, he spent the day in lengthy
prayers, thinking of holy rather than of mundane things. As a result, he sold nothing at all. When he returned home, his children
asked him: "Father, what did you bring us?" The father wept copi-
ous tears and said: "I have been away only a single day, and already
I am asked if I had brought anything. My soul went forth from
its place in Heaven twenty-five years ago. If I am taken back, what
reply could I make if I were asked: 'What have you brought?'"

Szlamovitz, p. 51.

6. *The Gift of Three Sons*

Rabbi Mordecai Neshkizer left a large sum of money in his home
in the belief it would be safe. But thieves broke in and made away
with the money. Seeing her husband's great distress, the Rabbi's
wife gave him her jewelry so that he might sell it and repay the
money to those who had left it in his custody. The Rabbi remarked:
"If ever I am able to repay you, I will give you gems worth three

thousand rubles." Later when his affairs improved, the Rabbi
wished to keep his promise. But his wife declined to accept repayment, saying: "You have already kept your promise. Have you not
given me three fine sons who are jewels without price?"

Kolbiel, p. 6.

7. A Holy Man's Submission

Rabbi Yehiel of Alexander wished to visit a Rabbi of greater
renown and invited his son, Samuel Zevi, to accompany him. The
son declined to do so. When asked later the reason for his refusal,
Samuel Zevi replied: "Of necessity my father would be required to
submit himself to the other Rabbi. I do not care to see a holy man's
submission to another mortal."

Zammlung, p. 91.

8. Study Yourselves

The Hafetz Hayyim said: "Do not say: 'and teach them (the
words) to your children,' but say rather: 'and study the words yourselves.' No one can be certain that his children will maintain their
father's eagerness to study and learn subjects of Torah."

Pupko, p. 20.

9. Satan and Our Youth

Said the Hafetz Hayyim: "The Psalmist says (127:4): 'As arrows
in the hand of a mighty man, so are the children of one's youth.'
Great indeed is our triumph over the Satan when we bring up our
little children in an atmosphere of dedication to Torah, thereby
building their loyalty to the Household of Israel. Great indeed is
our defeat, however, at the hands of the Satan when our children
desert from our camp. May the Almighty prevent it! Let us always remember that when our young people walk in the pathway
of the Torah, they are able to triumph over the Satan."

Pupko, ii, 66.

10. The Boy Within Himself

It is told that a Zaddik was visited by a guest late at night, and,
anxious to show him hospitality, went to his wine cupboard for a
bottle. But to his dismay he perceived that none was at hand. The
Zaddik remarked to his guest: "Be patient, my good friend; I will
send a boy to bring back some wine." When the host re-appeared,
the guest inquired of him: "Where is the boy to whom you referred?"
The Zaddik answered: "Within myself I have concealed the 'boy'

that I was in my youth. Whenever the need arises, I make good use
of him."

Rokotz, ii, 75.

11. Small Children Again

The Hafetz Hayyim once narrated the following tale: The Rav
Katzenelenbogen and his friend, the preacher Rav Feivel, were
walking one day in Vilna, discoursing together on the kind of judges
who would constitute the court at the Heavenly Tribunal. One of
the two Rabbis said: "I am confident that Rabbis of this generation
will be members of the court. For older leaders would judge too
harshly the sinners of the present day." A passer-by overheard
them and said: "I am sure you will have your seat at the Heavenly
Tribunal. Therefore won't you listen to my confession while I am
still able to correct my conduct?" Rabbi Saul remarked: "His plea
is convincing. I ask you, as the preacher, to listen to his confession."
Rabbi Feivel replied: "I am reminded of my school days. When
the teacher would step out of the room, the children would play
being soldiers in the army. Some enacted the role of officers and
passed judgment on the conduct of the ordinary soldiers. When,
however, the teacher returned to the room, all the pupils became
small children again. Merely to play at being judges does not help."

Pupko, p. 67.

12. Children and Prayer

The wife of the Hafetz Hayyim told her son that when she was
caring for her small children, her husband advised her not to
spend time in prayer, inasmuch as the care of little children is more
important for a mother than prayer.

Pupko, p. 13.

13. The Child and the Adult

The Hafetz Hayyim once saw a little girl in a village playing
with her doll. He remarked: "If we should conceal this toy and
give it back to her twenty years from now, she would be amused
at herself for having enjoyed so ragged a little plaything. Likewise
in the World-to-Come, a man will feel amusement at himself when
he is reminded of the inconsequential things he considered important while in This-World. We must always remember that Torah
and good works take precedence over all things."

Pupko, p. 97.

14. A Childish Excuse

Said the Hafetz Hayyim: "Oftentimes a foolish person, reproved
by a wise man, on the ground of impiety, will retort: 'Why is that

person impious?' It is comparable to a child who answers his mother when she scolds him for misbehavior: 'Why is that boy mischievous?' Such a retort, of course, is of no worth."

Pupko, p. 105.

15. Man Is Like an Infant

Said the Hafetz Hayyim: "An infant in his cradle imagines that he can do anything, but in reality he is helpless. The same is true of the grown man."

Pupko, p. 100.

16. The Locomotive

Said the Hafetz Hayyim: "The head of a family functions very much like a locomotive, which pulls uphill a number of cars loaded with goods. If he has enough fire and steam, he is able to draw all of them to the summit of the hill. If, however, he is without fuel and coal, the cars drag him backwards down hill to the very bottom, and both the locomotive and the cars are smashed into fragments." *

Pupko, ii, 41.

* This parable can be applied to the father who if he is vigorously religious succeeds in bringing up his family in the love of God; but if he is cold and without enthusiasm, both he and the family are dragged downwards.

17. "Where Is That Son?"

Said the "Yud": "I inquired from a hard-working merchant of wealth: 'have you not already acquired sufficient possessions? Why, then, do you continue to labor so strenuously to attain additional riches?' The merchant replied: 'I am doing this so that my son will not be required to work so hard.' Later I perceived that the son himself, on attaining manhood, acted in exactly the same way. For what reason, I inquired? He answered: 'For my son's sake.' Hundreds of generations have passed by, and fathers still work for their sons. When will I be privileged to behold that son for whose leisure and comfort countless forefathers have allowed themselves no rest?"

H. Hak., pp. 93-94.

18. Welcoming with Words

After a long absence a son returned to his father's home. The father, a very poor man, repeatedly asked his son how he felt; how things stood with him; how the journey was, and so forth. Finally the son exclaimed, with a show of impatience: "But, father, I've answered you already several times." "Yes, replied the father, "but I have no fatted calf to kill for your homecoming, nor any other festive viands. And so I wish to show my love for you through words."

Thus it is clear, we cannot often donate large sums to charity or to the House of the Lord, and therefore, we seek to express our love for Him through words.

Dubner, i, 60-61.

19. In Small Portions

Said the Dubner: "A rich man's son pursued his studies at a school distant from his home. His father was accustomed to send him money, but he selected as his agent a man who commuted between the two cities. This man was known to be a tight-fisted person. The father explained his choice as follows: 'My son is habituated to luxury and does not appreciate the value of money. A good-hearted man would succumb easily to my son's pleas, and would permit him to overdraw his weekly allowance in order to indulge himself. A hard-hearted man, however, would be adamant to my son's entreaties, and hence my son would lack the means to spoil himself with pleasures which would waste both my money and his health.'

"Sometimes a man receives his allotment of worldly goods in small portions, so that he may not stray from the straight road by over-indulgence."

Dubner, i, 88-89.

20. Advising a Father

Said the Dubner: "A wealthy nobleman sent his son away from home because of his profligate behavior. The son settled in a distant city but the father sent him money at regular intervals. Later the father yearned for his son's return. A friend advised him: 'If you invite him to come back, he will persist in his unseemly conduct. Moreover, as long as he receives an allotment of money from you, he feels no need to ask your forgiveness. Send him no more money, and he will return home contrite and ready for reformation.'

"From this we learn that the Lord exiled us but continued to provide for us a livelihood. When we find our livelihood is not forthcoming with ease, we come to understand that the Lord yearns for our return to Him, in a repentant and submissive mood."

Dubner, i, 162-163.

21. A Father Does Not Forget

Said the Dubner: "A father became angry with his son, and drove him out of the house. The boy took refuge with a neighbor. A few days later the neighbor advised the boy to go to his father and seek to appease him. The lad replied: 'I prefer to wait until my father comes to ask me to return to his house.' The neighbor commented: 'But what assurance have you that he will do so?' The boy answered: 'I looked through the window and I saw that my tutor was still living at the house. If my father did not care for me any more, why has he still kept the tutor?'

"From this story we learn: if God has indeed forgotten us, why does He support the nations whom He has appointed as our tutors at His expense? Why does He not permit the nations to become comrades friendly to us, so that we may become like them, instead of having them teach us we must remain a peculiar and distinctive nation?"

Dubner, i, 143-144.

22. The Two Celebrations

Said the Dubner: "Two neighbors lived in a certain city. The son of one of them loved to study; the son of the other loved to enjoy himself with unworthy pleasures. The first was a diligent student of the Torah; the second devoted himself diligently to money-making schemes. In time the first son graduated as a brilliant Rabbi; the second, however, went to prison as a swindler. A few weeks later both returned to their home town. Both fathers held celebrations: one, because his son had become the Rabbi of a prominent community; the other, because his son had been released from prison. An ironic person congratulated both parents and expressed the wish they might celebrate similar events in the life of their other children.

"From this we learn that there are celebrations and celebrations. There are some, however, which no one wishes to be repeated."

Dubner, i, 147-148.

23. The Tone of a Request

Said the Dubner: "A student wrote a letter to his father, asking for extra spending money. The father's secretary read the lad's letter to his employer in a loud, harsh voice: 'Father, send money immediately; I need shoes and an overcoat.' The father became incensed at the seemingly impolite tone of his son's letter and refused to answer him. Later he gave the same letter to his wife to read. She read it to him in a low tone of modest entreaty. The father, thereupon, wrote out a check and instructed his wife to mail it to his son.

"From this we learn that he who prays quietly makes a better impression than a noisy worshiper."

Dubner, i, 189-190.

24. A Son to His Father

Said the Dubner: "A father expelled his son from his home because of disobedience. The son went to the Beth ha-Midrash to pass the time, and sympathetic persons gave him food. The son learned that his father was inquiring about his presence in the House of Study. The son approached his father and said: 'Why do you not inquire if I have enough to eat and a place to sleep. Take me back, and I assure you that you will be satisfied with my conduct in the Beth ha-Midrash.'

"From this we learn: Grant us sustenance in the Land of Israel and we will be a worthy people."

Dubner, i, 258.

199. PASSOVER

1. The Afikomen and the Satin Coat

Rabbi Solomon Eger, the son of Rabbi Akiba, placed the following case before Rabbi Zalman of Nashelsk: His wealthy father-in-law had made a bequest in his will of a special fund to the first grandson who would bear his name. Rabbi Solomon chanced to have the first son to be given his father-in-law's name, and he therefore laid claim to the fund. The other heirs, however, objected, declaring that the infant boy had died before it was thirty days old and hence could not be considered for the bequest. Rabbi Zalman rendered a decision declaring that the other heirs, not Rabbi Solomon, had the correct opinion. Rabbi Solomon thereupon declared that his own father might have rendered a different decision. Rabbi Zalman laughed and remarked: "You remind me of the famous Rabbi Heschel of Cracow, known for his wit even as a youth. At a Seder Service, the boy Heschel captured the Afikomen and refused to surrender it until his father had promised him a satin coat. The father reluctantly made him this promise, but when he had been given back the Matzah he declined to give any to his son unless Heschel released him from his promise. Heschel laughingly took out of his pocket a piece of Matzah, ate it and said: 'I expected you to do exactly this, and therefore I provided myself with a remedy.' The circumstances are the same with respect to myself, and I anticipated this very argument by you. Therefore I placed the matter before my father and secured his response. His decision is the same as mine, and here it is in writing."

Sopher, p. 77.

2. *The Seder Symbols*

Said the Rachminstrovker Rabbi: "Follow the symbols of the Seder and you will not fall into error. The first symbol: *Kadesh u-rehatz* signifies: 'Sanctify yourself and wash away your sins.' The symbol: 'Karpas' has the initials of the words: '*Kelal Rishon: Peh setom*'; the first rule to adopt for the Sanctification of thyself is to keep thy mouth closed. '*Yahatz Maggid*' teaches us: 'Divide what you wish to say in two; namely, say but half of what you intended.' "

Twersky, p. 71.

3. *The Zealous Wife*

On the Eve of Passover a Rabbi had compassion upon his hard-working wife, and told her that she had cleaned the house with sufficient thoroughness to meet the requirements of the Shulhan Arukh. He begged her to desist and rest. But the Rabbi's wife who was known for her zeal replied: "Were I to listen to you and your Shulhan Arukh, we would be eating left-over Hametz on Passover."

Zlotnik, p. 82.

4. *Working for the Reward*

Said Rabbi Baruch of Medziboz: "In the Haggadah we read: 'The wise son asks: "what are the statutes," etc. . . .' By this he means to say: 'since the Israelites were redeemed without any effort on their part to merit their liberation, why are we today required to exert such strenuous efforts to merit the acquisition of further blessings?' The answer is as follows: 'God saw fit to liberate the Israelites from bondage in Egypt, though they were lacking in merit, because they were too deeply immersed in the mire of impurity to make it impossible for them to acquire merit. Later, however, the Lord restored the necessity of labor by men seeking their reward. The statutes of the Torah are the instruments by which God's blessings descend upon us.' "

I. T., p. 41.

5. *A Needle's Eye*

Said the Medzibozer: "It is customary for the Lord to require that a man take the initiative in turning to Him before He grants him aid. The Talmud indicates this in the words: 'Open to Me a door the width of a needle's eye, and I shall open unto you a door as wide as that of a palace.' Yet at the time of the Redemption from Egyptian bondage, God 'passed over' His requirement of the open door, as it is said: 'The Lord will pass over the door.' "

BDH., p. 55.

6. "Then Came the Dog"

Some impertinent youths stood outside the window of a Hasid and ridiculed his enthusiastic performance of the Seder ritual. Finally a youth entered and asked: "How far have you gotten in the Haggadah, Uncle?" The Hasid promptly replied: "Then came the dog." *

Zlotnik, p. 81.

* An item from the "Had Gadya," "One Only Kid." See also Isaiah 56:11: "Yea, the dogs are greedy."

7. Sanctification and Penitence

At his first Seder following his induction as a Rebbe, Rabbi Zevi of Alexander spoke as follows: "We read in the instructions of the *Haggadah*: recite the Prayer of Sanctification (Kiddush) and then wash the hands. Washing the hands is a symbol of penitence and ordinarily should precede Sanctification. In this instance, however, we know that there was no time for the Israelites to proclaim their penitence, since the Redemption came so swiftly upon them. Therefore they sanctified themselves first, being confident that they would surely find an opportunity to do penitence afterwards."

Zammlung, p. 93.

200. PATIENCE

1. The Two Watches

The Dubner Maggid told the following story: "A father bequeathed two gold watches of fine workmanship to each of his two sons. It chanced that both needed money badly and sold their watches. 'Did you get a good price?' asked the older son. 'No,' was the reply, 'I took it to a man who does not understand the value of watches, and he paid me a comparatively small sum.'

" 'I was wiser,' remarked the older son. 'I asked an expert to estimate the value of my watch, and then I sold it to a dealer for a handsome price.'

"The young son, however, remarked. 'I believe I did the more sensible thing. My purchaser is not aware of the worth of the watch and will gladly sell it back to me for a very small profit. When I am no longer in difficulties, I shall re-purchase it, and will be able to retain it as a remembrance of my father. You, however, will find that the person with whom you have had dealings will demand a large profit in addition to the large sum he paid you. You will see: you will find it hard to repossess yourself of your father's gift.'

"Thus it is clear that he who looks for an immediate profit may not be so wise as the man who looks towards a future benefit."

Dubner, i, 78-80.

2. Waiting for the Harvest

Said the Dubner Maggid: "Two brothers for the first time in their life visited a village surrounded by farms. The clean, grassy appearance of the field near their tavern pleased them exceedingly, and therefore they were vexed when the farmer who owned it, turned it into a black mass of earth with his plough, and then proceeded to sow it. It was not long, however, before the field became greener than before, and tall stalks grew up to furnish a beautiful adornment. When they later beheld the farmer mowing down the stalks and spoiling the field's fine appearance, they again were vexed. When, however, they visited the farm once more, they saw the grain being winnowed and placed in sacks. They then understood the purpose of all the work in the field."

The Dubner drew the moral, saying: "Frequently we mortals are dissatisfied with God's administration of the world because we see only His first actions. If we are privileged to witness the end results, we would come to understand the meaning of God's deeds at the beginning."

Dubner, i, 72-73.

3. The Value of Patience

Said the Dubner: "Two Yeshivah students, on their way home stopped to rest at an inn. The innkeeper was well-known as a kind and hospitable man, and the younger student, being hungry, wished to ask for some food. The older student, however, told him to have patience. Some travelers entered and ordered a meal in a hurry. Again the student wished to ask for some food, and again he was dissuaded by his older companion. Later the landlord wished to have his own meal and invited the students to eat with him. Since he was an epicure and selected the best of foods, the young men had a better meal than the travelers who had paid for their own.

"From this we learn that the wicked are impatient to enjoy all the pleasures of this world, and must pay dearly for them . . . The good men have patience to wait for their enjoyments until they are invited to the table of the Master of the Universe."

Dubner, i, 104-107.

201. PEACE

1. The Peacemaker

When the "Yud" was still in his childhood, his father, Rabbi Asher of Psedburz, and his uncle took him for a walk in the country. The boy observed several sheep fighting over morsels of food. He approached them, patted them gently, and divided the tasty food equally among them. The sheep munched their portion in quiet, and the peacemaker was delighted. "I prophesy," remarked his uncle, "that this child will grow up to to be a true shepherd in Israel. His action resembled that of Moses and David."

H. Hak., pp. 3-4.

2. Angels of Peace

The Zakilkover was a strenuous opponent of the "Yud." Once the "Yud" asked the Koznitzer Maggid to make peace between the Zakilkover and himself. The Maggid invited both for a Sabbath visit. When he returned home from the Friday Evening Services, the Maggid beheld his two eminent guests sitting at a considerable distance each from the other. He remarked: "How can I chant the 'Shalom Aleikhem' hymn which mentioned the welcoming of 'Angels of Peace' when you sit far apart from each other because of your enmity?" The "Yud" immediately shook hands with the Zakilkover. The latter offered no objection, but he remarked: "It is only until the Sabbath has passed."

H. Hak., p. 107.

202. PEDDLING

1. Peddling the Torah

A Rabbi called at the home of Baron Horace Ginsberg in the hope of selling a book he had written. The Baron remarked to him: "Is it not a profane thing for a Rabbi to peddle his Torah?" "On the contrary," responded the Rabbi. "Are we not told in Talmud Bavli, *Avodah Zarah*, 2, that God Himself peddled His Torah among all the nations before Israel accepted it?"

Zlotnik, p. 89.

203. PEDIGREE

1. Not Garments, but Adherents

Rabbi Hirsch of Rimanow met the Rabbi of Rizin, who immediately proclaimed his aristocratic lineage. Rabbi Hirsch commented:

"My parents were poor and pious. I was left an orphan at ten, and became a tailor's apprentice. Two things I learned: not to spoil new garments, and to repair old garments well. Thereupon the Riziner acknowledged the Rimanower Zaddik as his complete equal, for he understood that Rabbi Hirsch had meant not garments, but living adherents.

Raker, p. 135.

2. A Fine Rabbi

Rabbi Isaac of Ziditchov noticed among his visitors an eminent Rav who was known to take pride in his admirable lineage and his handsome appearance. The Zaddik called him over and said to him: "The Talmud, *Sanhedrin* 32, advises us to follow a fine judge. Such a judge is not a handsome judge, or one of noble descent. No, the fine judge is a judge who possesses a fine character and nobility of conduct."

Braver, p. 63.

3. Like an Umbrella

Said the Riziner: "Good birth is like an umbrella. It is useful only when there is a man under it."

Margulies, p. 7.

4. Unfulfilled Pedigree

A man repeated in the presence of the Hafetz Hayyim the proverb: "an apple does not fall far from the tree." The Rabbi commented: "Yes, this is true, if the wind does not carry it away." *

Pupko, p. 54.

* Let not the tempests of life's circumstances bear a man far away from the merit of his lineage.

204. PENALTIES

1. No Immediate Payment

Said the Hafetz Hayyim: "Greater than any debt which a debtor may owe you is your indebtedness to God. Yet we know that God does not exact payment for a long time by summoning your soul from your body. In similar fashion, do not demand a pledge of immediate payment when you aid the poor."

Pupko, ii, 48.

205. PENITENCE

1. The Nature of Penitence

Said the Karliner: "I am not in agreement with those who pre-
scribe fasting as a penance. Penitence is the feeling of sincere
contrition within a man's heart, and fasting weakens the heart. Let
the penitent eat well, strengthen his heart, regret his misdeeds and
perform acts of goodness. The Prophet Hosea's counsel to return
unto the Lord may also mean: return unto thy better nature, unto
the godliness within thee. Unto thyself restore thy self-respect,
thy peaceful conscience and whatever thou hast lost when thou hast
sinned."

I. K., p. 10.

2. Alive or Dead?

A Disciple of the Hafetz Hayyim secreted himself in the garret of
the Rabbi's home during the Penitential Period between Rosh ha-
Shanah and Yom Kippur. He overheard the Rabbi rendering an
account of his actions before the Lord. The Rabbi first enumerated
his deeds of piety and his endeavors to perform actions of moral
worth. Then the Rabbi began to give a roster of his shortcomings,
including his lack of concentration in prayer at all times. Finally
the Rabbi exclaimed: "I am regarded as an ordinary man, and therefore I may hope that God, in His pity, will judge me on the scale
of merit and mercy. But I hear a Voice asking: 'Is this man alive
or dead?' And I must answer: 'Alive.' And I hear the Voice con-
tinuing to say: 'Then why, O sinful man, dost thou depend upon My
pity? Go and repent.'"

Pupko, p. 84.

206. PERFECTION

1. Reward for Imperfections

Said the Bratzlaver: "The Creator permits the continued existence of so imperfect a world as ours because He foresaw that certain thinkers would be filled with doubt when they observed its
countless defects. Despite these imperfections, however, they would
still adhere to their faith in the Lord, and this would be sufficient
reward for the Creator."

Guttman, p. 16.

2. *Improvement and Repentance*

Said the Hafetz Hayyim: "When a physician examines a patient, he first instructs him regarding his diet, and then prescribes the necessary medicines. In the same way, it is essential that we first resolve to improve our behavior, and then to do penance for sins which we had previously committed."

Pupko, ii, 1.

207. PERSISTENCE

1. *Pray to the End*

Said the Bratzlaver: "If you perceive that God has answered your prayer and has already begun to send you the help you have sought, do not say to yourself: 'I do not need to offer prayer any longer; rather I should maintain silence and await developments.' On the contrary, you should pray again and implore God to help you even more. Keep up your entreaties until your wants are fully satisfied. Remember that after Mordecai and Esther beheld the punishment of Haman, they continued their petitions to the King that he utterly root out the villain's handiwork."

H. H. N., p. 40a.

2. *No Slack Time*

Said the Hafetz Hayyim: "In labors on behalf of God there is never any slack season. Nor is there ever any completion in the study of the Torah."

Pupko, p. 100.

3. *The Unwearying God*

Said the Hafetz Hayyim: "Do not hesitate to beg God to fulfil your needs at all times. He is not like a human being who wearies of frequent petitions."

Pupko, p. 99.

208. PERSUASION

1. *Skilful Persuasion*

Said the Hafetz Hayyim: "There are, oftentimes, merchants endowed with the talent of skilful persuasion, and who thereby are highly successful as salesmen. We in the domain of religion should study their methods and imitate them when we attempt to dispense spiritual values."

Pupko, p. 113.

209. PHILOSOPHY

1. The Inner and the Middle Garment

Said the Ladier: "Metaphysics is the inner garment of him who is engaged in the research of Torah. His middle garment is clear thinking regulated by the rules of grammar."

Teitelbaum, i, 18.

2. A Dangerous Path

In his youth Rabbi Leib Saras visited the Besht. The Besht noticed that at times his young visitor was deeply engrossed in metaphysical meditation, scarcely aware of his surroundings. The Besht said to him: "There are definite limits and boundaries for the human mind making research into metaphysical subjects. I counsel you to cleave to me and obey the restrictions I must impose, lest you suffer a breakdown."

G. A., p. 7.

210. PHYSICIAN

1. The Physician as Preacher

Said the Dubner: "A man who had suffered a heart attack called in a heart specialist. The doctor examined him but forebore to give him a prescription. He merely told his patient to avoid anger, to live in friendly and harmonious mood with everyone, not to be over-ambitious in money-making, and to avoid worry, whatever happened in his business affairs.

"A friend of the patient who was present remarked in astonishment: 'Why is it that the specialist wrote out no prescription, but merely offered good moral counsel. Why did he trespass on the domain of the preacher?'

"A second friend replied: 'There is a difference between the physician's counsel and the preacher's. The physician cares only for the bodily welfare of the patient, and the leading of a quiet life will save him from mortal illness. The preacher, however, cares for the spiritual welfare of his hearers, and a sound, quiet way of life will aid in the salvation of his soul.'

"From this we learn that frequently medicine for one's soul is also medicine for one's body."

Dubner, i, 185-186.

211. PIETY AND IMPIETY

1. Pious Deeds with a Blemish

Said the Hafetz Hayyim: "When the Satan perceives the futility of luring a great man into the performance of a sinful deed, he frequently makes an about-face and persuades him to perform a pious deed which contains within itself an unsavory element, and therefore brings no honor to God."

Pupko, ii, 50.

2. The Crown of the Torah

Rabbi Joshua Heschel of Komarna, son of the Leipniker, learned that an irreligious Jew was being held in prison because he lacked the money to pay a fine. He went to wealthy Jews of the community and asked them for donations so that the prisoner might be released. They refused to help because of the prisoner's evil repute. The Rav then went into the synagogue, removed the silver Crown from a Scroll of the Torah, pawned it, and paid the fine. The Jew thus benefitted was deeply moved by the Rabbi's act, and solemnly promised to better his ways. Later the Jewish magnates who had refused to rescue a Jewish soul in distress felt themselves compelled, however, to redeem the silver ornament of the Torah. When the man whom the Rabbi had freed became a reputable and excellent member of the community, the magnates perceived their folly, and honored their Rabbi still more.

Eibeshitz, p. 34.

3. The Inroads of Modernism

Rabbi Ber of Leova, a son of the Riziner Rabbi, grew weary of his role as a Zaddik. He resolved to acquaint himself with the culture of modernist Jews. But he found their worship of non-Jewish values to be more repugnant to his soul than the cult of Zaddik reverence. His nephew, the Rabbi of Bohush, visited him, displayed his deep sympathy and affection, and induced the rebellious Rabbi to return to Sadigura. Rabbi Ber never consented, however, to accept another call as a Rebbe.

Guttman, p. 11.

4. The Merit of Hasidism

The "Yud" said: "Hasidism is a guard. It guards the mind from the entrance of impurities in the same way that the eyelashes guard the eyes; the lips guard the mouth, and the lobes guard the ears." On another occasion he remarked: "A hair's breadth of pure Hasidism flowing from the heart contains more worth than This-World and the World-to-Come. He who is a genuine Hasid cares naught for This-World; he serves the Lord out of love for Him, not because of the 'Olam ha-Bah' (The 'World-to-Come.')" Again he said: "Of what avail is a visit to a Zaddik when the Hasid does not learn from the visit how to become a Zaddik himself; how to dig deeper his well of Hasidism, and to draw from it water of greater purity wherewith to quench his soul's thirst."

H. Hak., p. 87.

5. Irreligion Increasing

Said the Hafetz Hayyim: "It truly seems as if the spirit of irreligion is increasing with the rise of every new generation. An allusion can be found in the words in Deuteronomy (32:5): 'Is corruption his? (namely, the father's). No; his children's is the blemish; (and the next generation) is a generation crooked and perverse.'"

Pupko, ii, 39.

6. The Zaddik's Victory

Said the Hafetz Hayyim: "The impious scoffers imagine that they will draw to them the majority of the Household of Israel. But, lo, a single Zaddik appears and draws multitudes to the service of God."

Pupko, p. 100.

212. POVERTY

1. The Excuse of Poverty

Rabbi Joshua Belzer inquired of Rabbi Isaac Ziditchover: "I have been told that you offer prayer that your Hasidim may be blessed with wealth, health and offspring, but you never mention spiritual welfare. Is this report true?" "Yes, it is true," answered Rabbi Isaac. "But I ask you to take note that in the brief prayer: *Ana be-Koah*, the phrase occurs: 'prosper them; purify them.' Prosperity comes first. Therefore it is my belief that when my Hasidim can no longer plead the excuse of poverty and ill-health, I can then reprove them and instill in them the message of spiritual betterment."

Braver, p. 37.

2. Prosperity is Required

On Rosh ha-Shanah the Tzortkover said: "Thou, O God, art endless, and therefore Thy mercies are boundless. Of what significance, therefore, can the offenses of Thy people Israel be in Thine eyes? The people of Israel are like unto princes and they must have comfort, peace and joy. They cannot develop goodness in poverty. I beg Thee to ease their lot, to relieve them from penury, and then they will turn to ideals of life and serve Thee well."

Margulies, p. 26.

3. The Verdict of Poverty

Said the Hafetz Hayyim: "Many persons mistakenly believe that if a poor man works diligently, he will surely gain enough to support himself. They forget, however, the words of our Sages who tell us that before a man is born, it is decreed in Heaven whether he shall be rich or poor. How, then, can a man go against the decree of God?"

Pupko, p. 38.

4. Song Over Bread

Said the Dubner: "A man quarreled with his son. He gave him a sum of money so that he might leave town and settle in another community. There the son married and had children, but his enterprises proved unsuccessful. In every letter to his father, he besought him for financial help. The father sent the manager of his business to investigate and to report to him whether his son was as poor as he described in his letters. The manager returned and reported that the son was truly poor. 'Did you speak with him?' asked the father. 'No,' replied the manager. 'But I saw his child outside his home holding a piece of black bread in his hand, and singing a song of rejoicing that he had been given it to eat. This convinced me of your son's exceeding poverty.'

"From this we learn that the Lord understands the poverty of a Jew who chants praises unto Him after he has eaten a piece of dry bread and a potato."

Dubner, i, 100-102.

5. Acting a Part

Said the Dubner: "A poor man journeyed on his wanderings to a distant town in order to try his fortune there. He saw a drunken man dancing and singing in a foolish manner, while people crowded about him and threw coins into his hat.

"The poor man thereupon went to another town and imitated the antics of the drunkard. He also drew a crowd and collected a considerable sum from their contributions. Later, however, an acquaintance chanced to pass by, and observed the scene with surprise. He invited the dancer to speak with him, and said: 'I knew you in our town as a normal person. Since when have you lost your senses that you imitate a drunkard?' The man replied: 'I act in this non-sensical way out of dire want, whereas a true drunkard behaves as he does through exuberance of spirits.'

"From this we learn that a rich man sins through over-indulgence, whereas a poor man sins because of poverty."

Dubner, i, 206-208.

6. The Assets of Poverty

Said the Hafetz Hayyim: "I thank Thee, O Lord, for making me poor. For poverty has subdued my heart, and has given my enemies little opportunity to rejoice over my downfall. For are not our enemies created out of our sins?"

Pupko, p. 97.

213. PRACTICE

1. City or Town?

The Lubliner was asked by a Hasid: "Shall I take up my residence in a large city where my livelihood will come to me easily; or in a small town where my income will be less in amount, but where I will have leisure for study?"

The Rabbi replied: "The city offers more opportunities to give aid to poor Jews, but the town more time for study. It is for you to remember that practice takes precedence over study."

Walden, p. 90.

214. PRAISE

1. On Being Praised

Said Rabbi Sopher: "He who believes those who praise him is unworthy.

"He who hastens to deny the words of those who praise him is worthy."

Sopher, p. 35.

2. Proclaiming God's Name

Said the Hafetz Hayyim: "In Deuteronomy 32:1-3 we read: 'Give ear, ye heavens . . . and let the earth hear the words of my mouth.' Why? 'For I will proclaim the Name of the Lord.'"

Pupko, p. 102.

215. PRAYER

1. More Than Good Rations

Said the Hafetz Hayyim: "The Lord is prepared to grant our prayers, but we do not know for what to pray. This can be illustrated by a parable: 'a king inspected his army at maneuvers and pronounced himself satisfied. He proclaimed: "I am truly pleased, and any one may ask of me a favor, if he wish." A soldier stepped forward and asked for good rations. The king smiled and said: "Being a soldier it is expected that you receive good rations as a matter of course. Ask me for something more." In the same way, we pray for sustenance on every week day, like the modest soldier. Since we are His creatures, God gives us this benefit as a matter of course. On the Sabbath at least, we should pray that the Almighty raise up the honor of Torah. If he grants this petition, we will lack for nothing.'"

Pupko, ii, 38.

2. Awakening the Heart

A Hasid said to the Bratzlaver: "You say that one should pray much and recite many Psalms. But how can one compel his heart to be engrossed therein?" The Rabbi replied: "The recitation of prayers and Psalms has the virtue of awakening the heart. Make use of your lips and your heart will follow their lead."

H. H. N., p. 23a.

3. A Prayer is a Sword

Said the Bratzlaver: "Rashi comments on Jacob's statement that he took Shechem by his sword and bow, using the words: 'by his prayer and by his entreaties.' Since prayer is likened to a sword, the worshiper must learn how to use his weapon. He must stab straight, inclining neither to the right nor the left. Should he think: 'I have little faith in the efficacy of prayer; I have seen so many prayers remain unanswered,' he inclines to the left. No prayer is ever wasted. If he thinks: 'Since I will accomplish nothing by my prayer, were it not for God's mercies, why should I pray?, God's mercies will descend upon me without prayer,' he is inclining to the right. The worshiper should do whatever he is able to do, and God will do what He alone can do, and will speedily rescue him from all want."

H. H. N., p. 39b.

4. Prayer as the Only Weapon

Said the Bratzlaver: "Your only weapon in the warfare against the Satan and other adversaries is your prayer. If you earnestly wish to be a soldier in the army of defense; if you are not a weakling and do not care to desert, put your heart and your mind into your prayer. Every day learn how to improve it; how to discipline yourself against intruding thoughts; how to stand spiritual sentinel duty in order to challenge and refuse admittance to unwanted meditations; and how to escape the swift bullets shot at your prayers and devotions by your enemy, the Satan."

H. H. N., p. 24a.

5. Spontaneous and Prescribed Prayers

Said the Bratzlaver: "In wartime when the enemy is invading a country, it is safer to travel on the smaller roads that are less known than on the main highways which are clearly marked on the map. In the same way, when a man wishes to combat the Evil Impulse, he will find that foreign thoughts absent themselves from his spontaneous prayers, whereas they tend to be present in his regularly prescribed prayers."

H. H. N., p. 15b.

6. Advice on Prayer

Said the Bratzlaver: "If you cannot find any words to speak unto the Lord when your heart is surcharged, and you yearn to pour out your feelings before Him, it is wise for you to pray unto Him for mercy upon you so that you may be able to open your lips. Pray in the language you ordinarily use, for in this way you may place more sincerity in your petitions. Offer a complete prayer; explain in full what you desire, and place your hope in God. After such an intimate outpouring of the soul, forget your anxieties, and feel gladness in that you have so merciful a Patron who loves to hear prayers."

H. H. N., p. 14b.

7. The Heavy Stone

Said the Bratzlaver: "A prince asked his son to bring to his home a certain large and heavy stone. The son attempted to lift it but was unable to do so. The prince said: 'Take a strong hammer to it; break the stone into pieces and carry them to me one by one.' The Lord asks us to lift up our heart to Heaven, but our heart is heavy as a great rock. Through prayer and confession of our short-

comings let us break up our heavy heart, and then we shall be able
to lift it Heavenward."

H. H. N., p. 23a.

8. *Accepting a Prayer Today*

The Hafetz Hayyim was asked to pray on behalf of a sick child.
He did so, and was overheard, saying: "O Lord on High, many times
you have accepted my petitions.   I beg of you to do so this time as
well."

Pupko, p. 85.

9. *Prayer Without Payment*

Once a man with a basket of fresh fish came to the Premislaner.
"Weigh the basket and pay him, the Rabbi ordered.   "But it is a
gift," exclaimed the man.   "Nay, I cannot accept a gift from you,"
retorted the Rabbi.   "Yesterday you requested me to pray for the
recovery of your sick wife, the mother of six children.   When I
pleaded with God to cure her, I gave as my reason her children's
need of her for their upbringing.   If I should accept a gift, it would
be thought in Heaven that the reason for my prayer was in reality
to earn a gift; that I gave a false reason for my petition.   Hence in
the future my pleas would be distrusted and disregarded."

Szlamovitz, p. 40.

10. *Answering Our Prayers*

Said Rabbi Bunam: "I find among the Selihot a prayer which
reads: 'May He who answered Abraham on Mount Moriah answer
me.'   Had I been the author of this Selihah I would have worded it
thus: 'May He who has answered me until now answer me at present as well.'   There exists no person whom the Lord has not answered
many times."

Zammlung, p. 6.

11. *The Urim and Tummim*

Rabbi Abraham Kalisker said: "You, the Hasidim, believe that
your Zaddikim know as much as the Urim and Tummim of old.
Why, then, do you not display your respect for them by avoiding
trivial petitions on ever occasion?   Do you not know that the Urim
and Tummim were consulted only on matters of grave national
importance?"

Guttman, p. 7.

12. *No Intermediary*

A Hasid came to the great Maggid of Mezeritz and besought
him to pray in his behalf.   The Maggid responded: "Would it not
be better if you learned from me how to offer a proper supplication

to the Lord with your own lips? Thus you can save yourself the
trouble of coming to me to request me to do so for you."

Guttman, p. 8.

13. Over-Active Prayer

The Berditschever Rabbi once visited Rabbi Baruch of Medziboz.
The latter watched his distinguished guest as he prayed with many
gesticulations and energetic motions. When the Berditschever had
finally concluded, his host remarked: "Your fervent prayer does you
credit, since it demonstrates your enthusiastic service of the Lord.
But, sir, what would have happened if Aaron had behaved in this
way when he performed the service of kindling the Menorah? The
oil would have spilled over him, and how could he have performed
the service assigned to him?"

Guttman, p. 26.

14. Coming Without Fail

A wealthy Hasid invited the Karliner Rabbi to visit him at his
home the next day, adding the words: "without fail." The Rabbi
smiled and said: "Know, my friend, that I shall recite the Sh'ma this
evening with an offer to surrender my life for the sake of God. I
will repeat this tomorrow morning. Yet you ask my assurance to be
present without fail at your home tomorrow. Perchance the Lord
may accept the offer of my life, and I may not be in the land of
the living."

I. K., p. 9.

15. The Hour of Prayer

Said the Hafetz Hayyim: "When the clock is advanced an hour,
do not forget to offer your prayers at the right time. Let not the
clock serve the Satan."

Pupko, ii, 67.

16. Praying at Home

Rabbi Bunam once visited the home of the Radziminer Rabbi.
The latter was so deeply engrossed in reading a mystical work that
he did not notice the presence of his guest. When he became aware
of it, he was greatly distressed, but Rabbi Bunam calmed him, saying: "How goodly are thy tents, O Jacob!" The Rabbi, whose full
name was Jacob Aryeh Radziminer, accepted these words as advice
that he offer prayer in his handsome home. Henceforth he went
to the synagogue only on Sabbaths and Festivals, but prayed at home
on week-days. Thus he imitated the Talmudic Sages who recited
their prayers at the place where they were studying.

Zammlung, p. 50.

17. An Improper Prayer

Said Rabbi Sopher: "In *Betzah* 38 we find the story concerning Rabbi Abba who, on migrating to Palestine, prayed that his words might prove acceptable to the Sages. When, however, he offered his opinions, they were ridiculed. Why, then, was not his prayer acceptable? The answer is that it had been made in improper form. Rabbi Abba should have prayed in these words: 'May my words on a subject of Torah prove acceptable to the Lord!' Moreover, if he had a word to offer on behalf of the clarification of a Torah problem, he should have presented it without fear that he might be derided. His opinions would be acceptable to the Lord if they came from a pure heart, and were untouched by any self-concern or egotism."

Sopher, p. 34.

18. Prayers Without Effect

Said the Tzanzer: "In Psalm 115:3 we read: 'Their idols are silver and gold . . . they have mouths, but they speak not.' From this we learn that if men devote themselves to the acquisition of money and worship it as if it were an idol, their prayers and their holy learning fail to make any impression in heaven."

Tzanzer Hasidut, p. 241.

216. PREACHING

1. Borrowed Feathers

The Dubner Maggid once visited a town and went to the synagogue. There he heard a preacher adorning his sermon with parables borrowed from the Dubner Maggid and other Maggidim. The preacher, however, failed to give credit to the authors of his material.

When the preacher had concluded, the Dubner ascended the pulpit and asked permission to tell a story. When this was granted, he proceeded to tell the following:

"There was a certain bird in the wood that was entirely naked of feathers. Her neighbors came together for a consultation on a plan to aid her. It was decided that every bird in the forest should pluck out a feather and present it to the unfortunate bird. So many feathers were donated that the bird was thickly covered by them, and her own lack was no longer seen. She began to feel proud, however, of the many varieties of beautiful feathers she now wore and went about in a boastful mood.

"Another consultation took place, and as a consequence every

bird took back the feather which she had donated. The featherless
bird again appeared entirely bare of covering."

"This preacher," continued the Dubner Maggid, "is proud of his
parables and clearly is boastful of his alleged superiority over other
Maggidim. But if I should claim the first parable as one that I have
fathered, and other Maggidim should claim theirs—what will be left
over to the boaster?"

Dubner, i, 38-39.

2. *The Rays of Moses*

The Koznitzer Maggid said: "The Zaddikim are enabled to discover fresh ideas in the Torah because the soul of Moses illumines
them by the light of the rays surrounding his countenance. Therein
lies the secret of the 'beams' of Moses.

"Like unto Moses from whose mouth issued the discourse of the
Shekinah, the words of God issue from the lips of all inspired
preachers."

Rosenfeld, p. 5.

3. *Methods of Reform*

The Hafetz Hayyim was displeased by the fact that his son had
been appointed to institute reforms in the town where he had settled. He remarked: "To bring about reform in the institutions of a
community, even as few in number as fifty families, is almost beyond
a man's ability. Do as I do. Preach sermons to thousands of persons, advocating a wise program of social welfare, and many of
your hearers will be inspired and will themselves take the steps
necessary to put your ideas into action."

Pupko, p. 20.

4. *The Unwelcome Maggid*

Said the Dubner: "A Maggid who lived in a city known far and
wide for its corruption and dishonesty once came to a city renowned
for its integrity and righteousness. He began to lecture the local
inhabitants, enumerating various evil deeds. The townspeople
were incensed at such unfairness and exclaimed: 'Why do you not
admonish your own townsfolk?'

"Balaam came to curse Israel. Why did he not curse the cor-
rupt nation to which he belonged?"

Dubner, i, 139.

217. PREDICTIONS

1. False Predictions

An astronomer predicted that a comet would touch the earth and destroy a portion of it. The Tzortkover remarked: "Had he spent only five minutes in communion with the Lord, he would have understood that a human mind cannot predict with certainty God's will concerning nature."

Margulies, p. 32.

218. PREJUDICE

1. Automatic Prejudice

A Hasid asked the Berditschever to sanction a purchase he contemplated, but the Rabbi suspected it might be unethical. The Hasid brought arguments from Jewish law to justify the enterprise he planned, but the Rabbi answered: "Our codes prohibit a Jewish judge from accepting a litigant's gift, even though he asked no shading of justice in a case. Why is this gift prohibited? Because the mind of the judge would be automatically prejudiced. It is the same with you. The prospect of receiving a substantial gain has in anticipation distorted your viewpoint; the arguments you have brought forth do not apply to your case. You yourself would concede it if you were truly unprejudiced."

Guttman, p. 10.

2. Sinai and Haman's Downfall

Said the Hafetz Hayyim: "Although the Torah was received at Mount Sinai, it can be said that it was received with even more certainty after the downfall of Haman at Purim. Thus do we learn from the Talmudic tractate: *Megillah*. On Mount Sinai the Torah was received as a supremely significant Divine Law, to be observed in all ordinary circumstances. At Purim, however, it was received in an even more profound fashion: it not only grants to man a knowledge of the ways of life, but it also confers upon man the merit of receiving God's salvation from death. We should never forget that not only does the Torah lead us in the ways of life, but it also saves our life from destruction."

Pupko, ii, 64.

219. PREPARATION

1. Sharpening the Tools

Rabbi Leib Eger visited the Kotzker Rabbi. He observed with amazement the custom prevailing there that hours were devoted to the preparation for prayer, but that the actual time of praying was very brief. The Kotzker explained: "It is a Jewish regulation that a workman, preparing his tools, should sharpen them for hours. He then completes his appointed task with a few strokes. Nevertheless, he receives payment for a full day of work."

Sopher, p. 61.

220. PRIDE

1. Punishment for Pride

Long and earnestly did the Mezeritzer Maggid pray that the Redeemer come without delay. A Voice from Heaven called out to him: "Who is it that strives so zealously to bring about the Redemption before the predestined time?" The Maggid replied: "It is I, acknowledged by my holy companions to be the most illustrious Zaddik of this generation." Again the Voice cried out: "Ask your companions to confirm your assertion." The Maggid entered his synagogue and inquired of those present: "Is it true that I am the most illustrious Zaddik of this generation?" Thrice the Maggid repeated his question. But not a single person in the room said a syllable in reply.

Szlamovitz, p. 3.

2. Forsake Your Pride

Said the Hafetz Hayyim: "I once heard of a woman who was so filled with pride that she declined to accommodate any guest unless she could serve especially fine foods. Some persons likewise decline to study Torah unless they are in what they call the proper mood. The result in the first instance is that a poor man continues to suffer hunger, and in the second, the Torah is not studied."

Pupko, p. 104.

3. The Proud Mountain

Rabbi Abraham, the "Angel" visited Kremnitz. Instead of giving his attention to the crowd which had assembled to bid him welcome, the Rabbi gazed fixedly at a nearby mountain. A young Hasid made so bold as to inquire: "What does the Rabbi see in that mountain? Is it not a mere lump of soil?" The "Angel" replied: "I gaze and gaze at it, and it amazes me. Here is a lump of soil, whose pride has swollen it to the size of a mountain."

Margulies, p. 39.

4. Deliberation in Advice

A rich Hasid visited the Kotzker Rabbi and asked for immediate advice concerning a settlement on his daughter who was about to be married. The Rabbi replied: "I cannot give you advice instantly. It is not granted to me to ascend into Heaven and see the future decreed for a man and his family. When I am asked for advice, I feel a sense of pride. I find myself unable to reason correctly until my sense of pride has abated. When this has happened, I weigh the matter in the scales of ethics and law, and then I offer my advice."

Szlamovitz, p. 38.

5. Into the Deepest Abyss

Rabbi Schmelke and his brother, Rabbi Phineas, visited the Mezeritzer Maggid. "We came to you," the brothers said, "to receive instruction in a rule of conduct." The Maggid offered them this counsel: "The Holy Books tell us that it is proper for a man to meditate upon his actions of the entire day before he falls asleep. If he believes they contained no blemish whatsoever, he has permitted a spirit of pride to enter into him. Therefore the angels on high gather together all his excellent deeds, and, because of this pride, they hurl them into the deepest abyss."

Walden, Y. A., p. 76.

221. PRISONERS

1. The Poor Man's Offense

The Tzernobiler Rabbi came to a Jewish tax collector and besought him for a donation whereby he might pay the fine of a Jew who had been imprisoned. The collector exclaimed: "What! Should I give money to free a Jew who has been sentenced to prison?" The Rabbi answered: "The offense which the poor man committed resulted in a prison sentence only because he could not pay the fine imposed. A rich man would have paid the fine and immediately would have been released. Yet you aver that a prison sentence necessarily indicates that a serious crime has been committed." The tax collector bethought himself on hearing the Rabbi's words and he gave the Rabbi a sizable donation for the unfortunate man.

Twersky, p. 8.

222. PROGRESS

1. Progress in Spirituality

Said the Hafetz Hayyim: "The man who desires to advance in his piety must strive to imitate the ways of the Lord. He should have mercy, be kind, and so forth. This will lead him to possess the Fear of the Lord. If he wishes to make still greater progress, he must strive even more earnestly to imitate God's ways. Such a complete devotion will lead him to possess the virtue of the Love of God. This Love of God and increasing imitation of God in a multitude of other ways will guide him to the virtue of cleaving to the Lord and becoming His consecrated Servant."

Pupko, ii, p. 4.

223. PROMISES

1. Not Contradictory

Rabbi Isaac of Ziditchov made a promise to one Hasid, a farmer, that he would pray for rain. He also made a promise to another Hasid, a lumber dealer, that he would pray that no rain might fall, so that he might safely ship his lumber to its destination. The Rabbi's son asked for an explanation. Rabbi Isaac answered: "The promises I have made are not contradictory. Both can be fulfilled without deceiving my Hasidim. Underground springs and rain falling at the river's source may cause the waters to overflow. Thus the field of the farmer will be irrigated without injury to the lumber dealer's shipment."

Braver, p. 41.

224. PROSELYTES

1. A Figure of Clay

Count Potocki (Pototzki) of Wilna became a convert to Judaism and was burned at the stake in 1749. The clerics seized him and ordered that he be subjected to torture until he returned to his ancestral religion. Perceiving his obstinacy, one of the clerics said to him derisively: "In this world we are revenging ourselves on you. In the After-Life, I suppose you will petition the Lord to grant you revenge upon us." Count Potocki replied: "In my youth I was accustomed to play with some peasant children. Once I fashioned several clay figures and then went away to eat my lunch. When I returned I found that the peasant children had trampled my handiwork underfoot. I complained in anger to my father, but he refused to punish the offenders. When I grew up and became their master, I no longer cared to punish anyone for destroying my clay figures. Do you think, then, that I will seek revenge in the After-Life if you destroy a mere lump of clay—my earthly body?"

J. M. J., June 6, 1935.

225. PROTESTING

1. The Value of Protest

Said the Bratzlaver: "As long as you protest against the evil that tends to overwhelm you, the Prince of Evil cannot rob you of your share in the inheritance of Israel in 'the estate of the Lord.' For it is an axiom in law that a protest nullifies the rights of an unlawful possessor, no matter how long he has been in possession. Therefore, no matter how long your frailty has permitted evil to take possession of you, you cannot be deprived of your share in holiness if, at times, you break the chains of evil, and loudly protest that you are asking for aid to combat the evil. Each time the breaking of the chains will be achieved more easily, so that eventually you will conquer the Satan."

H. H. N., p. 37b.

226. PUNCTUALITY AND TARDINESS

1. Do Not Delay

Said the Hafetz Hayyim: "When you embark on an enterprise with the prospect of earning a few guilders, you are punctual and do not brook any delay. Do the same when you are on the way to the synagogue. Do not permit yourself any dallying with a friend or tolerate any other form of delay."

Pupko, p. 93.

2. The Balance of Credit

Rabbi Hayyim Auerbach of Luntzitz observed that a member of his congregation had fallen into the habit of tardiness at Morning Services. He inquired the reason, and received the following reply: "I imitate Rabbi Schmelke of Nikolsburg who also commences his morning devotions at a late hour." The Rabbi responded: "You are a man of wealth and Baron de Rothschild is a man of wealth. If the Baron should lose ten thousand thalers, it would not cut deeply into his fortune. But if you should lose such an amount, you would be impoverished. In the same way, even though Rabbi Schmelke loses the Mitzvah of early and prompt devotions, he is still rich by virtue

of his countless good and pious deeds; but, my friend, if you lose
the Mitzvah of punctual worship, how many Mitzvot would be left
to your credit?"

Walden, Y. A., p. 86.

3. After the Correct Time

The Hafetz Hayyim said: "I compare those who make long preparations for prayer and actually pray after the appointed hours, to
the villager who has collected money for his daughter's dowry and
with the money has proceeded to purchase government bonds.
When he wished to sell them, he went to the Sub-treasury building,
where he perceived that several persons brought in torn and dam-
aged bonds, which were accepted and redeemed in money. When
he gave in his new, carefully-preserved bonds, he was informed
that they had been called in a considerable time before. It was
necessary for the villager to go with them to a special window. In
the same fashion, it can be said that those who offer prayer with
poor attention to the words, but offer it at the appointed time, have
their words accepted on High. On the other hand, those who give
meticulous attention to the words, but offer them later than the
proper hour, find their prayers unacceptable."

Pupko, p. 15.

227. PUNISHMENT

1. His Own Judge

Said the Leover: "Before the Heavenly a soul is asked: 'What is
the correct penalty for this or that sin?' The soul describes the
penalty, and is then informed that it has committed the very offense."

Guttman, p. 24.

2. The Penitence of the Prince

Said Rabbi Samuel Zevi of Alexander: "The Talmud declares:
'Happy is the generation whose prince brings an offering for the
atonement of his sins.' Let me explain this by means of a parable
of the Besht. Once an official of the realm committed a crime. The
prince of the area, however, gave the offender a still higher position
in the royal court itself, where the offender had an opportunity to
reflect upon the gravity of his crime. Therein lay his punishment.
By the same token, the prince may be led to reflect that he himself
may have received his high rank as a punishment for transgressions,
and therefore he repents his sins with sincerity. Such is the prince
whom a generation is happy to claim as its own."

Zammlung, p. 97.

3. The Missing Sleeve

Said the Hafetz Hayyim: "Crimes can be punished and acts of virtue rewarded. Yet the man who has committed a crime can be spiritually cleansed by suffering and repentance. But the man who has omitted the performance of a meritorious deed has no way to make good his loss. We are reminded of a coat which may be washed, if it has become soiled. But if a sleeve is missing, washing cannot avail."

Pupka, p. 89.

4. Punishment by the King

Said the Dubner: "A king chose one of his servants as his favorite attendant, and ordered that he be given purple robes and the freedom of the palace. Later the king was given information to the effect that his favorite was spending considerable time at disreputable taverns and was associating with scoundrels. The monarch was greatly incensed, and ordered his servant to return the official garments given him, and to take leave of the country at once.

"From the place of his banishment the courtier wrote a long letter of penitence to the king, which so convinced the ruler of his subject's sincerity that he restored him to his former estate. Then the courtier asked his sovereign: 'Did I really deserve the severe disgrace you imposed upon me?'

" 'It was for your own good,' explained the king. 'Had I condoned your unseemly conduct, you would have become a confirmed drunkard; you would have proceeded to steal articles from the palaces in order to obtain liquor for your companions and yourself. Then, indeed, it would have been necessary for you to flee this country as a malefactor, without any opportunity ever to return.' "

"From this we learn that if the Lord had not taken away His 'vessels of holiness' and exiled us from His land, we would in time have so degenerated that we would have lost entirely the 'holy vessels' entrusted to our care. We would, of our own accord, have abandoned the Holy Land, never to return. Now we may hope that sincere penitence will bring us to our former estate."

Dubner, i, 203-205.

228. PURIFICATION

1. The Purifier

The Ropshitzer Zaddik spoke of his teacher, the Lubliner. He said: "My Master was an expert spiritual surgeon. When a new Hasid came to him for instruction, he would take out his soul, cleanse it of impurities, and restore it to its proper place as clean as it was at birth."

Walden, p. 110.

2. Purifying Oneself

Said the Hafetz Hayyim: "The laws regarding self-purification are identical with the laws governing the purification of vessels. If your offense has been performed in the heat of your emotions, it behooves you to repent with a similar warmth of feeling. Try to correct yourself by performing a Mitzvah with the same zeal you have shown in committing a sin. The study of Torah is the best form of penitence."

Pupko, ii, 61.

229. PURIM

1. A Warning and a Penalty

Rabbi Moses Sopher remarked in a sermon: "A teacher was accustomed to warn his pupils that if they continued their indolence, they would put him to shame and force him to give up his post as a teacher. An impudent boy retorted: 'Why don't you do so? Then we could enjoy a vacation.' The teacher thereupon gave him corporeal punishment and exacted a pledge from the lad that he would apply himself to his studies henceforth. In similar fashion, God warns us that if we disobey Him, His Name will be profaned. If we give no heed, He sends a Haman to force us to improve our conduct."

Sopher, p. 26.

2. Solidarity and Humility

In a Purim sermon, the Rabbi of Medziboz said: "Purim teaches us solidarity and humility. When Israel was liberated and left Egypt after the many miracles which God performed, all the nations stood in awe, except Amalek who tried to destroy Israel. God ordained that this proud and arrogant nation should be utterly eradicated as a sign that arrogance must be completely extirpated. The Tanna in *Ethics of the Fathers* declares: 'Be very humble of spirit.' We are also instructed that pride brings forgetfulness of God in its train. Haman, the Amalekite, possessed this vice of arrogance, and demanded that every person bow before him, a mortal.

"To a lesser degree, the Jews in the generation of Haman were guilty of pride. They seemed to be a people without unity, some wishing to lord it over others. Queen Esther recognized this shortcoming among her people, and ordered that the Jews, in order to

merit salvation, should attain to unity. In order to preserve this
unity and good will, she later instructed the Jews to send gifts to
each other. Her forefather, King Saul, was told by the Prophet
Samuel that he would deserve to become chief of Israel if he were
lowly in his own eyes."

Migdal David, p. 84.

3. A King Without a People

At a Purim banquet, the Turisker Rabbi discussed the verse in
Esther 4:14: "For if thou altogether holdest thy peace at this time,
then will relief and deliverance arise to the Jews from another place,
but thou and thy father's house will perish." He paraphrased the
verse as follows: "For if Thou, O Lord, altogether holdest Thy peace
now, and dost not redeem us, relief may arise to the Jews through
assimilation, and thus Thou shalt become a King without a people."

Twersky, p. 52.

4. Giving to God

In a Purim discourse, Rabbi Isaac of Skwira said: "The Riziner
has taught that a man should request God to grant him whatever
he needs, particularly on Purim. For the Sages laid down the rule
that whosoever stretches forth his hand as a suppliant on Purim
should receive that which he asks. It is my opinion that this rule
applies also to God's requests from us. For we read in the Neilah
Prayer *: 'Thy right hand is stretched out to receive the penitent.'
It is our duty on Purim to make our gifts to God when His hand is
outstretched. Hence we should be penitents, and return to the
Lord."

Twersky, p. 68.

* Singer, p. 267

5. Honoring Mordecai

Said the Hafetz Hayyim: "In the Book of Esther we read of the
great honor paid to Mordecai because the King, Ahasuerus, a mortal
monarch, delighted to show him honor. How much greater honor
will be shown to a man whom the King of Kings on High will delight to honor!"

Pupko, ii, 43.

6. "Who Will Imitate Me?"

Rabbi Isaac of Ziditchov held a Purim banquet in his home and
many affluent Hasidim were guests. The Rabbi entered and said:
"It is customary to make gifts to the poor in secret, but if giving in
public induces others to give as well, it is preferable. On Purim it

is the duty of every Jew to give gifts to the needy. I herewith donate all of my Purim contributions to a man of good family who needs a dowry for his daughter on her marriage. Who will imitate me?" All present emptied their purses at once. A dowry of handsome size was collected.

Braver, p. 80.

7. Reading the Megillah

Said the Medzibozer: "We read in the Talmud (*Megillah*, 17a): 'he who reads the Megillah *le-mafrea* has not fulfilled his duty.' *Le-mafrea* has two meanings: 'from later to earlier' and 'for pay.' We can interpret this as follows: he who believes that a Haman and a Mordecai could arise only in earlier ages, but could not appear again, does not understand the significance of the reading of the Megillah. Moreover, he who reads the Megillah or performs other Mitzvot 'for pay' receives no credit for doing so."

BDH., p. 71.

230. QUARRELS

1. Unselfish Quarrels

The Vishnitzer Rabbi rebuked the Mitnagedim who abused the Lubliner. He said: "You are like the farmer to whom a machinist presented an agricultural machine. Not understanding how it works, the farmer had it thrown out. Not knowing the source of the Holy Rabbi's wondrous acts, you wish to remove him from your midst." The Lubliner heard of this and said to the Vishnitzer Rabbi: "Your interest pleases me, but your rebuke displeases me. They quarrel with me for the sake of the Lord. Therefore why rebuke them?"

Walden, p. 118.

2. Delaying Redemption

Rabbi Shalom of Stripkov said: "Among the Jews of the generation before the advent of the Besht, there was a wealth of Torah, due chiefly to the labors of Rabbi Joshua of Frankfort and Rabbi Jonathan Eybeschuetz of Hamburg. The Satan feared that redemption would come by virtue of this abundance of Torah knowledge. He therefore succeeded in causing these two distinguished Rabbis to engage in a quarrel. Thus Redemption was delayed." *

Michelson, p. 56.

* The reference is to the controversy between Rabbi Jacob Joshua Falk (1741-56) and Jonathan Eybeschuetz (1690-1764), about the years 1751-2.

3. Ending the Quarrel

In the city of Radin, where the Hafetz Hayyim conducted his Yeshivah, a serious quarrel broke out among the members of the Burial Society. Much abuse was voiced, and blows were exchanged. Rabbi Israel Meir ha-Kohen ascended the speaker's pulpit and said: "In *Kohelet* we are warned that the Lord will bring every one of us to the Judgment Seat. Every person commits two types of sin: those he knows are sins, and those he commits unwittingly. By engaging in this quarrel you have committed this and this sin before my very eyes. Let my words serve as a warning. I can do nothing else for your souls. Know then that the warning makes every offense of grave importance for which you must bear the full responsibility." The quarrel ceased immediately.

Pupko, p. 27.

231. RABBIS

1. Visitors with Differing Missions

Rabbi Yekutiel of Siget paid a visit to Rabbi Isaac of Ziditchov. He observed that Rabbi Isaac would not take time to listen to the tribulations of his callers. He would bless each one of them in turn and immediately call over the next person. While doing this, he noticed the Sigeter and invited him to wait. When Rabbi Isaac had disposed of all the callers, he turned to the Sigeter and said: "Do not be distressed by the seemingly abrupt procedure I have followed. In Isaiah 65:24 we read: 'before they call, I will answer, and while they are yet speaking, I will hear.' As for those who come to me on a materialistic errand, I answer them before they finish. Those, however, who come to discuss Torah and ethics, I shall hear them while they are still speaking."

Braver, p. 45.

2. Removing the Dust

Rabbi Solomon Halberstamm, grandson of the Tzanzer Rabbi, accepted a call to become Rabbi of Wisnitza. In his first sermon he narrated a parable, as follows: a king engaged a famous painter to paint frescoes on the walls of his palace. When the work had been finished, he assigned to the artist the task of keeping the paintings in fine condition. After the artist's death, however, the caretakers were afraid to touch the beautiful paintings, and allowed the dust to accumulate on them. The king thereupon engaged an artist of lesser skill, saying: "I do not expect you to paint like the original artist. All that I wish of you is to cleanse the paintings and to retouch them if necessary." Rabbi Halberstamm continued: "The Jewish community of Wisnitza has had great Rabbis in its midst who delineated beautifully the ideas of the Torah. But ever since they have departed, you have allowed the dust to accumulate. My task will be to remove the dust so that these paintings may be seen in all their glory."

Eibeshitz, p. 58.

3. The Rav and the Driver

A Rav came to the Leipniker Rabbi. Before halting his wagon, the driver decided to play a joke on the Leipniker by pretending that he was the Rav, and that the Rav was the driver. Being a learned Jew, the driver easily passed the test as if he were in truth the Rav. The Leipniker gave them fine old wine to drink of which they freely partook. Before daylight he called out: "Awake, driver, it is time to move on." The authentic driver awoke but the Rav slept on. Thus the Leipniker uncovered the deception.

Eibeshitz, p. 65.

4. Avoiding Suspicion

A son of the Hafetz Hayyim wrote to the leaders of a small community inquiring whether they would consider him for the vacant post of Rabbi. At the same time, unknown to the son of the Hafetz Hayyim, another Rabbi wrote to the Hafetz Hayyim, asking if he would recommend the writer for the same post. The Hafetz Hayyim replied that he made it a point not to interfere in any choice of this kind. Then he instructed his son not to accept the call if it came to him, saying: "The other Rabbi will harbor the suspicion that you had heard of the vacancy from his letter to me, and God's Name would be profaned by what might seem to be an unethical action."

Pupko, p. 10.

5. The Rabbinical Call

Rabbi Yechiel, son of Rabbi Feivel Gritzer, did not choose to become a Rabbi. His friends, however, vigorously urged him to do so. Thereupon he sent an inquiry to two eminent Rabbis who replied: "He who is able to influence people to undertake the service of the Lord and does not make use of this ability is committing a grave sin." Rabbi Yechiel, on receiving this answer, purchased the house of Rabbi Henoch of Alexander, and became a Rebbe.

Zammlung, p. 60.

232. RAIN

1. Bringing Down Rain

The Berditschever recalled to his listeners the Talmudic statement that if the people are wicked, then rain descends for the sake
of the cattle. He added: "The cattle need grass on which to feed,
and there is no measurement of the adequacy or timeliness of the
rain to nourish the grass. Thus rain which descends for the sake
of cattle will do little to benefit people of wickedness. Only true
repentance will bring in its wake a rainy season to meet man's needs."

Guttman, p. 24.

233. REASONING; REASON

1. Decisions Without Deliberation

A son of Rabbi Moses Sopher asked his father how he was able
to render decisions on subjects of Jewish law with scarcely any de-
liberation. The Rabbi replied: "The Lord has set me up as a guide
to many of the perplexed in the Household of Israel. Therefore
I am confident he leads me on the right pathway. At times my
reasoning may be faulty, but I believe my decision is usually correct."

Sopher, p. 32.

2. The Power of Reason

Said the Rachminstrovker Rabbi: "Dedicate your actions to
God. Then He will endow you with the power of reason whereby
you may walk on the pathway of truth."

Twersky, p. 70.

3. Going Beyond Reason

Said Rabbi Samuel Zevi: "To have faith in God by using the
faculty of reason is merely to return to Him His endowment of
reason to us. But to go beyond reason and thus to believe in God
is an act of charity which brings closer the Redemption."

Zammlung, p. 97.

4. Faith Without Reason

Said Rabbi Feivel Gritzer: "In Psalm 119:66 we read: 'Teach
me good discernment and knowledge; for I have believed in Thy
commandments.' From this we learn: only if a man believes in the
validity of the commandments, even if does not comprehend the
reasons for them, may he pray to understand the reasons."

Zammlung, p. 33.

5. Comprehension Will Follow

Said the Hafetz Hayyim: "If you have commenced a study that is worth-while and do not comprehend the theme of your research, do not fail to continue your application, for in the end comprehension will come. Does the storekeeper who has sold nothing on one day fail to open his store the next day?"

Pupko, ii, 2.

234. RECREATION

1. The Absent Funds

The Hafetz Hayyim was about to leave for a vacation in a congenial village. Before leaving he asked his students if they, also, were able to take a vacation. One of the students remarked: "I imagine, Rabbi, that my fellow-students have the funds required." The Rabbi replied: "You have given yourself away by your words. Since you use the phrase: 'I imagine,' it indicates to me that you and your companions both are lacking in the necessary funds."

Pupko, p. 120.

235. REDEMPTION

1. A New Torah

Said Rabbi David of Talna: "When Redemption comes at last, the Torah will appear to us as if it were entirely new, unlike the Torah we know. For then it will be comprehended by all mankind by virtue of the light of the Lord which will shine upon it. The influence of the Torah will then be so powerful that freedom of the will no longer will exist."

Rosenfeld, p. 6.

2. Asking for His Wages

Said the Hafetz Hayyim: "Let us all petition God to grant us the Redemption. The laborer who fails to ask for his wages, must endure any delay."

Pupko, p. 95.

3. The Waking Heart

Said Rabbi Samuel Zevi of Alexander: "The Midrash appends the words: 'I am asleep, but my heart is awake' to the text in Exodus 3:2: 'And the angel of the Lord appeared unto him in a flame of fire, out of the midst of the bush.' The explanation is as follows: the bush was a plant that bore no fruit, thereby symbolizing the person who is bare of Mitzvot. Such was Israel before the redemption from Egypt. Yet the Angel of Redemption came in order to send a redeemer, Moses ben Amram. Why was this? Because potentially Israel was prepared to accept many Mitzvot. Therein lies the meaning of the phrase: 'At present I am asleep, and I perform no Mitzvot. But my heart is awake and ready to receive the Torah and the Mitzvot.' Thus it can be said that Israel was redeemed because of what Israel was destined to become."

Zammlung, p. 95.

4. No Delay in the Redemption

Said the Hafetz Hayyim: "We know that the moment the time had arrived for the liberation of Joseph, he was quickly taken from the pit. Likewise when the hour of the awaited Redemption arrives, there will not be a single moment's delay."

Pupko, p. 98.

236. REGRET

1. The Purpose of the Psalms

Said the Bratzlaver: "Understand, beloved Israelites, that every psalm has you individually in mind, as well as your particular struggles against evil inclinations. When you read a psalm, pray to your Maker in the words of that psalm." He also said: "When you read in the midst of your learning about an evil action, fill your heart with regret that thus you are near to it. When you read of an admirable deed, feel sorrow because you are far away from it. In this way your learning will become your prayer. Such a transformation is indeed pleasing in the sight of the Lord."

H. H. N., p. 5b.

237. REMINDERS

1. Continuing Reminders

Said the Gerer: "The commandment: 'I am the Lord thy God,' regarded as the First of the Ten Commandments, is not in the form of a command, but in the form of a statement. It states the fact that a Jewish soul is of necessity subject to the Lord. Moreover, even as God's declaration: 'Let there be light' brought light as a consequence, so, too, His declaration that He is the Lord our God can achieve our subjection to His Will. Lest we forget His Lordship, we say twice daily: 'Hear O Israel.' This means that we should hear God's declaration that He is our Lord, and therefore must receive our obedience. The Mitzvot and the Divine prohibitions remind us continually of our subjection to God's Will, and they aid us in our fidelity to Him."

Rokotz, ii, 37.

238. REPENTANCE

1. Forming Day

The Talner Zaddik said: "The Zaddik is like unto the morning, and the wicked man unto the evening. When the latter repents and attaches himself to the righteous man, together they form: Day."

Rosenfeld, p. 162.

2. "Return, O Israel"

The Tzortkover Rabbi explained the verse in Hosea 14:4 as follows: "With reference to the words: 'Return O Israel, unto the Lord, thy God,' Maimonides defined true repentance as regret over evil deeds so severe that the Omniscient will bear witness against their repetition. Whence did the great Rabbi derive this thought? Perhaps from the verse in Hosea, reading not 'Ad,' 'unto' but 'Ed,' 'a witness.' The verse thus interpreted would be translated: 'Return, O Israel' (with such sincerity) that 'a witness will be the Lord, thy God.'"

Margulies, p. 50.

3. Breaking Up the Bundle

A father instructed his son to bring in some kindling wood for the stove. The lad found the bundle of logs too heavy. "Break up the bundle and then you can carry it in," advised the father. From this we learn that oftentimes we find it too difficult to lift up our hearts to God. He then instructs us: "Break up your heavy heart through prayer and repentance and you will be able to carry your heart up to Me."

Ha-Nefesh, p. 23a.

4. Seasonal Repentance

Rabbi Mendel Vorker remarked: "We read in the Rosh ha-Shanah Service: 'If a man should repent, his repentance would be accepted at once.' From this we learn that if merchandise is offered for sale in season, it is taken without close examination. But out of season the would-be purchaser examines it closely for minor defects. The Ten Days of Penitence constitute the season for repentance, and therefore a repentance containing minor defects is accepted at that time."

Zammlung, p. 41.

239. REPROOF

1. No Reproof Needed

Rabbi Yekutiel Teitelbaum and a group of Hasidim came to Rabbi Isaac Ziditchover for a Sabbath visit. Rabbi Yekutiel had occasion to beg his host to reprove the Hasidim for their lack of enthusiasm in prayer. Rabbi Isaac replied: "Wait until tomorrow." When Rabbi Isaac went to the Reader's Desk and chanted the words: "All shall thank Thee; all shall praise Thee; all shall say: there is none holy like the Lord," ecstasy took hold of the Hasidim and tears poured forth from their eyes. No reproof was needed.

Braver, p. 26.

240. REPUTATION

1. The Barking Dogs

Said the Dubner: "A merchant was accustomed to take up lodgings at an excellent hotel when he made frequent visits to the city. Once, however, he engaged rooms at an inn of inferior quality. The proprietor of the fine hotel expressed astonishment at this, when he met the merchant on the street. The latter replied: 'My failure to stay at your hotel on this trip is really a high compliment to you. A certain young woman has been recommended to me as a wife for my son. I wish to discover her reputation in the city. I appreciate, however, that your servants refuse to engage in gossip and talebearing. I, therefore, purposely engaged rooms at an inferior inn, where I was convinced I would be informed in detail of any effect in the girl or in her character.'

"From this we learn that only inferior persons speak of other persons in derogatory terms."

Dubner, i, 112-113.

2. A Wise Change

Said the Dubner: "A pious man had a son of only mediocre attainments. He counselled his son to move to a place where his father's fame was but vaguely known so that his own accomplishments would not be obscured by his father's. The son did so, and soon he had gained a fine reputation by his own talents.

"From this we learn that in the Holy Land Israel's reputation was dimmed by the nearness of his great Father. Israel was therefore sent out among the nations, among whom Israel's greatness and excellent character stand out prominently on their own."

Dubner, i, 140-141.

241. RESPECT

1. The Feeling of Respect

A group of unbelieving Jews visited the Medzibozer Zaddik and later held him up to ridicule. On hearing of it, the Rabbi said: "Since they have no feeling of reverence for their Maker, how can I expect them to show regard for me?"

M. B., p. 20.

2. Heightening Their Respect

Said the Dubner: "A famous Rabbi had grown old and he requested permission to leave his position in a large community, saying it was too arduous for his advanced years. Inasmuch as this request seemed reasonable, the permission was granted. The Rabbi then wrote to a small town where there was a vacancy, informing its leaders that he was prepared to accept a call from them. The people of the little town were overjoyed and sent a committee to escort the Rabbi to their town. When the leaders of the large community beheld this Committee, they made several efforts to turn them back without seeing the Rabbi. Hearing the tumult which ensued, the Rabbi approached the combatants, and called the chief leader into his Study. 'Have you changed your mind about allowing me to leave you?' the Rabbi inquired. 'Nay,' replied the leader. 'There has been no change in our attitude. We merely wished to impress the Committee with the thought that we are parting with you most reluctantly. Thus they will respect you all the more.'

"From this we learn that when the Torah was given to Moses, the Angels, according to the Talmud protested vehemently, in order that men might regard it with greater reverence."

Dubner, i, 216-218.

242. RESPONSIBILITY

1. Leaving the Door Open

Said the Dubner: "A thief broke into a delicatessen store one night and stole some of the provisions. He left the door ajar, and others who chanced to pass by early in the morning also helped themselves. Then dogs and cats entered and added to the damage. The original thief was caught and offered restitution for what he had stolen. The owner refused the offer, however, saying: 'You must be punished severely because you left the door open and considerable loss resulted as a consequence.'

"From this we learn: 'the transgression of a man who points out the way or who is respected and imitated by others, must be expiated much more thoroughly than the offense of an ordinary person.'"

Dubner, i, 306-7.

2. Liable for the Full Amount

Said the Dubner: "Two men endorsed a note for an indigent friend. Soon after one endorser died. The second took it much to heart. 'Why are you so concerned over his death?' he was asked. 'Because,' was the reply, 'Now I remain as the sole guarantor and I can be liable for the full amount of the note.'

"From this we learn: When the Torah was given to us, according to the story in the Talmud, we offered our saints and our children as sureties that we would observe it. Now that we have no more saints among us, our children are the sole sureties to be held responsible."

Dubner, i, 293-294.

243. RETRIBUTION

1. Inevitable Payment

Said the Dubner: "A poor peddler came to a strange town and asked to be shown to a place where he could find lodging. He was shown the way to a hostelry. Under the impression that the owner was a hospitable man who entertained the poor without charge, the peddler accepted a good room and partook of good food. When, however, he was about to leave, payment was demanded. He explained to the tavern-owner that he was without money. Therefore his pack of merchandise was seized. He then told the owner that the merchandise was worth more than the amount of the bill. The host permitted him, therefore, to remain longer, until he had lodged there at a cost equal to the value of the goods.

"From this we learn that the Evil Impulse persuades a young man to transgress and leads him to believe there will be no penalty to pay. When in his old age, he learns to the contrary, the Evil Impulse urges him to continue on the road of wickedness, inasmuch as he will be punished anyway."

Dubner, i, 238-240.

244. REVELATION

1. Beholding Elijah

A Hasid boasted that his Rebbe had been granted a revelation of the Prophet Elijah. Overhearing this boast, the Gerer Rabbi said: "A sight of Elijah does not carry saintliness in its train. The wicked King Ahab beheld Elijah many times, yet he remained a wicked person."

Rokotz, ii, 29.

2. More Important Than Happiness

The Gerer Rabbi, questioned by his Disciples, was asked whether he had ever beheld the Prophet Elijah in a dream, a vision accounted as a happy lot in the Elijah song at the Conclusion of the Sabbath. He replied: "May I deserve a happier lot than even a vision of Elijah confers! May it be granted to me to be the happy man 'that hath not walked in the counsel of the wicked.'"

Rokotz, ii, 63.

245. REVERENCE

1. Seeking a Master

Rabbi Uri Strelisker was perplexed as to the choice of his Master. He visited the Lizensker, the Ostroher, the Koretzer and Rabbi Sussya. But no one of these Zaddikim inspired in him the reverence due a Master—a reverence he believed should be akin to the reverence due unto God. He continued his search until he met Rabbi Solomon of Karlin. His very first glance at the Rabbi inspired in him deep reverence, and he understood at once that he had discovered his Master.

I. K., p. 9.

2. The Fear of God

The "Yud" and the Lelever were on a walking trip. When they reached a certain village, the "Yud" sat down on the grass to rest. The Lelever, however, went away to pay a visit to the single Jew residing in the village. When he returned, the "Yud" inquired why he had been absent so long and what had kept him in the home of the Jew. The Lelever replied: "When I entered his home, I heard the farmer say to his son: 'Were it not for my fear of God, I would beat a lazy youth like you with this stick.' Since it was clear I had encountered a Jew who possessed the fear of God, I could not part with him hurriedly.'"

H. Hak., pp. 22-23.

246. REWARD

1. Without Thought of Reward

Said the Hafetz Hayyim: "Be sure to bear in mind the knowledge that when you perform a Mitzvah or study the Torah, without thought of gain, the deed stands above the Heavens, and it will be accepted at its full value. But the same action accompanied by the thought that it will bring a reward becomes worldly in character, and, as our Sages declare, it does not even reach to Heaven."

Pupko, ii, 62.

2. No Payment in Advance

Said the Dubner: "A coachman was engaged to take a passenger a long distance. At the first stopping-place, the coachman requested the fare. 'I never pay in advance,' replied the passenger. 'But I need money to buy feed for my horse,' answered the coachman. 'Very well,' replied the passenger. 'I shall pay you sufficient to buy the feed, but you will receive the balance when we reach our destination.'

"From this we learn that God provides the man of goodness only with the necessities of life. The balance will be paid after the final reckoning in the World-to-Come."

Dubner, i, 161.

3. The King's Gifts

Said the Dubner: "A king was accustomed to distribute gifts among his courtiers at stated intervals. Once his physicians jokingly asked him why they were not included among the recipients. The king replied: 'My courtiers serve me constantly and therefore I reward them on appropriate occasion. But you, my friends, serve me, I am glad to say only on infrequent occasions, and therefore I trust you will be satisfied with an occasional remembrance.'

"From this we learn: the Lord regularly grants joy of spirit and a 'higher soul' to those who serve Him and attend His House of Prayer every Sabbath. But those who attend His Sanctuary only two or three times a year cannot hope to enjoy throughout the entire year complete tranquillity of spirit."

Dubner, i, 271-272.

4. The Eskimo and the Watch

Said the Dubner: "An Eskimo received a watch as a gift. He made it a habit to go about the camp of the fur-hunters, asking for the time and moving the watch hands to the proper point. A hunter finally approached him, opened the back of the watch-lid, and showed to the Eskimo the many springs and wheels inside. The hunter remarked: 'Make use of this complicated machinery in the proper way by winding the stem daily. The moving of the hands to set the correct time should be done only occasionally.'

"From this we learn: do not live merely for yourself without asking or conferring favors. The world is organized to yield the proper results only if one aids others; if each man is a wheel or a spring to turn the marvelous mechanism of the universe."

Dubner, i, 229-230.

5. Recompense for Arduous Work

Said the Hafetz Hayyim: "Oftentimes I hear the complaint that it is hard in these days to preserve the Torah and to perform Mitzvot. We must remember, however, that when the task is difficult to accomplish, the recompense is commensurably large."

Pupko, ii, 37.

6. Forget the Reward

Said the Hafetz Hayyim: "When you perform a good deed, do not concern yourself with the reward you may receive. Make yourself like the tight-rope walker in a carnival. If he thinks of the rewards he may receive he will surely lose his footing and fall."

Pupko, p. 117.

7. Penalty or Reward

Said the Mezeritzer: "Your tongue can bring you either severe penalties or pleasing rewards. Penalties will be your portion if you utter words of gossip and slander. Rewards will come to you if you recite words of Torah and prayer."

BDH, p. 73.

8. A Share of the Gains

Said the Hafetz Hayyim: "Just as purchasers of shares in an enterprise derive a profit from the gains of the company, those who donate their rightful share to a Yeshivah shall receive a profit from the spiritual gains of the School."

Pupko, p. 121.

9. Reversing Their Roles

A woman came to Rabbi Meyer Premislaner and said: "Rabbi, though I lead the life customary for a woman, I am as yet childless." An aged porter entered and said: "Rabbi, I am too old to carry baggage any longer. I beg of you to send out an appeal for funds to provide me with a horse and wagon." The Rabbi then said: "Woman, I ask you to donate a sum sufficient to purchase a horse and wagon for this old man. Then I shall pray that your positions be reversed. Until now, you have led and he has carried; now, however, your roles will be reversed. You will carry (a child in your arms), and the old porter will lead (his horse)."

Szlamovitz, p. 40.

10. Easy Victory; Less Reward

Said the Hafetz Hayyim: "With the advent of the Messiah, the power of the Evil Impulse will be diminished. At present the Evil Impulse is inside of us; in Messianic Days it will be outside of us. The Evil Impulse always seeks to allure us into the worship of strange gods. But since resistance to this temptation is easy to overcome, the reward for this victory will be less."

Pupko, p. 96.

11. An Earthly Reward

Said the Hafetz Hayyim: "A brave soldier is given a medal for courage by his king. Inasmuch as the king is made of earthly substance, he cannot give much more. But God who is All-Powerful can reward his men of valor, as it is written: 'That I may cause those that love Me to inherit substance, and that I may fill their treasuries.' (Proverbs 8:21)."

Pupko, p. 113.

247. RICH AND POOR

1. The "Rich" Man

Two visitors came to Rabbi David Talner, one well-dressed, the other poorly-attired. The magnate was first received and remained in the Rabbi's Study for an hour. The other caller entered the Study, informed the Rabbi of his circumstances and received from him a benediction, to the end that God might improve his lot. The poor man thereupon asked: "Why did that magnate remain in your private reception room for an hour, whereas my affairs you completed in only five minutes?" "I will tell you," replied Rabbi David. "You explained to me your position in the first minutes of our conversation; I knew quickly what you wished and hence gave you my blessing. He, however, took an hour before I came to see that he was as poor as you. The blessing I gave him was identical with yours."

A. D. Ogoz, in *Jewish Morning Journal*, November 23, 1941.

2. The Gift of the Humble

Said the Hafetz Hayyim: "Why did not God accept the offering of Cain? It was because Cain believed himself to be an important person. But Abel, as his name indicates, felt himself to be as naught, and therefore the Lord accepted his gift." *

Pupko, ii, 45.

* Abel is thus linked to the word *Abel* which means a lowly mourner.

3. *The Poor Man's Torah*

Said the Hafetz Hayyim: "The Torah study of a poor man is especially esteemed and rewarded in Heaven."

Pupko, p. 113.

4. *The Two "Ki"*

The Strelisker Rabbi was exceedingly poor. Leib Mimiles once inquired as to his means of livelihood. The Strelisker replied: "I have two Ki." Mimiles interpreted the Rabbi's words to mean that he owned two milch cows (Kuehe, Ki). He therefore instructed his wife to buy milk only from Rabbi Uri Strelisker. The next morning the wife of Leib Mimiles told him that Rabbi Uri had no milk for sale. Mimiles went in search of the Rabbi and asked him for an explanation. The Rabbi answered: "I was referring to the two 'Ki' in Psalm 33:21, which reads in Hebrew: '*Ki bo yismah libbeinu, ki be-Shem Kadsho batahnu,*' ('For in Him doth our heart rejoice, because we have trusted in His Holy Name.')"

I. K., p. 8.

5. *The Ways of The World*

Said the Dubner: "A very charitable young man who loved the poor, resided with his wife at his rich father's home. A son was born to him, and the grandfather proposed that the circumcision be celebrated by a great feast, to which all the townspeople, rich and poor, would be invited.

"The son suggested: 'Let us not follow the usual custom of having the rich folk sit in front and the poor in back. Let us reverse their positions at the table.'

"The father, however, replied: 'It is better to follow the usual procedure. If the poor sit in front near the hosts and the Rabbi, they will be ashamed to eat. And it is for the food that they will come. The rich folk, however, do not need our food. They will have come to be honored. What enjoyment will they have by sitting in the back? Neither food nor honor.'

"The Gentile nations look for this world's material enjoyments; therefore they very properly have received as their share lands outside of Palestine. The Jewish nation, however, looks for spiritual enjoyment, and this is obtainable in Palestine. Hence Palestine was given to the Jewish people."

Dubner, i, 99-100.

248. RICH; RICHES; WEALTH

1. A Certainty

The Dubner Maggid was asked: "Why does a rich man prefer to aid a needy cripple more than a needy learned man?" "Because," replied the Maggid, "the wealthy man is not sure that he may not become a cripple himself some day. But it is a certainty in his mind that he will never become a learned man."

Dubner, i, 46.

2. Knowing What We Lack

A rich man asked the Dubner Maggid: "Why do you go to rich men, but rich men are never seen coming to you?"

The Maggid replied: "Because I have sense enough to know that I lack money, but the rich men do not know they lack sense."

Dubner, i, 47.

3. Wealth for the Soul

Said the Hafetz Hayyim: "Concern yourself with the acquisition of wealth for your soul, more than with wealth for your body. Only the first can avail you after death."

Pupko, p. 118.

4. Hesitation by the Vulgar

The Medzibozer said: "When Abraham sent his Canaanitish servant Eliezer to secure a wife for Isaac, he instructed him according to Rashi: 'I cannot permit the blessed Isaac to wed a Canaanitish girl, inasmuch as Canaan was accursed and could not associate himself with the blessed.' The question may be asked: 'Why did not Rashi phrase it in reverse, namely, that the blessed cannot associate with the accursed?' Rashi himself gives us a suggestion of the answer: if a Zaddik is anxious for his son to marry into a wealthy but vulgar family, it is usually the vulgar father who hesitates. The accursed does not care to associate himself with the blessed."

BDH., p. 53.

5. Wealth Without Harm

A wealthy man instructed his neighbor, the owner of a candy-store, to give to his son a few sweets every day and afterwards to submit the bill for the cost to him. The storekeeper, however, foolishly gave the child too much candy and the lad fell sick. The father thereupon refused to pay the bill. The matter was laid before a judge who rendered the decision that the bill need not be paid, since the storekeeper had disobeyed not only the father's instructions

but the dictates of good sense as well. "In the same way," said the
Hafetz Hayyim, "the Lord refuses to grant wealth to a man when
He knows it will injure his character. When a man prays for
wealth, he should declare: 'Grant me bodily comforts, O Lord, but
only if Thou knowest that such a gift will do me no harm.'"

Pupko, ii, 54.

6. An Orderly Method

Said the Hafetz Hayyim: "Those who wish to understand God's
ways in dealing with us should observe the Warden of a synagogue
distributing the honor of being called up the Reading of the Law on
the Sabbath. If a stranger should be led to inquire why the Warden
selects one person from this corner, and one from another corner
of the synagogue, he will be given the answer: 'there is order in
his method.' A similar method or system can be perceived in the
distribution of wealth by the Lord: in a former generation one
particular family has been affluent, but now riches are assigned to a
family formerly devoid of wealth."

Pupko, p. 59.

7. Refraining from Rights

The Vorker Rabbi visited a wealthy Jew in Warsaw and asked
for one hundred thalers for the wedding expenses of the magnate's
relative. The rich man declared he would have nothing to do with
Rebbes. The Rabbi made repeated attempts to persuade him, but
was pushed down the stairway for his pains by the magnate's servants. The rich man met a friend, himself a magnate, and narrated
the story. The friend was well acquainted with the Vorker and
advised the offending magnate to beg the Rabbi's forgiveness to
avoid a severe penalty. The magnate sent for the Rabbi, who said:
"Since he is extending an invitation to me, I may as well ask for two
hundred thalers and thus provide a sum sufficient for his relative
to arrange a finer wedding." He did so, and received the two hundred thalers, the magnate acting as if this sum meant little to him.
The Rabbi then said: "It is the custom in law that if a thing is repeated three times, it is regarded as a certainty. There is, however,
no hold-over right where a quarrel is involved. Though he had refused me three times, the rich man did not hold on to his discourtesy."

Zammlung, p. 24.

8. Garments Inside Out

Said the Dubner: "A rich man made a fine garment for his son.
The son, however, carelessly soiled it, and the father compelled him

to turn it inside out and wear it in this way. A friend inquired the reason, and the father replied: 'This will teach him the lesson to take care of the costly garment. When he has learned the lesson, I will turn it right again.'

"From this we learn: if we make improper use of our wealth, the Lord causes us to become poor in order to teach us a lesson."

Dubner, i, 150-151.

249. RIDICULE

1. Anticipating Ridicule

The Berditschever came to a town to deliver a series of discourses. Two unmannerly Rabbis, one the Rabbi of a synagogue of bakers, and the other the Rabbi of a synagogue of tailors, paid him a visit, but it was their intention to speak of him after their departure, in terms of ridicule. The Berditschever had word of this, and, since he did not relish ridicule, resolved to anticipate them. When the two Rabbis entered his presence, he said: "I do not know whom I should first greet; therefore I am giving to both of you *'ein shalom'* (In Yiddish: 'one greeting'; in Hebrew: 'no peace')." The two Rabbis did not comprehend the allusion and asked him for an explanation. The Berditschever replied: "In the Talmud, *Shabbat,* 30, there is a sentence which asserts that in the days to come the Land of Israel shall bring forth bread and clothing completely ready for consumption and use. Why are these only mentioned? Is it not because it would then be possible to abolish bakers and tailors, and as a consequence, to dispense with the Rabbis of the synagogues of bakers and tailors?"

Guttman, p. 6.

250. ROLES IN LIFE

1. Exchanging Roles

Said the Dubner: "A horse dealer made an agreement with a scholar that he would supply the needs of a student of learning, and the latter should divide with him the anticipated reward in the World-to-Come. One day the dealer grew very weary, and requested the scholar to watch his horses in the market-place, while he proceeded to the Beth ha-Midrash to study. Persons found it quite amusing to watch the scholar's attempt to take care of the horses. But they found it even more amusing to perceive the unlearned horse dealer's struggles with his studies.

"From this we learn: sometimes a man will undergo bodily fasts

and strike his breast in confession, whereas his mind and soul are
still engrossed with business affairs."

Dubner, i, 170-171.

251. ROSH HA-SHANAH

1. *Friend of the Satan*

One Rosh ha-Shanah the blower of the Shofar was unable to
bring forth a note. An irreligious man ascended the Bimah and
blew the ram's horn with smoothness and power. The Rabbi of
the synagogue remarked later: "The Shofar-blower is a pious Jew
who fights the Satan every day; hence on this day the Satan succeeded in obstructing his blowing. But the other man obeys the
Satan every day and regards him as his friend. Therefore the Satan
granted him the pleasure of blowing the Shofar well."

Zlotnik, p. 39.

2. *Watchers of the "Tscholent"*

A Hasid asked the Rav: "There are certain angels who have
charge of bringing forth the sounds of the Shofar. But, Rabbi, what
do these angels do all year round?"

The Rav smiled and answered: "Oh, they only work on the Sabbath, watching the special dish, called the 'Tscholent.'"

"How do you know this?" asked the Hasid.

The Rav replied: "Don't you know that when Rosh ha-Shanah
occurs on the Sabbath there is no blowing of the Shofar? Is it not,
because the angels are too busy with the 'Tscholent' to care for the
sounds of the Shofar?"

Zlotnik, p. 41.

3. *Confusing the Satan*

Rabbi Akiba Eger said: "According to the Talmud we blow the
Shofar many times on Rosh ha-Shanah. We thereby give evidence
of our love in performing a command of the Lord. This love con-
fuses the Satan and he does not bring forth his charges against us.
The Talmud leaves it to us to explain why the Satan becomes confused. There is another Talmudic adage which declares that he who
repents out of love of God beholds his sins transformed into good
works. And the Satan, observing how Jews love to obey God's command, fears that if he brings forth his charges, these, too, will be
transformed into good deeds. Hence he finds it more profitable to
refrain from bringing charges against us on Rosh ha-Shanah."

Sopher, p. 61.

252. SABBATH

1. *Three Excuses*

Three youths hid themselves on a Sabbath in a barn in order to smoke. Hasidim discovered them and wished to flog the offenders. One youth exclaimed: "I deserve no punishment, for I forgot that today is the Sabbath." The second youth said: "And I forgot that smoking on the Sabbath is forbidden." The third youth raised his voice and cried out: "I, too, forgot." "What did you forget?" he was asked. The lad replied: "I forgot to lock the door of the barn."

Zlotnik, p. 13.

2. *Friday and the Sabbath*

Near the city of Kutna in Poland there are two towns, the smaller of which is named: Piontek which means Friday, and the larger, Sobote which means the Sabbath. The Rabbi of Sobote died, and the townspeople inquired of the great Kutna Rav, Rabbi Joshua, whether he advised them to extend a call to the Rav of Piontek. Rabbi Joshua replied: "Our Sages declared: 'he who has labored Friday shall enjoy the reward of the Sabbath.'" (*Avodah Zarah*, 3).

Zlotnik, p. 5.

3. *Everlasting Sabbath*

The Hafetz Hayyim once wrote to a layman in Moscow that he was coming to visit the city with reference to the affairs of his Yeshivah. The Rabbi invited him to meet him at the railroad station but not to inform others of his coming. When another prominent layman heard that the Hafetz Hayyim had already arrived, he grumbled at the fact that he had been denied the honor of meeting the Rabbi. The Hafetz Hayyim said to him: "Honor is comparable to Sabbath dish known as Kugel. It is reserved especially for the Sabbath meal, namely, for life in the World-to-Come, which is an everlasting Sabbath."

Pupko, p. 60.

4. *Diminishing the Blessing*

When the Hafetz Hayyim was in Moscow, he heard of a Jewish storekeeper who kept his store open on Fridays after sunset and opened it on Saturdays before sunset. He visited the Jew and said to him: "I once heard of a farmer who brought some grain to the city for sale. He asked the grain merchant to give him a silver coin for every one hundred pound weight of the grain. Thus, he believed, he could count the coins and know how many one hundred pound weight portions, for which he was to receive payment. When the foolish farmer, however, felt himself weighed down by the silver coins in one pocket, he placed some of them in another pocket. When the weighing of the grain was over, he forgot about these transferred coins, and submitted only those in his large pocket. Thus he deprived himself of a large sum to which he was entitled. It is the same folly of which you are guilty. Instead of benefitting from the Sabbath blessing for the full twenty-four hours of the day, you are diminishing the blessing by slicing off a number of hours after the Sabbath has begun and before it has ended."

Pupko, p. 62.

5. Not Idolaters

When the Hafetz Hayyim heard that the Jews of Moscow had been banished, leaving their property behind them, he remarked: "It is true that these Jews had profaned the Sabbath by keeping their stores open. But they cannot be described as idolaters, in the same way that we classify other wilful and public Sabbath-breakers. For the banished Jews of Moscow abandoned their properties and refused to be converted to Christianity."

Pupko, p. 10.

6. The Outward and the Inward

The Alexanderer said: "When I studied Hasidism with the 'Yud,' and the first Sabbath Day arrived, the 'Yud' taught us that the holiness of the Sabbath did not rest in the fur-hat worn on the Sabbath or in the 'Kugel' dish served on the Sabbath. Sabbath holiness must be perceived in the enkindlement of the mind. When the strict piety of the Radishitzer was brought to the attention of the 'Yud,' the latter remarked: 'Not his outward observance makes him a man of piety, but rather his inner cleaving to the Lord with all his heart and soul.'"

H. Hak., p. 88.

253. SALESMANSHIP

1. Refusing to Compete

The Hafetz Hayyim in his younger days travelled from place to place to sell his own works. Whenever he discovered another solicitor in a town, seeking funds for a worthy institution; or if he found a Maggid there, he would decline to enter into competition, and would leave the city, even if he had arrived first. Once the leaders of a community besought him earnestly not to take his departure; the Maggid also assured him that he had already received his honorarium, and the Hafetz Hayyim consented to remain. His sales, however, were few in number, and the Hafetz Hayyim considered it a punishment from Heaven for remaining. He never repeated the experience. When the pious men of another town begged him not to take his departure, he nevertheless did so, promising to come again. And the number of his sales in the end proved thoroughly satisfactory.

Pupko, p. 3.

2. A Too Successful Agent

Rabbi Israel Meir ha-Kohen, the Hafetz Hayyim received a letter from an agent who had volunteered to sell his works in the city of Ostrolenko. The agent succeeded so well that he sold books to the amount of one hundred rubles. When the Rabbi heard this, he sighed deeply and remarked: "He has taken out too much money from so small a city. Who knows what exaggerations my agent used to mislead the purchasers!"

Pupko, p. 3.

254. SALVATION

1. Hope for Salvation

Who can hope for salvation? He who is never self-satisfied.

Yehudi ha-Kadosh, p. 20.

2. Salvation Through Faith

A Hasid visited Rabbi Samuel Zevi of Alexander and told him that his wife who was about to give birth to a child had fallen ill, and that he had no money to give her hospital care. The man continued: "I don't see what I can do about it, Rabbi. I leave the matter entirely in your hands." The Rabbi thereupon offered prayer in the woman's behalf, and her child was born with so little difficulty that her health was not injured. The Rabbi explained: "Her husband's faith brought him salvation from Heaven."

Zammlung, p. 95.

3. Salvation Brings Honor

Rabbi Bunam was engaged in a discussion with his son, Abraham Moses, a close student of the Psalter. Rabbi Bunam said: "We read in Psalm 119:146: 'I have called Thee; save me, and I will observe Thy testimonies.' Does the Psalmist mean to say that a man must observe the injunctions of the Torah, *only* if God saves him; otherwise he is immune, since salvation is not granted him?" Rabbi Abraham Moses replied: "By no means! When a mortal king shows

favor to a suppliant, the latter enjoys the favor and nothing else.
But when it is known that a man's prayers have been answered
by God, he not only enjoys the Lord's favor, but he also gains
honor and respect as a man of saintliness."

Zammlung, p. 13.

4. The Trunk and the Branches

Said the Hafetz Hayyim: "In these dangerous times it behooves
us to imitate a drowning man. We should cling fast not to the
branches but to the trunk of the tree if we would be saved."

Pupko, ii, 39.

255. SANCTIFICATION

1. Kiddush and Havdalah

When Jews fail to make Kiddush (namely, to sanctify their lives),
invariably the non-Jews make Havdalah (discrimination) against
Jews.

Zlotnik, p. 33.

256. SATAN

1. Battling the Satan

Said the Hafetz Hayyim: "The Psalmist says (Psalm 127:4): 'As
arrows in the hands of a mighty man, so are the children of one's
youth.' From this we learn that if we give our children the advan-
tages of a religious home and a fine religious education, they will
be equipped to give sturdy battle to the temptations of Satan, and
they will be able to gain the victory."

Pupko, ii, 66.

2. The Satan's Brother

In a certain city there lived a wealthy Jew who was thoroughly
without piety, but who insisted on his right to blow the Shofar.
One Rosh ha-Shanah the Dubner Maggid visited the particular city.
The rich man tried to exercise his right to blow the Shofar but the
proper sounds would not come forth. Another person had to take
his place. The Maggid delivered his sermon immediately after the
ceremony of the Shofar-blowing, and told this story. "A long-drawn-
out battle greatly wearied both sides in a struggle, and it was decided
to pit the best marksman of each side against one another. The
decision would hinge upon the outcome of the duel. The chosen
champions on encountering each other recognized that they were
brothers who had long been separated. They consulted in whispers

and resolved to use blank cartridges in their rifles. As a result, nothing happened, and they were eventually relieved of their assignment."

"We must be careful," continued the Maggid, "lest we recognize the Satan as our brother. Otherwise we will puff and puff and no sound will emerge from the Shofar. How can you expect a man to blow away the dignity of his brother?"

Dubner, i, 41-43.

3. The Cow in the House

One day a cow found the hall door open and entered the house of the Hafetz Hayyim. The Rabbi's wife drove the cow out. The Hafetz Hayyim, hearing of this, remarked: "This reminds me that the Satan always stands near a man and awaits his opportunity. When the man opens his mouth to speak, the Satan at once injects a word of slander or malice. Do not talk unnecessarily and you will avoid the temptation to sin."

Pupko, ii, 23.

257. SCOFFERS

1. The Scoffers

The Hafetz Hayyim said that he sought to imitate Moses ben Maimon in speaking only good of scholars. But he always explained to his pupils his view of the evil nature of the scoffers. He said: "Thus I seek to obey the injunction in the verse (Psalm 139:21): 'I hate those who hate Thee.'"

Pupko, p. 73.

2. No Debates with Scoffers

The Hafetz Hayyim said: "My counsel to you is to engage in no debates or disputations with scoffers on matters of religion. You will become involved in endless arguments, and your own warmth in the service of God may abate."

Pupko, p. 99.

258. SECRECY

1. Emphasizing His Secrecy

Said Rabbi Israel Isaac (Yerachmiel) of Alexander: "I have been informed that a certain Zaddik serves the Lord in secret. He emphasizes this secrecy by giving the impression that he is transgressing the laws of good behavior. This is a wrong thing to do. It is excellent to conceal one's good deeds, but not in the disguise of impurity."

Zammlung, p. 86.

259. SELF-CONTROL

1. Secretly, Not Publicly

Said the Leover: "We read in *Ethics* 4:1: 'Who is mighty? He who subdues his passions.' I declare this to mean that a man should subdue both his passions: his passion to do good, as well as his passion to do evil. Both should be done secretly, not publicly."

Guttman, p. 25.

2. The Habit of Self-Control

Rabbi Mordecai Neshkizer's son, Isaac, ate fish for dinner and became exceedingly thirsty. His father requested him to wait a bit before taking a drink. The boy, however, declined to wait and went outside to secure a drink. When he returned, his father said: "If you do not habituate yourself in your youth to control your desires, what will you do in your later years when it becomes your duty to combat them?"

Kolbiel, p. 6.

260. SELF-IMPROVEMENT; IMPROVEMENT

1. Using Life Aright

Rabbi Moses of Ohel remarked to his grandson, Yekutiel: "After my demise, when I am called before the Heavenly Tribunal, I will see before me angels acting as judges. But I will have no fear, for I can offer the excuse that I was not created an angel. But if I see judges like Rabbi Ezekiel Landau and Rabbi Abish, I shall feel great fear. For they were flesh and blood like myself, but they made so much more out their life on earth."

Michelson, p. 41.

2. An Empty Barrel

A Hasid of the Lubliner Zaddik once visited the Rabbi of Ziditchov and told the latter much regarding the behavior and preaching of his teacher. The Ziditchover became enthusiastic at the Hasid's words and exclaimed: "I feel in truth like an empty barrel. I must go to Lublin to fill myself with spirit."

Walden, p. 83.

3. The Swift Messenger

Said the Dubner: "A swift messenger brought to a wealthy merchant the news that his house in town was afire. The owner inquired from the messenger the identity of the person who had sent him and was given the name. Immediately the merchant ordered his servants to harness his horses and to drive to the city without delay. 'Will it not be too late to do anything when you reach town?' inquired his wife.

" 'Not at all,' replied her husband. 'Were there no hope to rescue anything, my neighbor in the city would not have taken the trouble to dispatch an especially swift messenger.'

"From this we learn: If the Lord had not cherished the hope that Israel would improve his ways, He would not have sent him such eloquent prophets and preachers."

Dubner, i, 259-260.

4. Sinners into Saints

Said the Hafetz Hayyim: "We read in Numbers 15:39-40: 'That ye go not about after your own heart and your own eyes . . . and be holy unto your God.' Our Sages comment: 'after your own heart' means that our heart leads us to deny God. 'After your own eyes' means that our eyes lead us into impure behavior. Therefore the question arises: 'How can we associate holiness with persons who oftentimes descend into sins of such gravity?' The anwer is to be found in the text which teaches us that even a serious transgressor may transform himself and become holy before God and man."

Pupko, p. 105.

5. Self-Improvement and Repentance

Said the Hafetz Hayyim: "Repentance consists in self-improvement according to one's rank and occupation. Every one of us is expected to make the utmost use of his abilities. For example, a Cantor asked Rabbi Israel Salanter how he might repent. The Rabbi answered: "Endeavor to improve your singing, and earn your emolument by an effort, even worthier than heretofore."

Pupko, ii, 40.

261. SELFISHNESS

1. The Governing Condition

Said the Dubner: "A wealthy man who owned a block of houses was compelled to leave his city for reasons of health and to take up his residence in an area with a better climate. He made out a document in which he left his properties as a gift to a friend. A few years later, the man's health had improved so much that he returned to his home town. He asked his friends to allot to him one of his houses, but the alleged friend refused. The former owner summoned him to a civil court. The judge, however, decided that the deed was clearly worded, and that the former owner had no rightful claim. The man answered: 'There is a clause, sir, which you have over-looked.' The judge read the document aloud, including the words: 'This gift shall be valid on condition that the beneficiary does not prove to be a false friend to me.' By virtue of this clause, ownership was restored by the judge to the former proprietor.

"From this we learn that the selfish man punishes himself by his own selfishness."

Dubner, i, 119-121.

262. SELF-RELIANCE

1. *Mastering Knowledge for Oneself*

Said the Dubner: "A merchant prince once summoned his sons into his presence and said to them: 'I would like to train you in the conduct of my extensive and demanding business affairs. Who of you cares to undertake this training course?' Only one of his sons consented. His friend asked this son: 'Why do you need to work your way up the ladder from the bottom when, being your father's son, you can enjoy a life of leisure?' The young man answered: 'A practical business training is worth more than all the money which my father can bestow upon me. If it should happen—Heaven forbid —that my father's business should collapse and his fortune disappear, I shall at least know how to proceed in the acquisition of another.'

"From this we learn that knowledge is more precious than pearls."

Dubner, i, 280-282.

2. *Undiminished Fire*

Said the Hafetz Hayyim: "In your love of God rely upon your own spiritual resources. Do not depend for help upon circumstances outside yourself. Never forget that even in the midst of a severe winter, when everything else is frozen, a fire retains its flame throughout."

Pupko, ii, 37.

3. *Depend Upon Yourself*

Said the Hafetz Hayyim: "There are two kinds of heat: the heat of the fire, and the heat of an object near the fire. The latter will grow cold if it is removed from proximity to the fire. From this we can learn that a man should not depend upon his Rabbi to kindle his warmth of devotions; he should be a Rabbi by virtue of his own enkindlement, and he should maintain his religious observances even in the absence of a Rabbi."

Pupko, p. 103.

263. SERENITY

1. Zeal and Serenity

Said the Bratzlaver: "A man without zeal cannot offer perfect service to the Lord." Said the Leover: "Serve God with both zeal and serenity. Both are included within the command to love God with all our heart."

Guttman, p. 19.

264. SERVANTS

1. Sprinkling the Sand

Rabbi Wolf of Grodno asked Rabbi Akiba Eger to inscribe a recommendation of his commentary on *Pesikta Rabbati* so that its sale might be enhanced. Rabbi Akiba went into his garden, perused the manuscript, and then wrote a few prefatory remarks on the fly-leaf. Having done this, he bent down and picked up some sand to dry the ink. Rabbi Wolf inquired: "Why did you not order your servant to give you the sand?" Rabbi Akiba answered: "I engaged my servant to perform the usual services. I did not engage him to perform an unforeseen service, such as blotting my words of approval for a book, as if to indicate that I am really important enough to give a worthwhile recommendation."

Sopher, p. 63.

265. SERVICE

1. Tasting the Sweetness

The Psalmist (34:9) declares: "O taste and see that the Lord is good." In other words, it behooves you to partake of the sweetness of serving the Lord, and then you will know that He is good.

Dor Deah, p. 263.

2. Forgetting Our Comfort

We can become God's Children not by choosing the easy and enjoyable ways of serving Him, but only by being unmindful of our own comfort. We have not beheld the Divine Light if we think only of ourselves when serving the Lord.

Dor Deah, p. 107.

266. SHAME

1. Without Cause for Shame

Said the Hafetz Hayyim: "We say in the Grace after Meals: 'That we may not be ashamed nor confounded for ever and ever.' * These words mean: 'we should have no cause for shame when our good deeds are reviewed in Heaven, for they should be deeds of significant goodness.'"

Pupko, ii, 42.

* Singer, p. 281. Edition, 1908.

2. The Source of the Shame

Said the Hafetz Hayyim: "The Talmud tells us that 'the worthiness' of Joshua compared to that of Moses was as the moon compared to the sun. The Elders of the generation exclaimed: 'Woe unto such shame!' Wherein does the shame lie? Perhaps a parable will illustrate the point: a man was about to depart for the diamond fields in South Africa. When he invited his townsfolk to accompany him, only one man consented. In a few years both men returned, one with great, the other with less, wealth. The townsfolk exclaimed: 'Woe, the shame! Had we accompanied them, we, too, would have become wealthy.' Joshua acquired worthiness by clinging to the tent of Moses. The Elders then said: 'We also have had the same opportunity as Joshua, yet we took no advantage of it. It is of this that we are ashamed.'"

Pupko, p. 48.

267. SHAVUOT

1. Not for Ingathering

The Kelmer Maggid visited the city of Koenigsberg to deliver a sermon in the synagogue. Very few persons, however, came to hear him. The Sexton explained to the Maggid that he had come to preach on the day when it was customary to make collections of the sums owed for merchandise sold during the week. The Maggid commented: "Oh, but they have made an error. Today is Shavuot, not the Sukkot, the Feast of Ingathering!"

Zlotnik, p. 91.

2. "Tikkun Shavuot"

In accordance with their custom, the Disciples of Rabbi Ber of Leova came to the Rabbi's synagogue, after they had finished the Shavuot evening meal, in order to recite the compilation, known as the *Tikkun Shavuot.* The Rabbi, however, spent the entire night talking of other matters. When daylight arrived, Rabbi Ber remarked: "There is a better *Tikkun* than the printed book. Search your souls thoroughly, to discover whether since last Shavuot you have performed everything which God has commanded you. And resolve to perform that which you have omitted to do. To this we also give the name: *Tikkun,* for *Tikkun,* as you know, means improvement—improvement of your character."

Guttman, p. 21.

268. SHEKINAH

1. The Shekinah's Departure

Said the Riziner: "We read (Genesis 49:1): 'And Jacob called unto his sons, and said: "Gather yourselves together, that I may tell you that which shall befall you in the end of days.' Rashi makes this comment: 'Jacob desired to reveal the time of the Messiah's advent, but the Shekinah departed from him and he was unable to do so.' If we inquire the reason for this, the answer is as follows: 'The Sages teach us: "If Israel manifests merit, the end of our captivity will be hastened. If not, it will come in its proper time."' Now Jacob could alone reveal the proper time, as it is predestined. It would indicate that he lacked the belief that Israel merited the advent of the redemption before this appointed time, and such an uncharitable view caused the Shekinah to depart."

Nissanzohn, Royal Hasidut, p. 272.

269. SHEMINI ATZERET

1. A Remarkable Generation

On Shemini Atzeret the Hasidim in the synagogue of the Tzortkover Rabbi exhibited a very merry mood. The Rabbi exclaimed: "How much more remarkable is this generation than the generation of the Exodus! At the time of the Going Out from Egypt Moses our Master was present as the Holy Leader; Prophetic revelation and wondrous events abounded. Yet, again and again, God's manifestation of loving care was required to arouse faith and confidence in Him. Today, however, we have no revelation; no great leader is present; no assured source of strength. Yet the Holy Day itself lifts Israel unto the Source of Holiness on High, and causes the people to rejoice. Yes, it is true: remarkable is this generation!"

Margulies, p. 28.

270. SHOFAR

1. God Is Disqualified

The Lubliner "Seer" delayed his entrance into the synagogue on
Rosh ha-Shanah though the time had arrived for sounding the Shofar. Rabbi David Lelever entered the "Seer's" private room, and
inquired as to the reason for the delay. The Lubliner answered:
"With the eyes of the spirit I have perceived Israel being sternly
accused at the Judgment Seat in Heaven; therefore I cannot enter
the synagogue. Pray tell me, however, the name of the youth who
is with you." The Lelever replied: "It is Israel Isaac of Vorky, my
adopted son." The Lubliner turned to him and said: "Tell me, my
lad, what have you learned recently." The boy replied: "I have
studied the law of testimony. I have turned over in my mind the
question as to the invalidity of a near-relative's testimony if it is
unfavorable to his relative. Then, I argued, we look for the testimony of ordinary people. If a man, however, testifies voluntarily
against a near kinsman, he is out of the ordinary." The Lubliner
remarked: "We need an ordinary judge to judge us. But God is our
Heavenly Father, and His judgment against his own children would
be both extraordinary and invalid. He, therefore, is under the
necessity of rendering a decision in our favor, and to refuse to give
heed to the accusations against His children." This conversation
proved calming to the Lubliner, and he entered the synagogue to
sound the Shofar.

Zammlung, p. 19.

2. A Weak Note on the Shofar

When the Rabbi of Ziditchov blew a blast on the Shofar, only a
weak sound would emerge. Paraphrasing a passage in the Rosh
ha-Shanah *Piyyut: "Unethanneh Tokef"* his Disciples declared:
"When a great man's Shofar is blown, and a still small voice is heard,
the angels quickly assemble and trembling seizes them." (See
Amos 3:6)

Braver, p. 82.

271. SICK

1. Gifts for the Sick

When the son of the Rabbi of Lelev was seriously ill, scores of
people brought him gifts of strengthening food. The Rabbi wept.
He was asked: "Why do you shed tears?" He answered: "Every ill

person should receive the same attention at your hands. But because he is my son, you show him special consideration."

Yehudi ha-Kodosh, p. 17.

272. SILENCE

1. *Silence Is Restful*

Hasidim loyal to the Tzortkover Rabbi implored him to defend himself against the attacks of the Rabbi of Tzanz. The Tzortkover answered: "Silence is so restful."

M. B., p. 20.

2. *The Virtue of Silence*

Rabbi Akiba Eger visited Rabbi Mordecai Bennett at Nikolsburg. Rabbi Mordecai invited him to deliver a discourse before a gathering. When the guest had concluded, the host remarked: "We appreciate the depth of Rabbi Akiba's arguments, but I trust he will not mind my saying that they awaken questions in our minds." Later Rabbi Akiba inquired: "What are the questions to which you referred, my friend?" Rabbi Mordecai enumerated them, and Rabbi Akiba explained what seemed to him the correct answers in each instance. Rabbi Mordecai listened with amazement, marvelling at the ease with which Rabbi Akiba disposed of his questions." Finally he exclaimed: "Tell me, my dear Rabbi, why did you not disprove my statement in public as soon as I made it?" Rabbi Akiba replied: "I did not do so, because you are the Rav of this community. As for me, I am merely a passer-by. By my silence you gained respect in your own community, while I suffered no harm whatsoever." Rabbi Mordecai, however, narrated the entire conversation before his congregation in his next discourse.

Sopher, p. 73.

3. *The Silence of the Hafetz Hayyim*

At the wedding of his grandson, many Rabbis delivered orations, but the Hafetz Hayyim remained silent. Later he gave an explanation, saying: "When I wish to speak, I gather together my own audience who wish me to be the sole speaker. But I do not care to speak in a company. If my speaking is appreciated more than any other's, this person feels as if I had robbed him of his honor."

Pupko, ii, 30.

4. *Why Be Inarticulate?*

Said the Hafetz Hayyim: "Open your heart to God and tell Him your worries in any language you choose. Since you possess the right to petition Him, why remain inarticulate?"

Pupko, p. 96.

273. SIMHAT TORAH

1. Partners in All Things

A workingman was dancing with a Scroll of the Law in his arms on Simhat Torah; he displayed religious joy above all the other worshipers.

The Dayyan asked him: "Have you devoted yourself particularly to a study of Torah?"

"Even if I have not zealously studied Torah, you have done so," replied the workingman. "When my partner has a feast, shall it not be my feast as well?"

"But suppose your partner has not extended you an invitation," remarked the Dayyan.

"That is impossible," was the workingman's rejoinder. "You urged me to offer earnest prayer on Yom Kippur, and include in my Confession the words: 'For the sin we have committed in the taking of bribes.' If I am your partner in your sin, I am also your partner in your feast."

Zlotnik, p. 56.

274. SIMPLE FAITH

1. The Two Hasidic Systems

The Medzibozer Rabbi offered the opinion that Rabbi Schneour Zalman of Ladi had wandered away from the system of the Baal Shem Tov by creating again a privileged class of profound thinkers, instead of teaching a simple faith for simple people.

M. B., p. 25.

2. The Constancy of Simple Faith

Said Rabbi Samuel Zevi of Alexander: "The Midrash comments on verse 23:15 in Leviticus, which reads: 'And ye shall count unto you from the morrow after the day of rest, from the day that ye brought the sheaf of the waving; seven weeks shall there be complete.' It interprets the words: 'when they are complete,' namely, when Israel fulfils God's will. I say, however, that it is God's will that His commands be fulfilled without subjecting them to the influence of mortal reason. Only then are they complete, for the judgments of human reason vary from time to time, but simple faith is constant and unchanging."

Zammlung, p. 96.

3. Tradition and Research

Said the Rabbi of Dinov: "Traditional teaching was received in the Revelation from God on Mount Sinai. Inasmuch as God is limitless, belief associated with the Revelation on Sinai is without limit. Research, however, is linked to the human intellect, and since the mind of mortal man has its bounds, therefore belief founded upon it is limited."

Kaufman, p. 61.

275. SIMPLICITY

1. How to Argue with God

The Bratzlaver advised a young man to make frequent visits to a place of solitude and implore God to bring him nearer to His Presence. "Speak in the vernacular," the Rabbi counselled the youth. "Use simple words. Say to God: 'Is it right that my days should pass amid vanities? Was it for such a purpose that Thou hast made me?' The Rabbi thereupon went to his room. The young man placed his ear at the keyhole and heard the Rabbi use these self-same words in his own prayer."

H. H. N., p. 9a.

2. Service Without Sophistry

The Bratzlaver cherished great love for those who performed the simple services before the Lord: those who recited the many additional prayers found in the thickest prayer books; those who sang many hymns on the Sabbath and on Saturday Nights; those who recited many Psalms. He would say: "The paramount thing in Judaism is to serve God with simplicity and sincerity, and without any sophistry."

H. H. N., p. 17a.

276. SIN; SINNERS

1. "In the Sight of All Israel"

"The Torah," said a Rabbi, "ends with the words: 'in the sight of all Israel.' From this we can take the meaning that for the Jew who sins, unashamed 'in the sight of all Israel,' the Torah has ended. He has no further association with it."

Zlotnik, p. 57.

2. Painting Sin as Goodness

Said the Besht: "The Talmud teaches us that he who slaughters an animal on the Sabbath is guilty also of engaging in the act of dyeing, for some of the skin is dyed by the blood of the animal when slaughtered. We must remember this when we give heed to the teaching that in the days to come God will condemn the Satan to death and extinction. The question arises: since the Satan was created to tempt man, and by tempting him, he fulfils his appointed mission, why, then, does he merit extinction? The answer is to be found in the fact that the Satan is guilty of dyeing, namely, of painting sin in bright and alluring colors. This can be construed as over-zealousness on the part of the Satan, since he was not authorized to depict sin as goodness."

Kaufman, p. 41.

3. A Record of Our Offenses

Said the Hafetz Hayyim: "The Talmud narrates that when Rabbi Ishmael was reading before a lamp on a Sabbath Evening, he inadvertently cleansed the wick. Thereupon he wrote in his diary: 'when the Temple is rebuilt, I shall bring an offering as atonement for this offense.' From this tale we can learn that we should always keep our offenses in mind. It is as if a creditor requests payment for the money he declares is owed him. If the debtor shows the record of his debts which he is keeping, and makes clear that he intends to repay them, the creditor may not be averse to waiting. But if the debtor denies the debt, the creditor can show him the document of his indebtedness and is justified in demanding immediate payment. By the same token, we can express the hope that if we acknowledge our transgressions, God will be patient on High."

Pupko, ii, 67.

4. Keeping Your Ledger

Said the Hafetz Hayyim: "Be sure to keep an account of your deeds, in the same way that you keep a record of your business transactions. While you are alive, you can endeavor to counteract an evil deed with a good deed. After your demise, this will no longer be possible."

Pupko, iii, 7.

5. The Names of Sinners

The Neshkizer Rabbi remarked of the verse in Exodus 32:33: "Whosoever hath sinned against Me, him will I blot out of My book;" "I interpret these words as a question. God really said to Moses: 'Why ask Me to blot thy name out of My book? Do I ever blot out the names of sinners? Do I not forgive transgressors?'"

Kolbiel, p. 13 (Rishpe Esh).

277. SINCERITY

1. The Use of a Mirror

A visitor to the Tzortkover Zaddik noted a large and handsome mirror in the reception room. The visitor thought to himself: "Is then the Zaddik so vain of his looks?" The Rabbi read the Hasid's thought, and remarked: "The mirror was presented to my father, the Riziner. He had been overheard by my father, saying: 'The Zaddik, also, wishes to gaze upon the face of the Zaddik.' My father, the Riziner replied: 'Nay, this is not true. But I wish those who come to visit me to observe with what manner of a countenance they come to me.'"

Margulies, p. 31.

2. Without Hearing or Feeling

Rabbi Ber of Mezeritz said: "When I am discoursing on a subject of Torah I neither hear nor feel the words I am speaking. They issue from my mouth without my knowledge or help. As soon as I hear myself talking, I stop."

Braver, p. 31.

3. Grain During Drought

Rabbi Leib Libavitz spoke to the Hafetz Hayyim with considerable distress of spirit because he felt himself insufficiently sincere in his recital of prayers by reason of the business worries which harassed him. The Hafetz Hayyim replied: "When grain-merchants purchase their supplies during a regular season, they scrutinize with close attention the samples of grain submitted to them. But during seasons of drought, their examination is by no means so thorough. Likewise among generations of God-fearing men, the quality of the prayers offered is carefully scrutinized. But during the present generation the examination is by no means so searching. Blemishes are overlooked if only the heart is turned to God."

Pupko, p. 58.

4. A Prayer That Is Heard

Said the Bratzlaver: "When you are filled with regrets over the multitude of your sins; when you are filled with anxiety over your lack of the necessities of life; when you seek to strengthen yourself and pour out your heart unto God, then you have His Divine Assurance through the words of the Psalmist (22:25) 'That He hath not despised nor abhorred the affliction of the poor; neither hath He hidden His face from him; but when he cried unto Him, He heard.'

The words: 'despised' and 'abhorred' demonstrate that as a matter of strict justice, this suppliant, by reason of his evil ways, deserves to be despised and abhorred by the Lord. Nevertheless, the Lord hears him and answers him."

H. H. N., pp. 52-53.

5. The Nature of Genuine Prayer

Said the Bratzlaver: "If, when you pray, you feel that there is another person near by, it is not authentic prayer. Moreover, if you feel that you exist and remember your own being, at the moment of your praying, it is not authentic prayer. If your prayer is to be real, you must remember and feel the existence of God only, and of no one or nothing else."

H. H. N., p. 17a.

6. Writing With Blood

Rabbi Isaac of Ziditchov said: "When I do my writing, I dip my pen twice, once in ink, and the second time in my heart's blood."

Braver, p. 75.

7. Sincere Repentance

Said the Hafetz Hayyim: "We are fortunate indeed that the Lord accepts sincere repentance."

Pupko, p. 107.

8. Genuine and Insincere Tears

Said the Dubner: "A storekeeper suffered the loss of his entire stock through a fire, and had no insurance whatsoever. He owed a thousand thalers to a wholesaler and was beside himself with anxiety as to the debt. Finally he went to the outer office of the wholesaler's company, and began to weep unrestrainedly. Thereupon the wholesaler came out, and taking pity on his plight, he tore up the storekeeper's promissory note, and thereby cancelled the storekeeper's indebtedness.

"Another merchant, hearing of this, came to the wholesaler and tearfully besought him to make him a gift of a thousand thalers as he had done before.

"The wholesaler laughed, however, saying: 'The other storekeeper has given me a great deal of profitable business over a period of many years, and I, therefore, was willing to cancel his debt when he proved he could not pay it. But why are you, a stranger, entitled to such a sum?'

"A good man who has transgressed and repented of his sins deserves forgiveness, inasmuch as he has performed good deeds before,

and his repentance is sincere. But a man of wickedness who seemingly repents on Yom Kippur—why does he merit forgiveness?"

Dubner, i, 89-92.

278. SLANDER

1. The Law of Slander

The students in the Yeshivah of the Hafetz Hayyim divided into
two camps, one favoring, the other opposing the superintendent of
the School. The half who were critical of the superintendent spoke
of him in highly derogatory terms. The Hafetz Hayyim thereupon
said: "In the Code of Maimonides, a law from the Tosefta, *Peah*,
1 is inserted, reading: 'Slanderers have no share in the World-to-
Come.' The very fact that the great codifier introduced this statement into his code has made it obligatory on the Heavenly Tribunal.
As for me, I refuse to countenance your slander, even if it means
closing the Yeshivah." Later, however, the superintendent moved
to another city with his adherents.

Pupko, p. 81.

2. The Prohibition Against Slander

The work: *Hafetz Hayyim* deals, as a code, with the prohibition
against slander in far-reaching detail. Rabbi Israel Meir brought
this work to Rabbi Baruch Mordecai of Novgorodek, asking him to
recommend the volume. Rabbi Baruch Mordecai was surprised to
see a codebook concerning a single prohibition, and instructed his
Disciples to make sure the work was not filled with casuistry. The
Disciples studied the work with great care, and reported to their
Rabbi that the code was completely useful and practical. The Rabbi
then inscribed his recommendation of the volume.

Pupko, p. 4.

279. SONG

1. The Merit of Song

Said the Ladier Rabbi: "The harmony of opposites make for
artistry and beauty.

"Intense love and longing burst forth from our lips transformed
into song.

"Song reminds the soul that it has its origin in Heaven where the
singing of angels fills all space. Therefore song transforms prayer
and study into the sounds of holiness.

"The Kabbalah declares that there are mansions in Heaven which
open only to song.

"It has been well said that whatever reason cannot comprehend

because of its profundity can be understood through the medium
of song."

Teitelbaum, i, 19.

2. *The Hymn and the Sermon*

The Ropshitzer entered the synagogue of Rabbi Hirsch of Zidit-
chov and discovered there Rabbi Issachar Ber, brother of Rabbi
Hirsch, chanting a hymn in a most remarkable and moving manner.
"Ah," exclaimed the Ropshitzer, "Now I understand the secret of
Rabbi Hirsch's admirable sermon. After hearing such superb hymn-
singing, the spirit is truly uplifted."

Braver, p. 5.

3. *The Distracting Melodies*

A king gave to one of his subjects permission to behold his
treasure-chambers for six hours and to take for himself whatever
he desired. When the king's subject had left his presence the monarch ordered the royal musicians to follow him, and when he was
inside the treasure-chambers to play a variety of melodies. The subject listened with rapture to the exquisite music and forgot to take
with him a single object of treasure. Hence when the six hours had
ended, and he was escorted out of the chambers, he had nothing
whatsoever in his hand. From this we can receive the following
instruction: we are sent into this world to acquire the treasures of
good deeds, but we give ear to the alluring voice of temptation.
When we are ready to depart from this life, we have nothing to
show for having lived."

Siat Hullin, chapter 14.

280. SOUL; BODY

1. *A Message to the Soul*

Said the Hafetz Hayyim: "We read in *Ethics of the Fathers,*
3:1: 'know whence thou camest.' These words are addressed to the
soul, that it may know that it has come from the Upper World. 'And
reflect whither thou art going.' These also are directed to the soul,
that it may give a suitable answer to the question: 'Art thou ascending, as thou shouldst do, or art thou descending?'"

Pupko, p. 94.

2. *The Soul's Mission*

Said the Gerer: "God has appointed a mission for every soul.
If it does not fulfil this mission in one lifetime, the soul is reborn.
Do your best to give to your soul Eternal Rest."

Ha-Nefesh, p. 50.

3. Body and Soul

The Hafetz Hayyim said to a member of the Zeirei Zion group: "The Torah is the soul of Israel, and Palestine is its body. We must always remember that the healthiest body is in the midst of death unless its soul is vital and alive. If your group believes in God and in the Thirteen Articles of Faith, you belong in our company; otherwise, you stand outside it."

Pupko, ii, 28.

281. SPEECH

1. The Locomotive's Lesson

Rabbi Leib of Ger was about to leave the city on the train. A Hasid in the farewell group invited the Rabbi to say something to him which he might cherish in his memory during the Rabbi's absence. Rabbi Leib said to him: "Behold the locomotive of this train! Its power lies in its ability to hold its steam in check until desired. Therein also resides the power of a Rabbi. He likewise should be able to hold back his words until a suitable moment."

Rokotz, ii, 59.

2. The Heart Will Follow

A Zaddik was asked: "Of what benefit would our attendance at divine worship be? How can a man compel his heart to be in them?" The Master replied: "Make use of your lips and in time your heart will follow."

Ha-Nefesh, p. 23a.

3. Speech and Memory

Said the Bratzlaver: "Great is the power of the spoken word! We find in the Talmud that when a man is worried because of an evil dream, he should narrate it to three persons, who should tell him: 'you have dreamed a good dream.' Thus a word can change the dream from evil to good. In the same way a man's words of prayer are able to transform an evil man into a good man. Another power resident in the spoken word is in its ability to impress a matter on one's memory. A man remembers something if he speaks of it several times. Therefore we should read aloud many ethical books and speak worthy words to our own heart. In this way the moral instruction will be impressed upon his mind. The Prophet remarks that when God spoke of Ephraim, He remembered him well."

H. H. N., p. 44a.

4. Responding Quickly

Rabbi Moses Sopher gave a second reason for his rapidity in responding to questions on subjects of Jewish law. He said: "The phrase in the *Ethics of the Fathers* (5:10): 'The wise man . . . is not hasty to answer' is presented by Moses ben Maimon in a different version, namely, 'The wise man is not afraid to answer instantly.' Both versions are correct. While an informed person is still engaged in the process of learning, he should not offer a hasty opinion; without doubt this is the wise course. But in the later period of his Rabbinical career, the wise course is to avoid delay in rendering opinions. The Rabbi should handle all matters with self-confidence."

Sopher, p. 33.

5. Useless Speech

Said the Riziner: "The preacher who is interested only in making a pretty speech will fail to make an impression with his words. We read (Psalm 141:6-7): 'and they shall hear my words, that they are sweet, as when one cleaveth and breaketh up the earth.'" *

Nissanzohn, R. H., p. 276.

* For a similar item see the *Hasidic Anthology*, 136:6, p. 346.

6. A Peddler's Knapsack

Rabbi Nahum of Tzernobil would often say: "My mouth is like a peddler's knapsack. It can offer adornments as well as needles. That which you wish to receive depends upon your behavior."

Twersky, p. 2.

7. Not a Profane Syllable

Two Disciples of the Hafetz Hayyim resolved to listen carefully to the conversation of their Rabbi to discover if any word not associated with piety ever escaped his lips. They listened a long time, and also heard thirty discourses by their Rabbi, but not a profane syllable were they able to discover.

Pupko, p. 82.

8. Alternating Silence With Speech

The son of the Hafetz Hayyim visited his father on Sukkot, 1887. He encountered at the Rabbi's home a man whose actions seemed to him highly eccentric. One day the man would speak volubly, and the next day he would not utter a syllable. When the son of the Hafetz Hayyim inquired of his father the reason, he received the following reply: "A certain farmer experienced considerable trouble with goats and pigs which would jump over the low fence and damage his garden. He made the fence higher, but the damage continued. He then closed the gate with bars and made the holes of the fence smaller by crossing wooden planks over the openings. Thus the goats and pigs which, if the gate was left open by error or the fence was unattended, were prevented from entering the garden. We have here a comparison with the person you are discussing. Probably he perceived his error in talking too much, thereby committing the sin of tale-bearing; therefore he took upon himself the precaution of talking only every second day." Later the man who alternated silence with speech proved himself to be a holy person who left for the Holy Land where he spent his last years until his death.

Pupko, p. 70.

9. Gentle and Stern Words

Said Rabbi Samuel Zevi of Alexander: "In Exodus 19:3 we read: 'Thus shalt thou say to the house of Jacob, and tell to the children of Israel.' Rashi makes the following comment: 'By the words: "to the house of Israel," namely, to the women, speak gently; but to the "children of Israel" speak stern words. If it be asked: but did not the Lord speak the same words to the women as to the men?, the explanation can be given: God told them that they are a holy people, sons and daughters of holy Patriarchs. The women felt themselves complimented to be addressed in this way, but the men interpreted these words as a rebuke. 'What sort of people are we?' they inquired. 'Can we compare in piety with the Patriarchs?' "

Zammlung, p. 88.

282. SPIRITUALITY

1. The Inmost Entrance

Said the Radziminer: "He who delights in laboring in matters spiritual should always behold in front of him more and more doors, through which it is necessary for him to pass before he can reach the inmost entrance."

Zammlung, p. 48.

283. STEALING; THIEVES

1. "Do Not Steal"

A prominent Jew inquired from his Rabbi whether he might conceal from his non-Jewish partner an unexpected profit. He added: "My donations for charity are much larger than his."

The Rabbi replied: We read in Exodus 20:13: '*Thou* shalt not steal.' But in Leviticus 19:11 we read: 'Ye shall not steal.' This teaches that whether you are an insignificant person addressed as 'thou,' or a prominent person, addressed as 'ye,' you shall not steal."

Zlotnik, p. 92.

2. Removing Foreign Garments

Said the Dubner: "A thief watched a clerk every day as he carried bags of money for deposit in a bank. He went in to a clothier and said: 'I wish to order an expensive suit of clothes for an out-of-town friend. I shall watch for a man of his build and shall ask him to allow you to fit the garment according to his size.' When the clerk passed by with his money for deposit, the thief approached him and promised to pay him if he would step in for a moment to have his measurements taken. The clerk agreed, and while he was being fitted, the thief seized the bags of money and started to run away. The clerk wished to pursue him, but the clothier said: 'First take off this expensive suit which belongs to me, and then you can run after him.' In the meantime, of course, the thief had disappeared.

"From this we learn that the soul of man is eager to ascend to Heaven, but the Satan has placed on him the garments of worldly desires. The Guardians of Paradise therefore say to the soul: 'Remove the foreign garments you are wearing before you ascend to Heaven.'"

Dubner, i, 102-104.

284. STRENGTH

1. The Source of Strength

A Disciple of Rabbi Leib Saras wished to carry his Zaddik's trunk for him, but found it too heavy to lift. But the Rabbi picked it up and carried it without difficulty. He explained: "In Psalm 103:20 we read: 'Ye mighty in strength that fulfil His word.' Both physical and spiritual strength is essential for those who desire to fulfil God's word."

G. A., p. 15.

2. Keeper of the Law

An especially heavy Sefer Torah was presented as a gift to the Tzortkover Rabbi. The Zaddik carried it around and offered it to be kissed by all present. A Hasid remarked: "Let me hold it, Rabbi; it is very heavy!" "Nay, my friend," replied the Rabbi. "It is not heavy at all for one who keeps it." *

Margulies, p. 25.

* who performs its injunctions.

285. STUDY

1. Prayer and Study

Rabbi Uri Strelisker said: "There are some authorities who declare that the study of Torah is more important for a man of piety than prayer. I am of a different opinion. Do we not perceive that on the holiest days of the year, namely on Rosh ha-Shanah and Yom Kippur, we are not enjoined to study more than on other days of the year, but to pray more?"

I. K., p. 40.

2. A Thread of Favor

After devoting most of the night to the study of sacred books, Rabbi Issachar Ber of Ziditchov discovered that he had no money whatsoever for food. The Rabbi remarked to his son: "Do not our Sages teach that if a man studies by night, the Lord will cover him with a thread of favor by day?" Rabbi Isaac replied: "Perhaps, father, the Lord's favor consists in vouchsafing to us the strength of character to devote the night to study, even though we have no sustenance by day."

Braver, p. 6.

3. The Blessing by Jacob

Said the Hafetz Hayyim: "When Jacob beheld before him the sons of Joseph, he inquired: 'Who are they?' By these words he meant: 'Are they students of Egyptian or Hebrew schools?' Joseph replied: 'They are my sons and they study the Hebrew religion.' It was then that Jacob called them over and gave to them his blessing."

Pupko, ii, 40.

286. SUFFERING

1. Suffering by Others

A Rav and his wife visited the Hafetz Hayyim. The wife complained: "Much do I suffer because of my husband's goodness." The Hafetz Hayyim replied: "When both of you arrive in the World-to-Come, you will prefer by far to have known that your husband and you underwent sufferings because he was so good, than to know that others suffered because he was wicked."

Pupko, p. 72.

2. Courage Amid Suffering

The Hafetz Hayyim said: "He who suffers yet keeps his courage alive is more to be praised than the man who continually complains. We are reminded of a man who, on being arrested, is placed in chains. If he behaves calmly, his chains hurt him but slightly, but if he attempts to wriggle out of them and escape, the chains twist themselves about his body, and he undergoes great pain."

Pupko, p. 11.

3. Salvation Through Suffering

Said the Hafetz Hayyim in the name of Vilna Gaon: "Without the chastisement induced by sufferings no one has a chance to gain salvation in the World-to-Come."

Pupko, p. 13.

4. Suffering for God's Honor

Said the Hafetz Hayyim: "How profound is the Tannaitic injunction to the effect that we should prepare ourselves in the vestibule (*Ethics of the Fathers*, 4:21)! My interpretation of these words is as follows: 'Prepare thy acts of piety in a proper mood. Offer perfect merchandise to the King of Kings so that He may deem it acceptable. Thus wouldst thou do with respect to an earthly monarch.'"

Pupko, p. 93.

5. Suffering for the Honor of God

The son of the Hafetz Hayyim told his father that a certain Jew had been imprisoned for compelling irreligious persons to conform to religious rites. The Rabbi remarked: "I envy the prisoner immensely. I have always wished to undergo suffering for the sake of God's honor."

Pupko, p. 92.

287. SUKKOT

1. Unworthy of Trust

At a Sukkot celebration the Tzortkover declared: "We are assembled here in order to celebrate the Joy of Drawing Water to be poured upon the altar. Today, however, we have no altar, but we do have the Well, to be found in the Zaddik. Come, all of you, and draw forth the waters of holiness. But it is necessary that you bring your own vessels." A Hasid exclaimed: "But we have no vessels, Rabbi. Cannot we borrow them from the owner of the

Well?" "Nay," replied the Zaddik, "None of you in this assembly may be trusted with them."

Margulies, p. 24.

2. The Four Minim (Species)

Said the Hafetz Hayyim: "The Agada reminds us that the Etrog must associate with the other three lesser species to win forgiveness. But whereas in the Lulab the Myrtle, the Willow and the Palm are tied together, the Etrog (or the Learned Sage) associates with the three species only for the time required to perform the Mitzvah. Then the Etrog stands by itself."

Pupko, ii, 35.

3. Jealousy Over a Lulav

During World War I a Lulav and an Etrog could be obtained only for the Hafetz Hayyim. He held them in his hands for a moment, and waved them a bit. But he refused to hold and wave them during the recitation of the Hallel. He declared: "To cause others to envy me is a sin sufficient to nullify the reward I might obtain for performing the ancient rite of waving the Lulav during the recitation of the Hallel."

Pupko, p. 83.

288. SUPPLICATION

1. Opening the Gates

Said the Dubner: "A rebellious city was besieged by the armies of the king. An ultimatum was issued that the city would be burned to the ground if it did not surrender within a stated time. The starving people opened a loophole in the gates, and said to the king: 'Sire, we abandoned all thought of further rebellion some time ago. But we are so exhausted from hunger that we lack the strength to unlock the city gates. If you will first give us and our families nourishment, we will come to you to implore your pardon.'

"From this we learn: we are too weak to open our hearts unto God. Therefore we ask that the Messiah come first in order to strengthen us for the task."

Dubner, i, 260-261.

289. SURPRISE

1. "I, too, am Amazed"

Elijah, the fourth son of Rabbi Isaac of Ziditchov, was of a retiring nature and never anticipated that he would receive a call to

become a Hasidic Rebbe. His father read to him a parable from
Midrash, Shir ha-Shirim to chapter 6, verse 12. "A prince was playing with other boys in a field. The royal coach passed near by.
The king recognized his son and called him over, inviting him to
ride in the coach. The lad's playmates exclaimed in amazement:
'What, you are a prince?' The boy replied: 'Yes, I am a prince, but
I, too, am amazed that my father should pass this way and call me
over.'" Rabbi Isaac then continued: "It is for you, Elijah, my son,
to keep this story in mind." Years later, long after Rabbi Isaac's
death, Hasidim recognized in Elijah qualities entitling him to become
his father's successor. They extended a call to him to become their
Rebbe at Ziditchov. A friend visited him, and exclaimed: "You,
Elijah, a Rebbe?" Rabbi Elijah answered: "My friend, I, too, am
amazed!"

Braver, p. 94.

290. SYMPATHY

1. The Greater Pain

Rabbi Mendel Vorker underwent an operation on his finger
without taking an anesthetic. To the surgeon's amazement he
uttered not a sound. Later he explained: "If a Jew comes to me
and tells me he is unable to earn a livelihood, I feel greater pain
than when a surgeon cuts into my finger."

Zammlung, p. 100.

291. SYNAGOGUES

1. The Main Portion Missing

A visiting Rabbi was shown the rich, artistic decorations of a
wealthy synagogue. A figure of a leopard had been painted above
the inscription: "Be strong as a leopard." An eagle was pictured
above the words: "Light as an eagle." A hart and a lion were shown
to him next, above the appropriate words of Tanna Judah ben Tema.
The Rabbi commented: "Yes, you have here all of the words illustrating the counsel as given in *Ethics of the Fathers,* 5:23. But
the main portion of the lesson I do not see here, namely, 'to do the
will of Thy Father who is in Heaven.'"

Zlotnik, p. 28.

292. TESTING MAN

1. Satan and Jacob

Said the Radziminer: "With reference to an interpretation of the
Sedrah: *Way-yeshev,* we find a contradiction in the views of the

Midrash and of Rashi. Rashi writes: 'Jacob wished to leave in peace. God remarked: "the Zaddik can have peace in the World-to-Come, but he cannot also have peace in this existence."' The Midrash says: 'The Satan asked: "Can, then, Zaddikim have peace in both Worlds?"' The answer is as follows: 'The Midrash has in mind Zaddikim like Job who may fail when placed to the test. Rashi, however, has in mind Jacob. And the Satan knew he was too weak to be victorious in any temptation of Jacob. It, therefore, remained for God Himself to test Jacob.'"

Zammlung, p. 51.

2. Failing the Test

The Besht once heard a Voice from Heaven declare that all his achievements were to be removed from him. He exclaimed: "If this be so, I shall serve the Lord even as a child who has as yet achieved nothing." The Talmud tells us that the Elisha ben Abuyah also heard a Voice from Heaven, speaking these words: "Return, ye mischievous children, except Elisha ben Abuyah." Elisha, on hearing this, was plunged into despair, and did not repent. Rabbis in later centuries were convinced that the Besht acted more wisely than Elisha, the Tanna. They argued as follows: "If it were true that God did not really wish Elisha to return unto Him, why should He have permitted him to hear the Voice of Warning? This was merely a test of Elisha's perception and good sense. The Besht was victorious in the test, but the Tanna failed."

Zammlung, p. 104.

3. A Parable Concerning the "Yud"

An old Hasid related the following story: "Once there was a wholesale merchant who bought and sold on credit; as a consequence he rarely engaged in any cash transactions. He desired to secure some ready cash for his personal needs. He therefore took part of his stock of goods and with it opened a retail store. Soon, however, the store also resolved itself into a wholesale concern. He opened still another store, using the least popular articles as stock. Even this did not avail him, for the articles became popular and a new wholesale firm developed. So it was with the 'Yud.' The Satan tempted him with general obstacles so that he might pay more attention to his bodily desires, but the effort was unsuccessful. The Satan then tempted the 'Yud' by subjecting him to abject poverty and a nagging wife. But the 'Yud' broke through all obstacles and still cleaved unto the Lord."

H. Hak., p. 56.

293. THE PAST

1. *"Thou shalt see My Back"*

Rabbi Sopher told a story to illustrate the verse in Exodus 33:23: "And thou shalt see My back." He said: "In my youth a French officer was quartered in the home in Mayence where I was a boarder. We became friends, but we lost sight of each other when we both left the city. In 1809 the French Army under Napoleon conquered Pressburg, where I lived. I was arrested on suspicion of aiding the Austrians, but the military judge proved to be my friend of Mayence days, and I was acquitted. Thus I came to understand the meaning of the words in Exodus: oftentimes we can see the consequences of something that has happened far back in former years."

Sopher, p. 21.

294. THIS-WORLD

1. *Sojourning for a Night*

The Hafetz Hayyim once visited a town on behalf of the distribution of his books. The local Rav observed him studying by candlelight, and remarked: "You should give your eyes a rest at night." The Hafetz Hayyim replied: "I am reminded of a town where I once stopped overnight. When I awoke in the morning, I said to the innkeeper: 'your inn is satisfactory, but you have placed the stove too near the beds; moreover, your windows are too small and narrow.' The innkeeper answered: 'Is it your intention to remain with me for long?' 'No,' was my reply; 'I must leave within a few hours.' 'Since this is so,' was the rejoinder of my host, 'why comment on the layout of my house?' In the same way, I can say to you, my friend: 'Since my sojourn in the world is of brief duration, why should I try to take pains to preserve or improve my eyesight.'"

Pupko, p. 74.

2. *Furniture is Unnecessary*

A wealthy man came to visit the Hafetz Hayyim. He observed a room in which there stood an unpainted table and unpainted benches. He therefore imagined it was a corridor and was surprised when the Rabbi welcomed him in this room. He exclaimed: "But where are your furnished rooms?" The Rabbi answered: "I regard myself as a passer-by in this world, and like yourself, I do not concern myself with the furniture when I am passing through a place."

Pupko, p. 76.

295. THOUGHTS

1. The Holy Thought

The Besht offered this teaching: "Sanctify your every act by cleaving in your thoughts to the Source of Holiness. It must be remembered that not even a holy deed, the performance of a Mitzvah, is holy in and of itself. It is the accompaniment of a holy thought that makes the deed a holy one."

Teitelbaum, i, 26.

2. As a Man Thinks

Said the Hafetz Hayyim: "The indolent storekeeper does not bother if his merchandise is thrown hither and thither in confusion. The diligent storekeeper, however, keeps everything, even of small size, in perfect order, and therefore sells his entire stock to advantage. Thus it is with piety. One man thinks that everything he does must be in the spirit of an act of piety. Another man thinks of his deeds merely in worldly terms. As a man thinks regarding his actions, so do they oftentimes become."

Pupko, ii, 26.

296. TIME

1. Sleeping Away Time

Rabbi Abraham Sopher said: "One Amora has declared that the night is for sleeping; another, that it is for studying. I say that sleeping is suitable for those who are not students, for by sleeping they do not disturb those students who spend the night studying. As for myself I deplore the necessity of sleep. A man wishes to have a long life, yet by setting aside too much time for sleep, he virtually commits suicide, a lengthy portion of his life. When he is asleep, a man is not really a human being, but is comparable to an animal."

Sopher, p. 83.

2. The Best Time to Study

Said Rabbi Aaron Tzernobiler: "The best time for the study of Torah is the time, usually neglected by others; for example, Friday afternoons or on the Eve of Festivals when Jews are busying themselves with affairs other than study. The Psalmist indicates this in words: (119:126) 'It is time for the Lord to work; they have made void thy Torah.'"

Twersky, p. 35.

3. Using Free Time

Rabbi Leib Gerer inquired from a Hasid the nature of his occupation. The young Hasid replied: "I am still without an occupation, and I eat my meals at the table of my father-in-law." "This is truly a fine occupation," said the Rabbi with a smile. "How about devoting your free time to the study of Torah?"

Rokotz, iii, 62.

4. The Use of Time

Said the Hafetz Hayyim: "I dislike spending money on articles for the house, or even on books which I do not need at the moment. To obtain money time is required; time is life, and life was granted to men to be used in serving the Lord."

Pupko, p. 22.

297. TIMIDITY

1. The Unsigned Agreement

Two hares were resting peacefully in the forest, when suddenly they heard the sound of hounds baying in the distance. One of the hares became frightened, but his companion re-assured him, saying: "Don't worry! The hares have made an agreement with the hounds. We won't run away from them, and they won't run after us." At that moment, however, the baying of the hounds showed that they were drawing nearer rapidly, and the first hare started to run. The second hare caught up with him, and asked: "Why are you running? Don't you know about the agreement?" "Yes, I know," answered the first hare. "But I'm afraid those particular hounds haven't signed that particular agreement."

Aryeh ben Pinhas commented on this story, saying that non-Jews may make an agreement not to discriminate against and persecute Jews, but when anti-Semitism arises somewhere, it is clear that the non-Jews responsible for the specific outbreak of prejudice may not have signed "that particular agreement."

Selected.

298. TOBACCO

1. A Mixed Value

Said the Tzortkover: "The yearning for tobacco is undoubtedly without merit. Yet, it must be confessed, it is often the instrument by which acts of kindness are performed. Hence it almost acquires an element of holiness. And what are these acts of kindness: the wealthy and the poor alike freely offer a cigarette to others, and both the wealthy and the poor are unashamed to ask for it."

Margulies, p. 25.

299. TOLERANCE

1. Tolerating Distasteful Actions

Rabbi Aryeh Leib ha-Cohen in his discourses often spoke critically of Rabbi Isaac, the Lubliner "Seer." The latter's Hasidim retorted by belittling the honor of the Gaon, Aryeh Leib, who, on hearing of this, placed them under a ban for thirty days. The Hasidim went to Lubliner, but he declined to admit them because of the ban. Later, when they were admitted, the Lubliner explained, saying: "We read in Numbers 12:8 that the Lord spoke unto Aaron and Miriam, and said: 'Wherefore, then, were ye not afraid to speak against My servant, against Moses?' From this verse we receive instruction to the effect that there are two types of Rabbi we are in duty bound to honor; one of these is comparable to Moses, namely, the Gaon, distinguished for his knowledge of the Jewish Law. We must respect him as a servant of God who is deeply sincere in his service to the Lord. Inasmuch as you belittled the honor of a Gaon, you have deserved the ban he issued. Be sure to safeguard a Rabbi's honor, and do not interfere with his actions, however distasteful they may be to you."

Raker, p. 188.

2. Tolerance and Evil

Rabbi Ber Lubavitzer paid a visit at the home of the Gaon Akiba Eger. The latter extended to him a cordial welcome and accepted with thanks the works of the Ladier Rabbi and of his visitor, Rabbi Ber. Then the host began to expound interpretations of Halakah but took care that each was phrased in simple words so that it would not be beyond the comprehension of the visitor. On returning home, Rabbi Ber remarked: "Now I understand the remark of Rabbi Israel Polotzker to the effect that on his visit to communities in Germany he discovered no evil. By this he meant that where there is tolerance, evil may be overlooked."

Sopher, p. 62.

3. No Two Minds Alike

Said Rabbi Moses Sopher: "We read in the *Ethics of the Fathers* (3:13): 'He in whom the spirit of his fellow-creatures takes delight, in him the spirit of the All-Present takes delight.' Why does the Tanna say this? Unless the spirit of the Lord takes delight in a man, it cannot be expected that the spirit of many of his contemporaries will take a similar delight in him. No two minds are exactly alike, and it requires a special favor from Heaven to induce a multitude of minds to agree on anything."

Sopher, p. 6.

4. A Minute Measure of Untruth

Said the Koretzer: "Both the Pulnoer and I love the truth ardently, yet our ways are dissimilar. The Pulnoer disseminates truth in ample measure. And if, by misadventure, a little exaggeration, or even untruth, becomes mingled with it, it does not disturb him. As for me, I must declare that I dislike even a tiny portion of untruth. Therefore I do not speak overmuch, even about matters which I know to be true, lest a minute measure of falsity inadvertently creep into my words."

Twersky, p. 70.

5. The Whims of the Adherents

The Rabbi of Lublin was inclined to accept as adherents any Jew, even though he might know little of Judaism and have at the moment little faith. The "Yud," however, declared: "My learned and deeply religious adherents do not wish to lower their minds to the standards of the common people." And lo, the common people deserted the Rabbi of Lublin, the democrat, and flocked to the "Yud," the aristocrat, who really did not want them.

Selected.

6. The Group is Unimportant

The Hasidim and their Opponents were being discussed by a number of men in the presence of the Hafetz Hayyim. The Rabbi remarked: "The Holy Sages of the Talmud once taught that in the World-to-Come the Lord will be seated on High with a Scroll of the Torah in His hand, and he will declare: 'Whosoever has fulfilled the precepts of the Torah is to come near to Me and receive his reward.' From this we learn that it does not matter in the eyes of the Lord, to which group a Jew belonged, whether Hasidim or Mitnagedim. If he has kept the injunctions of the Torah, his lot will be satisfactory; if not, his membership in any institution of the community will not avail them. Neither can a brother save a brother, if he has failed to save himself."

Pupko, p. 62.

7. Many Pathways to Salvation

The Hafetz Hayyim once visited a physician who inquired of him: "In what way can I gain salvation and inherit a share in the

World-to-Come?" The Rabbi replied: "The Torah describes the location of the Tree of Life as being in the center of the Garden of Eden. This indicates that there are many pathways to reach it. The Talmud tells of a physician in the time of Raba who daily heard a message of greeting from Heaven, whereas the Rabbi received such a message only once a year. This physician always respected the modesty of his patients, and with regard to his fee, he hung up a box in an inconspicuous place. In this way his poor patients need give little or nothing without being identified, and the well-to-do may contribute as much as they wished. It is clear from this that a physician of merit can earn a larger share in the World-to-Come than the most illustrious Rabbi."

Pupko, p. 57.

300. TOOLS

1. The Workman's Tools

Said the Dubner: "A workman had been engaged to work steadily at the court of the king. He was well paid and, as a consequence, was able to furnish a beautiful home for himself. Later he fell ill and could not work for a long time. The king paid him his wages in part. Inasmuch as this was insufficient for the workman's needs, his wife proceeded to sell the costly articles of the home. Finally she wished to dispose of her husband's tools. The workman protested, however, saying: 'Leave them here. As long as I retain my tools, I am still a workman for the king, even though I may be temporarily incapacitated, and I receive from him a part of my wages. If you sell my tools, the king will believe I shall never work again for him, and will halt the payment he is still making me.'

"From this we learn that in Exile we have been compelled to abandon many forms of service to the Lord, but as long as we retain the Torah, our tools of the spirit, the Lord sends us a livelihood, however sparse."

Dubner, i, 164.

301. TORAH

1. Two First Things

Said the Rabbi of Medziboz concerning "Bereshit," the first word in the Hebrew Bible: "I read this word as meaning: 'B,' the number 'two,' 'reshit,' 'first thing.' In the scheme of creation there were two things. The Torah, requiring obedience to God and His commandments, is the first 'first thing.' Israel, the only nation to accept Torah and to study it, is the second 'first' or 'fundamental' thing."

Migdal David, p. 86.

2. Torah is Light

Said the Hafetz Hayyim: " 'Torah is Light' according to the Biblical word. (Proverbs 6:23) Therefore it is evident that the more profound the Torah, the stronger is the light it gives forth."

Pupko, p. 94.

3. The Power of the Torah

Said the Hafetz Hayyim: "We read in Exodus 17:11: 'when Moses held up his hand, Israel prevailed; and when he let down his hand, Amalek prevailed.' Moses is thus symbolic of the Torah. When the Torah is upheld, we shall in truth prevail over our foes."

Pupko, ii, 46.

4. A Share in Torah

Said the Hafetz Hayyim: "Occupation in the study of the Torah is a profitable enterprise. Do not neglect to acquire a share in it."

Pupko, ii, 39.

302. TRANGRESSION

1. Regaining Goods

Said the Dubner: "A wholesaler and a distributor had two assistants. One traveled from place to place to buy merchandise, and the other traveled in order to sell it. The two never met each other in their travels and were therefore unacquainted. Once the salesman received his employer's permission to sell a lot of unsatisfactory merchandise which had been left over, at a low price. The assistant who was the employer's buyer chanced to be in the same town as the salesman and he bought the lot of merchandise at the low price when the salesman disposed of it. Thus, the merchant, unwittingly, had bought back the very goods of which he wished to rid himself."

"In the same way we mortals are eager to rid ourselves of our transgressions on Yom Kippur, but immediately after we re-acquire a large store of them."

Dubner, i, 83-84.

303. TRAVELING

1. The Traveler's Disadvantages

The Lubliner Rabbi remarked that the traveler is at a disadvantage compared to the person who remains at home. The traveler must look upon unseemly sights; he must be satisfied with faulty places for study and prayer. Moreover, he must be careful lest he show his purse in public, and, as a consequence, there are times when he must refuse to give aid to the poor.

Walden, p. 95.

304. TRIBULATIONS

1. For the Sake of Torah

Said the Leover: "If tribulation overtakes you, examine the record of your life, to discover, if you can, some meritorious deed you may have performed. For the sake of this good deed, you may petition God for clemency. If, however, you cannot discover an outstandingly good deed in your past, then you may invite God's compassion for the sake of Torah, which, because of your suffering, you have been unable to learn."

Guttman, p. 25.

2. Pitying a Thief

The Ropshitzer Rabbi once remarked: "A thief stole my house coat. Its pockets were bulging, and the thief doubtlessly expected to find in them a considerable sum of money donated to me by my visitors. But I keep in my pockets only the slips of paper on which they write down their troubles for my attention. Thus all the thief secured for his pains was a bundle of other people's tribulations. I pity that thief."

Walden, p. 31.

3. A Change of Tone

Said the Hafetz Hayyim: "The word: 'Mah,' namely: 'what' can be uttered in either a sad or an exalted tone of voice. In evil times, we say: 'what hath God wrought for His people? Why has he meted out to us so many misfortunes?' But the tone of voice will change in the future. As Balaam prophesied in Numbers 23:23: 'Now it is said of Jacob and Israel: what hath God wrought!' "

Pupko, p. 46.

4. Serving God Amid Tribulation

Said the Hafetz Hayyim: "Frequently a man says to himself: 'When God improves my circumstances, I shall study the Torah and other books teaching me the way to reverence the Lord.' This seems to me a false approach. It may well be that the Lord prefers you to serve Him even under adverse conditions. The Torah says: 'The place whereon thou standest is holy ground.' (Exodus 3:5) And the Sages have taught us: 'of greater import is your service to the Lord during your troubled hours than a hundred hours of service during your days of prosperity and peace.'"

Pupko, ii, 45.

5. A Troubled Life is No Life

Two men called on Rabbi Abraham, known as "The Angel." One said: "My creditors are harassing me; shall I sell my land to pay them?" The other man said: "My wife treats me badly, and gives me no peace. Shall I divorce her?" In both instances "The Angel" refused to countenance the remedies suggested. The first man disobeyed and sold some of his land for the benefit of his creditors. Soon after he became dangerously ill. When the man's friend came to the Rabbi beseeching him to pray in his behalf, the Rabbi replied: "I understand the matter thus. The man has already lived beyond his allotted span of life. As long as he led a life of tribulation, it was not considered in Heaven as a true life, and he was allowed to live on. But when he sought a remedy for his troubles, he forfeited his life."

Szlamovitz, p. 71.

6. Only Mental Torment

Said the Bratzlaver: "I have only pity for the philosophers. They never meet with their ideal world in this existence, and they refuse to believe in existence beyond this life. Throughout their entire allotment of years, they experience only mental torment."

Guttman, p. 16.

7. Our Indebtedness

Said the Hafetz Hayyim: "Do you wish to know why there is so much tribulation in the world now? A parable can make the problem clear. A storekeeper had always been willing to sell his goods on credit. But in his old age when he wished to retire, he began to collect the amounts due him. To his customers, who still wished to buy on credit, he would say: 'I am sorry, my brothers; but now it is necessary for me to collect the money owed to me.' In the

TRIBULATIONS 229

same way, we must understand that we are approaching the Messianic Era. The prevailing order is now being terminated, and no delays in the payment of our debts to God can be tolerated."

Pupko, ii, 40.

8. Fresh Misfortunes and Old Ones

Said the Dubner: "A wealthy man suffered severe reverses in business and was forced to undergo bankruptcy. His creditors seized his house, his costly furniture and his jewelry, but left him a comfortable home with a field and a garden. He had sufficient for a moderate livelihood, but he bewailed the loss of his costly house. A fresh misfortune overtook him, and his home burned to the ground. He sold his land and bought a horse and wagon to transport men and goods from place to place. He bewailed the loss of his comfortable home and garden. But his horse died and he was compelled to become a porter. Upon his back he had to carry heavy boxes and crates. Now he bewailed the loss of his horse. A friend of his youth met him and expressed sympathy for the loss of his splendid house with its costly grounds.

" 'I have long since forgotten these,' exclaimed the unfortunate man. 'Now I am bewailing only the loss of my beloved horse.'

"From this we learn that fresh misfortunes cause us to forget old ones."

Dubner, i, 121-123.

9. Good From Tribulation

Said the Dubner: "A small boy saw some woodcutters chopping down trees. He asked his father: 'why are they destroying these fine trees?' The father replied: 'The lumber will be made into furniture which is finer still.'

"From this we learn that many a tribulation which overtakes us becomes the cause of an improvement in our circumstances."

Dubner, i, 235-236.

10. Tribulations Before Redemption

Said the Hafetz Hayyim: "The tribulations prior to the advent of Redemption have already come. It is now our duty to prepare for the Redemption itself."

Pupko, p. 106.

11. Prayer Amid Tribulation

During the war of 1914-1918 the Hafetz Hayyim would be urged by the wives of soldiers in battle to pray for the safety of their husbands. The Rabbi would say: "Open the Ark of the Covenant and talk to the Lord in the simple language which comes to your own lips. Your sobs and petitions are worth far more than mine where your happiness is concerned."

Pupko, ii, 22.

12. The Reason for Tribulations

Said the Hafetz Hayyim: "Why do tribulations occur among us? They arise in order to lay bare the crookedness of the heart, and to bring about its banishment through repentance."

Pupko, p. 100.

13. "Through the Front Door"

When visitors came to the Hafetz Hayyim and related to him their tribulations, he was accustomed to say: "Why walk through the kitchen door? Walk through the front entrance. Daily you recite the Sh'ma, and you are instructed to believe that piety and obedience to the laws of the Torah will bring to you prosperity, length of days and offspring. There you have the means of fulfilling your needs."

Pupko, p. 6.

305. TRUTH

1. Truth Belongs to God Alone

A Hasid requested Rabbi Mordecai of Tzernobil to explain the phrase in the *Zohar Hadash* which reads: "Because God is One, the conjunctive letter *Vav* is omitted in Psalm 145:18, in the second part of the verse, namely, 'to all that call upon in truth.' Every other verse in Psalm 145 has the *Vav* to connect the two parts of each verse." The Rabbi gave this explanation: "The *Vav* has the property of adding. We may add the Zaddik to all the attributes of God, except the attribute of truth. In this respect God is One. No one possesses absolute truth except God."

Twersky, p. 13.

2. The Meaning of "Emeth" (Truth)

"Emeth" (truth) contains the Hebrew letters: Aleph, Mem and Tav. These are, respectively, the initials of the following phrases:

1. "Al Tirhak mimeni"—"keep not far from me."
2. "Matai tavo elai"—"when wilt Thou come to me?"
3. "Al tashlikeinu mi-le-fanekhah"—"Do not cast us away from Thee."

The lesson contained in this presentation is as follows: "Be truthful, and the Lord will be near unto you." "He will appear and will not cast you away."

Kaufman, p. 216.

3. Walking With Truth

Said the Dubner: "A man was persuaded by a marriage-broker to see a prospective bride for his son. Another man whispered to him that the girl's father was very poor and that the promised dowry would not be forthcoming. Nevertheless the man wished to see the girl. On his way, he thought to himself: 'they are expecting me; so I suppose they will borrow good clothes and houseware in order to create an appearance of being well-to-do.' When, however, he arrived, he found the family to be poorly-dressed and the home very plain. He thought: 'since they are so truthful and honest, the maiden will surely make an admirable wife.'

"From this we learn: the Lord did not cause the Spies who came to investigate Canaan to see only that which was good. He did not conceal the obstacles which stood in the way of Israel's acquisition of Palestine. For this reason, Israel appreciated the land more than ever."

Dubner, i, 141-142.

306. TU BISHVAT

1. The Fruit of Torah

On Tu Bishvat, the Fifteenth Day of Shevat or the Jewish Arbor Day, Rabbi Isaac of Ziditchov perceived that the number of visitors at his home was larger than anticipated, and that he lacked sufficient fruit for all present. Therefore he said: "Those of you who do not celebrate the New Year for Trees by eating semi-tropical fruits like those in the Holy Land, can still commemorate the festival day. The Mishnah declares that above all Mitzvot, the fruit of which we enjoy in 'This-World' the study of the Torah is uppermost. Go then, my friends, and devote yourselves to the study of Torah. You will enjoy this fruit, and at the same time, lay up a goodly store for yourselves in the 'World-to-Come.'"

Braver, p. 77.

307. UNBELIEVERS

1. Superstitions

The Bratzlaver Zaddik once said: "Better is the man who believes in both superstitions and in the words of truth as well, than the man who denies both superstition and truth. The scoffer at superstitions oftentimes derides all belief."

Rosenfeld, p, 154.

2. The Unbelievers

The Leover once exclaimed: "How can anyone say that there is wisdom in the words of unbelievers? Do not their efforts tend to lower man to the status of animals?"

Guttman, p. 26.

3. Icicles

A grandson of the Rimanover Rabbi told the Tzortkover Rabbi that his grandfather was accustomed to refer to the impious as icicles. The Tzortkover Rabbi remarked: "If they are icicles, then there is a way to reform them. It is by fiery reproof, for icicles thaw out when the air round about them is sufficiently heated."

Margulies, p. 25.

4. Gifts from Unbelievers

The Hafetz Hayyim would not accept money for his Yeshivah from persons who did not believe it necessary to study Torah.

Pupko, p. 42.

308. UNDERSTANDING

1. Knowledge and Understanding

Said Rabbi Sopher: "We read in the *Ethics of the Fathers* (3:21): 'Where there is no knowledge there is no understanding.' Knowledge is acquired from a man's teacher, understanding from his own mind. Understanding, however, must be based upon knowledge to be correct. Very seldom are original ideas correct unless the thinker has learned the rules of logic and the laws of derivation formulated by experienced Sages."

Sopher, p, 7.

309. UNITY

1. The Long Arm

The Vorker Rabbi declared: "If all Israelites were united, they could take each other by the arm. Thus they could form a long arm which would reach to the Throne of Glory. Then of a truth the Household of Israel would lack for nothing."

Zammlung, p. 20.

2. Joy in Unity

Said the Hafetz Hayyim: "If all Jews worked together in true unity, they would feel greater joy in their lot."

Pupko, p. 123.

310. UPPER WORLDS

1. The Upper Worlds

Rabbi Hayyim of Tzanz heard that the Hasid, Fischel Gorlitzer, was accustomed to write down his "dinner talk." The Tzanzer asked: "Are you, then, with me in the Upper Worlds?" "To be sure," responded the Hasid. "Where the Rabbi sits and utters his interpretations of Torah verses, there the Upper Worlds are to be found."

Raker, p. 101.

311. VALUES

1. Unloading the Unessential

Said the Dubner: "A storm arose at sea, and the ship on which a merchant was traveling with his merchandise was exposed to great danger. The captain ordered all the passengers to drop overboard all belongings which could be spared. The frightened merchant was about to cast overboard his Tallith and Tefillin, together with some holy books. A Rabbi on board stopped him and said: 'Such an act will not really lighten the ship. It will only deprive you of the tokens of your spiritual life. Throw over the side of the ship the less valuable merchandise instead.'

"From this we learn: when an economic depression occurs, many persons begin to halt their charitable and religious donations. They forget that they need spiritual consolation even more than before. They should really economize on their luxuries and non-essentials."

Dubner, i, 277-278.

312. VISION

1. Seeing Too Clearly

Rabbi Isaac of Lublin, the "Seer," once asked Rabbi Mordecai of Neshkiz to pray in his behalf. He said: "Heaven endowed me with the power to penetrate completely a man by the sight granted me. Such a power is detrimental to my love for my brother Israelites. Will you entreat the Lord to divest me of this power of insight?" Rabbi Mordecai replied: "I cannot do this, for do we not learn in *Taanit*, 25: 'Heaven grants gifts, but never takes them back.' "

Kolbiel, p. 8.

2. "A Sun and a Shield"

The Tzortkover thus explained the verse in Psalm 84:12 which reads: "For the Lord is a sun and a shield," saying: "To see the sun we need a smoky glass as a shield for our eyes. In the same fashion, in order to see God, we must look at nature, which is the shield of His magnificence."

Margulies, p. 50.

3. Unveiling the True God

Said the Hafetz Hayyim: "When the Redeemer makes his advent, he will of a surety remove from the eyes of all men the hindrances to true insight. Then they will have perfect vision and all mankind will be granted a view of the true and only God and will bow down in worship before Him."

Pupko, ii, 19.

4. The Power of Pre-Vision

The Hafetz Hayyim believed in swift action when a compulsory breach of Jewish laws was impending. He said "This is the meaning of the words in the Talmud: 'Whoso is wise? He who perceives that which is coming.' The consequence of a situation is already clear beforehand to the eyes of the wise."

Pupko, p. 92.

313. WANDERING

1. Aiding the Wanderer

Rabbi Isaac of Ziditchov said: "I have cherished in my memory and heart the name of every single donor who gave me aid in the course of my wanderings during my early years. In my estimation a thaler given to me then counts for more than a hundred thalers given to me now."

Braver, p. 97.

314. WEAKNESS

1. The Weakling

The Lelever saw a man running away from a crowd which pursued him shouting: "Stop thief; stop thief!" The Rabbi gave refuge to the fugitive in his own home, and placed before him food and drink. When the crowd demanded the culprit's surrender, the Rabbi exclaimed: "Have mercy on a poor weakling! He is unable to control his impulses!"

H. Hak, p. 18.

315. WIDOWS

1. Evicting a Widow

A poverty-stricken widow could not pay her rent and the heartless landlord ordered her eviction, though it was the middle of winter. Everyone was shocked at this inhumane behavior and waited to see if he would be punished. The Hafetz Hayyim expressed his confidence that in due time punishment would follow. It chanced that soon after the landlord was bitten by a mad dog, and a few weeks later died from the effects of the wound. The Hafetz Hayyim made it a practice to warn people against bringing pain to orphans or widows, and would often mention the above occurrence.

Pupko, p. 40.

316. WIFE

1. The Influence of a Wife

Said the Hafetz Hayyim: "It depends upon you whether the influence of your wife leads you into merit or demerit. If you fail to take care, you may lose your world."

Pupko, p. 96.

2. The Understanding Wife

The Lubliner counselled the young Vorker Rabbi to become a teacher in a village. The Vorker taught his pupils for two terms and received one hundred thalers in payment. On his way home he stopped at an inn, and was distressed to see the innkeeper and his wife in tears. They related to him that they were planning to marry their daughter that very night to her betrothed. The owner of the inn, however, was insisting that the parents pay him one hundred thalers in settlement of their debt to him. The father and mother feared that the wedding would be indefinitely postponed as a consequence. The Vorker, hearing this story, immediately gave them the money he had earned, and the wedding took place as planned. When he arrived in Vorky, he feared to face his wife on coming home penniless. But he explained to her the entire matter, and she comforted him by her understanding.

Zammlung, p. 22.

317. WISDOM

1. Wisdom of the Besht

Said the Besht: "Just as a man cannot fully appreciate the taste of a new article of food until he has tasted it, so he cannot comprehend the estate of being attached to God in reverence and love before he has attained this estate. No amount of explanation in words will avail."

"An unclean thought breeds an unclean view of life. It is a spiritual hybrid."

"Your body was given to your soul as a gift. Keep it clean and do not castigate it."

"God has sent you into this world on an appointed errand. It is His will that you accomplish your errand in a state of joy. Sadness implies an unwillingness on your part to do God's will."

"A man is in error if he declares that this world is without meaning. On the contrary this world is beautiful and good if you behave properly therein."

"If a man engages in severe fasting and imagines that thereby he has achieved much, he is mistaken, for the soul becomes no purer by such conduct."

"Your prayer is worthier if you do not move your body during it. But you are permitted to pray thus if no foreign thoughts assail you."

"There are two ways to serve the Lord. One is to separate yourself from people and from mundane affairs, and to devote yourself wholly to a study of religious books. This is the safe way. The other way is to mingle with people, to engage in the affairs of the world, and, at the same time, to seek to teach godliness by example. This is the dangerous way, but it is by all means the worthier."

The Besht observed a man completely absorbed in studying a religious book. He remarked: "This man is so deeply buried in his studies that he forgets there is a God in the world."

Said the Besht: "My Disciples will be as numerous as the leaves on a tree, and each one will act differently from the other. Yet every one will maintain that he truly imitates and follows my ways."

Srebrak, p. 18.

2. The Wisdom of Rabbi Baruch of Medziboz

"1. The Lord has endowed us with a part of Himself, namely, our soul. Therefore it has transpired that we have become divine beings only in part."

"2. The Lord declares: 'I give Myself to you. If you accept Me, you will receive My Blessing by gaining the power to understand the divine element residing in every Mitzvah.'"

"3. Torah may be either an offering unto the Lord or an offense in His sight. Everything depends upon the student's motive in learning it."

"4. The Shekinah has its abode with every person. If the latter is coarse, the Shekinah has the unpleasant duty of donning coarse garments to care for him. The finer a man becomes, the more pleasure the Shekinah gains in being able to don fine garments."

"5. Since the Shekinah is in exile in company with Israel, it follows that Israel's redemption will achieve as well the redemption of the Shekinah."

Migdal David, p. 79.

3. Sayings of the Lubliner Rabbi

"1. When you pray, simply ask God to send you out of His abundance. Enumerate no details, for God's abundance includes provision for both material and spiritual needs.

"2. It follows that the best gift from Heaven is the knowledge how to pray.

"3. Repent in your heart before you commence to study Torah, for "unto the wicked God saith: 'What hast thou to do to declare My statutes?' "

"4. The best cure for a mind that feels itself to be unbalanced is the study of ethical ideals. This gives to a man an appreciation of his own insignificance and tends to balance his sense of failure.

"5. Remember that fire purifies, even as water. If there dwells within you a feeling of impurity, cleanse yourself by means of a fiery yearning for spirituality."

Walden, pp. 55-56.

4. The Wise and the Unwise

Said Rabbi Sopher: "This is the way of a wise man: be silent, listen carefully; remember what you hear, and then proceed to teach."

"This is the way of an unwise man: be hasty in giving advice on all matters."

Sopher, p. 35.

5. Wise Sayings of the Koretzer

Said the Koretzer:

"1. If you are guilty of offenses, you can offer excuses to a human judge. But what can you say to the Divine Judge?

"2. If you labor diligently in your study of the Torah, you will discover faith. If you labor indifferently, you will discover only unbelief.

"3. It is easy for you to behold seeming injustice in God's providence for the world, but if He should relax His providence for the world a single moment, you would declare this even less justifiable.

"4. One category of Zaddikim lift their minds to Heaven; another category bring down Heaven into their minds.

"5. Better is the Sage than the Prophet. The Prophet speaks chiefly of one phase of experience, whereas the wisdom of the Sages embraces a multitude of phases."

Rokotz, ii, 26 and 93.

6. *Mire and Gold*

Said the Hafetz Hayyim: "A fool turns gold into mire, whereas a wise man transforms mire into gold."

Pupko, ii, 39.

7. *Wise Sayings of the Gerer*

Said the Gerer:

"1. It behooves us to work untiringly for the benefit of our soul all the days of our life. This is the meaning of the words of the Tanna (*Ethics of the Fathers*, 2:21): 'It is not thy duty to complete the work, neither art thou free to desist from it.'

"2. God does not hasten to redeem the Household of Israel, inasmuch as He appreciates their study of the Torah and their performance of Mitzvot even under unfavorable conditions.

"3. God cannot divorce His bride, Israel, for she insists again and again on returning to Him. This would invalidate any divorce.

"4. Pious men may belong in two categories: one includes those who adhere strictly to every rule of piety; the other includes those who are misled by their love and reverence for God into the making of unintentional errors. Both categories are worthy."

Rokotz, ii, 50-56.

8. *Sayings of the Alexanderer Rabbi*

Said the Alexanderer Rabbi: "Good manners and gentlemanly conduct are not discussed in the Torah, inasmuch as an ill-mannered person usually does not study the Torah."

When the Rabbi's son became Bar Mitzvah at the age of thirteen, his father said: "Remember, my son, that I have been freed of my formal obligations to you according to Jewish custom, inasmuch as you are no longer a religious minor. It behooves you, however, to remember that, despite this, you are not free of your spiritual obligations to me, your father."

Said the Alexanderer: "I consider the fact that I am your Rabbi as a form of penalty for you. And since both men and women share equally in penalties, I cannot discourage women from visiting me for guidance, as other Rabbis regrettably do."

Rokotz, ii, 52.

9. Words of Wisdom

A man made a comment in the presence of the Rabbi on the unusually hot weather. The Rabbi said to him: "Your comment indicates to me that you have no worries about your livelihood. Do not the Sages say that he who, like a donkey, bears the burdens of sustenance, feels cold, even in July."

A Hasid begged the Gerer to offer prayer that his young wife might be able to nurse their new-born infant at her breast. "I will do as you wish," answered the Rabbi, "but I also wish your promise to give of the milk of kindness within you to the poor and needy."

A Hasid complained to Rabbi Leib that his fur hat had been stolen. The Rabbi exclaimed: "I have never heard you complain that your head had been stolen by impure thoughts."

Rokotz, ii, 61.

10. Wisdom of the Neshkizer

Said the Neshkizer Rabbi: "Be not like water that flows on the way of least resistance. Have courage and strive to vanquish all obstacles."

"Dost thou wish to elevate thyself? Remember to make yourself lowly and bear in mind that only God is lofty."

"The Tree of Life grows in the Garden of the Torah."

"To every man creation is a constantly fresh occurrence, and he is in duty bound to acknowledge the Creator constantly and with constancy."

"God created the universe in order to house free-will therein."

Kolbiel, p. 12 (Rishpe Esh).

11. Wisdom of the Karliner

Said the Karliner: "Fear without love is imperfect; love without fear is worthless."

"This world is the lowest of all, and the highest of all."

"Conversation among good friends is an indication of mutuality, but so, too, is silence."

"Prayer and study are best undertaken in company with one's fellows."

I. K., p. 10.

12. Nine Imperatives

Said the Hafetz Hayyim:

"1. You must always run away from a quarrel.

"2. You must always strive to prevent the Profanation of God's Name.

"3. You must repent of your sins every day.

"4. You must pray daily for progress in spiritual insight.
"5. You must be pious, wise and good.
"6. You must give close thought to your spirit, not your body.
"7. You must remember that gains of the spirit are yours for ever.
"8. You must bear in mind only the day at hand, the matter at hand, and the immediate cultivation of your soul.
"9. You must be convinced there are penalties for every foolish deed."

Pupko, p. 110.

318. WOMEN

1. Bearing an Interruption

At the Vienna Conference of 1923 a delegation of women asked permission to sit in the galleries in order to hear the speeches of distinguished orators. Some of the adherents of the Hafetz Hayyim and some Hungarian participants fervently objected to the petition. The Hafetz Hayyim sat calmly by and took no part in the discussion. The Gerer Rabbi thereupon ascended the speaker's platform and said: "The Talmud relates that when Jonathan ben Uzziel was interrupted during his concentration upon his studies, it seemed as if a consuming fire issued from him. Nothing of this nature, however, is related concerning his Master, Rabbi Hillel. Why was this? Because the greater the man, the better able was he to bear an interruption. Thus it is with Rabbi Israel Meir ha-Kohen (the Hafetz Hayyim) and his truly representative adherents." In the light of these remarks, it was decided that the women should have the right to sit in the galleries and hear the speeches.

Pupko, p. 79.

319. WORDS

1. Lessons from Words

Rabbi David Mirapoler enjoyed teaching truths by utilizing words as the initials of ethical phrases. Here are a few examples:

1. *"Hokhmah"* (Wisdom) has the initials of *"Hillu mi-panov kol-haaretz,"* "tremble before Him, all the earth."

2. *"Hamah"* (Wrath) has the initials of: *"Hesed Yah malah ha-aretz";* the mercy of God fills the earth." (For God's wrath is truly mercy).

3. *"Mishnah"* (Mishnah) has the initials of: *"Haalita min-Sheol nafshi";* "Thou hast brought up my soul from Sheol." (A student of the Mishnah is granted salvation).

4. *"Karvah"* (Approach) has the initials of: *"Kumi roni ba-hatzi*

*ha-layelah"; "*arise and chant at midnight." (The performance of
the Midnight Services brings the soul near to the Shekinah).

Kaufman, p. 216.

320. WORK

1. Making It Too Easy

Rabbi Baruch Frankel of Leipnik wrote the work: *Baruch Taam,*
wherein he explained a multitude of unclear Talmudic items. Later
he issued the work in an abridged form. He explained this as follows: "I do not wish to eliminate all the questions which arise. I
prefer to have students discover the questions and then labor to
develop the answers. Thus they will understand far better the
points involved."

Eibeshitz, p. 9.

2. Doing the King's Work

The Hafetz Hayyim learned that some laborers were doing work
for the armed forces which freed them from the necessity of serving
as soldiers. He remarked: "This is true concerning man in relationship to God. A cobbler who sustains his family, pays tuition for
his sons at the Hebrew School and donates to the Yeshivah, may be
compared to one who has devoted his entire life to the study of the
Torah."

Pupko, ii, 26.

321. WORLD-TO-COME

1. Reward for a Moment

The Mezeritzer Maggid said: "In *Avodah Zarah,* folio 13, we
read that Judah, the Patriarch wept, saying: 'This person acquired
a share in the World-to-Come as a reward for a moment's service to
the Lord.' Rabbi Judah wept at the thought that perhaps the dying
person had only a moment to serve the Lord before he expired.
Thus he was able to acquire only an insignificant share in the World-
to-Come."

Walden, p. 110.

2. Storing Our Goods

Rabbi Baruch Leipniker's sister-in-law told this parable: "A
cattle-dealer was accustomed to sell the meat of his cattle to a
butcher and to place the hides in his garret which he used as a store-
room. Once he became short of the cash he required to buy cattle.
He had forgotten his store of hides and wondered that the cash at his

disposal was so small an amount. One day he remembered the hides he had hidden away, and, by disposing of them, secured the money he required. So it is with many mortals. When their last hour of life is at hand, they think: 'What Mitzvot do I bring with me?' Later, however, they recollect various generous and pious deeds they have performed. Thus they gain the confidence that they will not enter the World-to-Come with empty hands."

Eibeshitz, p. 6.

322. YAHRZEIT

1. Banquet on Yahrzeit

The Tzortkover explained why the Hasidim celebrate the Yahrzeit, or anniversary, of a Zaddik's death with a joyous banquet. He said: "The soul of a Zaddik is of a lofty quality and does not require residence in This-World to exalt it. It is sent from on High to elevate other souls of lesser quality. But while the Zaddik's soul is within its body, there is always the danger it will fall into a lower status. Therefore, when its mission is done and the soul is liberated, it is filled with joy because it returns to Heaven in purity. For this reason we also joyously celebrate the anniversary of a Zaddik's death."

Margulies, p. 49.

323. YOM KIPPUR

1. One Plus Zeros

An adherent of the Lubliner Zaddik asked him: "Am I not guilty of pronouncing God's Name in vain when I offer prayer, but am unable to concentrate?" The Rabbi responded: "Offer your daily prayer despite this. When Yom Kippur comes, you, like other Jews, will find that you are able to pray with the proper concentration. Your prayer on the Day of Atonement will count as: One; the prayers of the other days of the year will count as: Zeros. But if you write down the figure: One and place to the right all the Zeros, together they will form a vast number."

Walden, p. 40.

2. The Sage Waits

Rabbi Moses Sopher advised his sons to refrain from interfering in community quarrels, even though they were invited to do so. He paraphrased a Yom Kippur hymn as follows:

> "The Hasid profanes at the right;
> The Heretic throws off his yoke at the left;

And the Sage in the middle?
He keeps silence and waits."

Sopher, p. 100.

3. Prayers for Erev Yom Kippur

The Hafetz Hayyim once asked the printers that they change the order of Confessions in the introductory Prayer of Purification (*Tefillah Zakah*)* for the Yom Kippur *Mahzorim*. He requested that the Confessions of sins against our fellow-men be placed ahead of the Confessions of sins against the Lord. When asked the reason he replied: "It is known to all of us that our sins against our fellowmen are not forgiven on Yom Kippur unless the offended persons have stated their forgiveness. Hence it is clear they are the more important sins for which the penitent needs pardon. If printed at the end of the long prayer, it usually occurs that the time to recite the *Kol Nidrei* arrives before the *Tefillah Zakah* is completed. Thus the important portion of the prayer remains unuttered." A number of the printers complied with the Rabbi's request.

Pupko, p. 22.

* The wording in the *Tefillah Zakah* is: "I forgive all who harm me."

324. YOUTH

1. Too Presumptuous

At his Bar Mitzvah banquet, the son of the Hafetz Hayyim discoursed on Halakah and gave his answer to a difficult question in the *Shaagat Aryeh*. Exhilarated by the applause, the lad exclaimed: "In a short time I will be able to give the correct answers to all the difficulties in the book." The Hafetz Hayyim was incensed at his son and declared: "I see that you will never become a great scholar." This prediction proved correct, but the Hafetz Hayyim never referred to the matter again.

Pupko, p. 13.

325. ZADDIK

1. An Habitual Visitor

Said Rabbi Isaac Ziditchover: "When a man visits me for the first time, I give him my blessing and I bid him farewell. When he visits me a second time, I allow my gaze to penetrate his inmost being, and I scrutinize him thoroughly. When he visits me a third time, I carry him on my shoulder."

Braver, p. 40.

2. Tzanz Versus Sanz

A Hasid from Sanz once visited Rabbi Meyer Premislan and handed to him a written petition, wherein he stated that he came from Sanz. Rabbi Meyer exclaimed: "Do not write: Sanz, but Tzanz, for it is the abode of the Tzaddik (Zaddik) of this generation." The Hasidim obeyed their Rabbi.*

Raker, p. 75.

* In the *Hasidic Anthology,* the name is spelled: Tzanz. The word: Tzaddik begins with a Tzadeh, as in the word: Tzanz.

3. A True Center

Said Rabbi Akiba Eger: "In *Talmud Bavli, Taanit,* 31 there is present an allegory saying that God will enjoin the Zaddikim (the Righteous)* to dance round about him, point their fingers at him and exclaim: 'Behold, He is our Lord!' In our own day there are different fashions of serving God among pious persons of different views. In the future, however, it will become clear to one and all that every fashion of serving the Lord is the true fashion, if the service be performed under the guidance of the spirit of piety. All Zaddikim dance about one true center."

Sopher, p. 62.

* "Zaddikim" in this statement refers to pious religious leaders in general, not necessarily Hasidic Rabbis. Rabbi Akiba himself was a Mitnaged, an Opponent.

4. Greater Than an Angel

The Rabbi of Rizin said: "A genuine Zaddik is greater than an angel. An angel cannot ascend to a higher status, but a Zaddik can do so. My father, Abraham, was an angel in his body, but a Zaddik in his soul."

Szlamovitz, p. 71.

5. The Zaddik's Responsibility

Rabbi Johanan of Rachmistrovka said: "Let us reason together on the subject: why does the Hasid harass the Zaddik when his business affairs are not succeeding? We can draw an answer from the story in the Talmud to the effect that the Tribe of Zebulun entered into an agreement with the Tribe of Issachar as follows: Issachar was to labor in the study of the Torah while Zebulun was to engage in business and furnish Issachar with a livelihood. The merit of Isaachar's endeavors in Torah was to benefit Zebulun's enterprises. Zebulun continued to hold up his end of the agreement in a conscientious and diligent manner. Issachar, however, was not always devoted and faithful: he would arrive at the House of Study at a late hour and leave early. This conduct proved hurtful to Zebulun and hindered his efforts to succeed. Naturally Zebulun was critical of his partner Issachar. In the same way, the Hasid assists the Zaddik and hopes to be successful in business as a consequence of the Zaddik's merits. If the Hasid's affairs are not crowned with success, naturally he complains to the Zaddik who may have been neglectful in the performance of his share in the agreement."

Twersky, p. 69.

6. The Zaddik and the Hasid

The "Yud" said:

1. "Hasidism cannot be judged by its Zaddikim but by the rank and file of its adherents."

2. "A Zaddik who does not strive to acquire disciples, but merely to gain adherents is of little consequence in the long run."

3. "The Zaddik should not constantly read the soul of his Hasidim, but he should teach them to read their own inmost souls by their own insight, and to eject from themselves everything that is false."

4. "Hasidism does not consist of recognizing the greatness of Zaddik, but to be aware of the duties of a Hasid."

5. "Hasidut rests not in visits to the Zaddik for counsel regarding things material, but in visits to him for advice regarding matters spiritual."

H. Hak., p. 94.

7. The Scholarly Conscript

A man came to the Hafetz Hayyim, bringing his scholarly son. He besought the Rabbi to offer prayer that his son escape conscription. The Rabbi disliked to offer such prayers, knowing that if one man is not drafted, another is conscripted in his place. In view of the fact that the man's son was a scholar, the Rabbi agreed to make an exception. He blessed the youth, voicing the hope that he might be freed from the impending peril. Nevertheless the father remained in the room and refused to depart. Then the Rabbi understood that the supplicant was a Hasid, accustomed to more specific promises. "Very well, then, I give you the promise that the Almighty will free your son from conscription. Yet you consider me to be a Zaddik? Where do you behold in me sufficient love and reverence for God to warrant me to be called a true Zaddik?"

Pupko, p. 7.

8. A Visit to the Zaddik

Rabbi Kalonymus of Cracow has written in his book: *Maor ve-Shemesh:* "Each one believes himself to be a just man, a pious man, a learned man, a person who possesses nothing but good traits. Let him, however, visit the Zaddik on a Holiday. He will meet there some of the most eminent people; some young men striving to serve the Lord appropriately; some elderly persons of noble mien. All of them submit themselves to the authority of the Zaddik and look up to him for guidance in service to the Lord. He finds there distinguished merchants, who, despite all their wealth, are humble of heart and reverential towards the Zaddik. He sees poverty-stricken men who turn their mind away from their anxieties and needs; and thereby fortify themselves for service in joy to the Lord. Seeing all this, a man's flinty heart melts like water; he becomes reverential towards everyone. He acquires the wish to enter the heart of his fellows with gladness and with love. His heart within him breaks into tiny shreds at the recollection of all his previous foolishness in regarding himself as a perfect man. And when he beholds the Zaddik himself, he becomes as naught in his own eyes. All his vanity disappears; all his unsatisfactory traits are separated from him; he steps out from the limitations of earthliness and thereby is enabled to serve his Maker."

H. Hak., pp. 81-82.

326. ZEAL

1. Earnest Recitation

Rabbi Hayyim of Tzanz passed by a synagogue and heard the voice of someone reciting passages from a volume of Jewish Codes. He was captivated by the student's earnestness, and remained at the door, until his son prevailed upon him to leave. The Tzanzer remarked: "I was so attracted by a voice reciting Torah for its own sake that I was unable to move from the spot. Had I received an invitation to enter Paradise, I would not have budged a single step."

Braver, p. 14.

327. ZIONISM

1. The Balfour Declaration

The Hafetz Hayyim was overjoyed when he read the Balfour Declaration. He remarked: "Now if the Zionists do not spoil this historic opportunity by irreligious policies, this may result in the approach of Redemption."

Pupko, ii, 28.

BIBLIOGRAPHY OF BOOKS USED
(With Abbreviations)

Berditschevsky
  M. J. Berditschevsky, *Sefer Hasidim*, Warsaw, 1900.
BDH
  R. Margulies, publisher, *Butzina D'Nehora Ha-Shalom*, Bilguray, 1926.
Braver
  M. Braver, *Pe'er Isaac*, Lwow, 1928.
Dor Deah
  Y. A. Kamelhar, *Dor Deah*, Bilguray, 1933.
Dubner
  Israel J. Zevin (Tashrak), *Alle Meshalim von Dubner Maggid*, New York, 1925 (Hebrew Publishing Company) Yiddish.
Eibeshitz
  J. Eibeshitz, *Ohel Baruch*, Lodz, 1903.
G. A.
  R. Margulies, publisher, *Geburat Ari*, Lwow.
Guttman
  M. E. Guttman, *Rabbi Dov Leover*, CLUJ, 1925.
Ha-Nefesh
  (see *H.H.N.*)
H. Hak.
  Z. M. Rabinovicz, *Ha-Yehudi Hakadosh*, Piotrkov, 1932.
H. H. N.
  R. Nachman Bratzlaver, *Histapkhuth Ha-Nefesh*, Mukacevs, 1932.
I. K.
  R. Margulies, publisher, *Imre Kadosh*, Lwow.
I. T.
  R. Margulies, publisher, *Imrot Tehorot*, Lwow.
J. M. J.
  A. D. Ogoz, *Jewish Morning Journal*, November 23, 1941.
Kaufman
  Rabbi Samuel Kaufman, *Tiferet Samuel*, N. Y., 1926.
Kolbiel
  N. C. Kolbiel, *Shibhe Mordecai Neshkizer*, Lodz.
M. B.

R. Margulies, publisher, *Mekor Baruch,* Lwow, 1931.
M. E. H.
Abraham Alter, *Meir Einei ha-Golah,* Vol. I, Piotrkov, 1928; Volume II, Warsaw, 1931.
Michelson
A. S. Michelson, *Ohel Abraham,* Lodz, 1911.
Nissanzohn
S. Nissanzohn, *Royal Hasidut: Rizin Dynasty,* Warsaw, 1938.
Pupko
Aryeh Leib Pupko, *Mikhtevei ha-Rav Hafetz Hayyim,* Warsaw, 1937.
Raker
Yeshua Raker, *Der Sanzer, Reb Hayyim Halberstamm,* New York, 1927.
Rosenfeld
A. J. Rosenfeld, *Hatzofeh le-Bet Jacob,* Warsaw, 1883.
Rokotz
J. K. K. Rokotz, *Siach Sarfei Kodesh,* Lodz, 1929. (S.S.K.)
Sopher
S. Sopher, *Hut Hameshulash,* Drohobycz, 1908.
Srebrak
Z. S. Srebrak, publisher, *Sippure Zaddikim,* Vilna, 1909.
Szlamovitz
Szlamovitz, publisher, *Sifthei Zaddikim he-Hadash,* Lodz, 1933.
Teitelbaum
M. Teitelbaum, *Ha-Rav Mi-Ladi,* Warsaw, 1914.
Tzanzer Hasidut
S. Nissanzohn, *Tzanzer Hasidut,* Warsaw, 1938.
Twersky
A. D. Twersky, *Yachas Tzernobil,* Lublin, 1933.
Walden
M. M. Walden, *Niflaot Ha-Rabbi,* Warsaw, 1911.
Y. A.
M. M. Walden, *Yekhabed Ab,* Piotrkov, 1923.
Zammlung
Eser *Zekuyot Zammlung,* Warsaw, 1937.
Zlotnik
Isaiah Zlotnik, *Yomim Tovim Folklore,* Warsaw, 1930.